IMPERIAL COMMUNISM

Imperial Communism

ANTHONY T. BOUSCAREN

*Associate Professor of Political Science,
University of San Francisco*

Public Affairs Press

TO BARBARA, TONY AND MICHAEL

INTRODUCTION

This is an extraordinarily timely book. If we are to be realistic—and not merely journalistic—about Soviet Russia's so-called "peace offensive" we must consider it in the cold, clear light of what Prof. Bouscaren points out.

Time was when we used to view with alarm practically everything that happened in Moscow. Nowadays we seem to be going to the other extreme. Some of us—all too many of us, in fact—tend to see silver linings in every report, no matter how inconsequential, from behind the Iron Curtain. This is true not only of the uninformed layman, but also of comparatively well informed students of international affairs, journalists, and even government officials who sometimes indulge in wishful thinking. The other day the *New York Times* reported, for example: "Diplomatic observers said yesterday that the Soviet Government's decision to send a team of chess masters here next month for a match against this country's best players was a significant move in the Kremlin's current 'peace offensive' as well as an effort to dispel United States belief in Soviet anti-semitism." Surprisingly enough, the story was judged of such importance that its details were set forth in a full column conspicuously displayed toward the front of the paper.

Considering that American lives continue to be lost in Korea, that Communist troops have invaded Laos, that Congressional investigations are daily revealing the nefarious operations of Communists in the United States, it is exceedingly hard to believe that Soviet Russia has seen the error of its ways one whit.

As this book shows, irrefutably and penetratingly, Soviet Russia doesn't make a single move without cold-blooded calculation of how it will advance international Communism. Prof. Bouscaren makes it crystal clear that world domination is the Kremlin's be-all and end-all. In the light of his evidence, the current "peace offensive" is nothing more than a delaying action designed to give Stalin's heirs more time to consolidate their position. It's an old story. Deception has long been one of the major weapons in the Communist arsenal.

Prof. Bouscaren has no illusions about Soviet Russia for the simple reason that he has spent ten years studying its machinations. He knows what makes it tick and why. His book is a tract for our times which all should read and ponder.

M. B. Schnapper, *Executive Secretary*
American Council on Public Affairs

Contents

Soviet World Outlook

The Soviet Union is a sovereign state in a world of sovereign states. It differs from other states in its attitude towards and its relationship with other states and peoples. What that difference is, and what the true Soviet attitude is towards the non-Soviet world, are matters on which opinions differ violently. These opinions differ also in the extent of the knowledge, or the depth of the ignorance, or the strength of the prejudices, on which they are based. This is an unhappy situation, because Soviet foreign policy, ever since the revolution of 1917 and especially since 1939, has had a direct bearing on the life of every individual and nation in the world today.

The responsibility for the ignorance and prejudice about the nature and purposes of Soviet foreign policy is twofold. First, the Soviet Government maintains throughout the world an elaborate organization designed to present a plausible but distorted picture of Soviet policy as one designed to serve the interests of the working classes all over the world. Secondly, there continues to exist, in some of the circles at which Soviet propaganda is chiefly directed, a tendency, based on wishful thinking or historical and theoretical preconceptions, to accept the Soviet explanation of Soviet policy as credible.

The first task of anyone seeking to form an accurate opinion about Soviet foreign policy is to discover the facts on which to base his judgment. These facts should be looked for in the writings and statements of the Soviet leaders, and in the actual behavior of the Soviet Union on the international scene. The alternative is to form a superficial judgment based on partisan pronouncements, on brief and carefully stage-managed visits to selected areas of the Soviet Union, and on wishful thinking which emotionally wishes to accept Soviet explanations at face value.

Marxist theory holds that the capitalist economic system has long ceased to be "progressive" in that it hinders the development of productive forces. According to this theory, the Socialist organization of society is required for further "progress". Therefore, the industrial working class, under the leadership of a "vanguard" (the Communist Party), is the only class whose economic interests coincide with the general interests of this "progress". Marx taught that in any state, power is in the hands of a ruling class, against which other economic classes conduct a struggle. Thus follows the doctrine of class struggle and violence. Tied up with this concept is that of economic determinism. History is inevitably following the path caused by the mode of production of a given era. A "dictatorship of the proletariat" (in effect the dictatorship of the Communist Party) must result through a violent process, first in one country, and ultimately throughout the world.

Lenin's development of Marxist theory held that the working class could only attain a monopoly of political power if it is represented by a small, highly organized and highly disciplined political party, a party which itself might not be proletarian in character. In the name of the working class this party, militarily organized and directed, would gradually Communize the world. Leninist theory also taught that in the "present epoch of imperialism" the capitalists of the more highly industrialized states exploit not only their own working classes, but also entire nations of the less developed areas, as in Asia, the Middle East, and Latin America. Not only that, but the leading "imperialist states" are inexorably marching towards struggle amongst one another for world markets. Lenin taught that the Communist Party, as the "vanguard" of the proletariat, must take advantage of this situation, in order to ultimately lead the Soviet Union to victory over the capitalist-imperialist states.

Stalinist theory teaches that the interests of the working class all over the world are indistinguishable from those of the Soviet Union. Stalinist practice has shown that the interests of the ruling group of the Soviet Union should override all other interests including those of other working classes and Communist parties: any action is justifiable if it serves Soviet ends. Any policy that strengthens the Soviet state and advances the cause of World Communism should be pursued. This consideration has resulted in the conversion of the Soviet state, internally, into a rigid hierarchical caste system, militarist in tone, in which all initiative comes from the top, and in which the workers and others have become simultaneously mere instruments of increasing production, and cannon fodder in time of war.

Soviet policy towards national groups and movements, and towards the independence of states, is that the interests of the Soviet Union, as the incarnation of the interests of the world, should override local interests. National aspirations should be encouraged when they prove of assistance to Soviet policy, and suppressed when they oppose Soviet interests. Meanwhile, in the U.S.S.R., a system of unreal local autonomy gives such superficial satisfaction to national feelings as is compatible with the simultaneous existence of a rigid centralism.

Soviet foreign policy regards the great industrial states, especially the United States, as its main opponents. It attempts to exploit differences between these states, as for instance in the case of the United States and Great Britain, and it seeks to oppose against these states the colonial and semi-colonial peoples of Asia, the Middle East, and Latin America. It makes use of all forms of economic strife and racial friction which might strengthen the Soviet Union, weaken non-Soviet states (and especially leading anti-Soviet states), and forward the cause of World Communism to promote the end result: a world U.S.S.R. (See Stephen King-Hall, *Soviet Foreign Policy*, 1952.)

The world Communist movement is required to give unquestioning obedience to Soviet leadership. The Soviet Union as the bastion of world revolution, has the task of imposing its will on the world through a combination of military power, diplomacy, and the assistance of Communists and their allies in non-Soviet states. When, after the first world war, the expected revolutions in non-Communist states failed to materialize, Lenin determined to build up the Soviet stronghold in order that it might become a mighty base for world revolution, a center from which ultimate Soviet victory throughout the world might be achieved. Increasingly this meant that the Soviet Army and Soviet diplomacy must succeed where local and spontaneous Communist revolutions had everywhere failed. As Stalin himself said: "Lenin never regarded the Republic of the Soviets as an end in itself. To him it was always a link needed to strengthen the chain of the revolutionary movement in the countries of the proletariat of the whole world over capitalism." (Stalin, *Works*, Moscow, 1947, vol. 6, pp. 50, 51.) Stalin also made it clear what strategic role the Soviet Union would play in the struggle to achieve World Communism: "The victory of Socialism in one country is not a self-sufficient task. The revolution which has been victorious in one country must regard itself not as a self-sufficient entity, but as an aid, a means for hastening the victory of the proletariat in all countries. For the victory of the revolution in one country, in the present case Russia, . . . is the beginning of and the groundwork for the world revolution. . . . There can be no doubt that the development of world revolution. . . . will be quicker and more thorough, the more thoroughly Socialism fortifies itself in the first victorious country, the faster this country is transformed into a base for the further unfolding of the world revolution, into a lever for the further disintegration of imperialism . . ." (Stalin, *Problems of Leninism*, Foreign Languages Publishing House, Moscow, 1941, p. 113). In this work, Stalin stated Communist objectives as follows: ". . . to consolidate the dictatorship of the proletariat in one

country, using it as a base for the overthrow of imperialism in all
countries. The revolution is spreading beyond the borders of one
country; the epoch of world revolution has commenced. The main
forces of the revolution: the dictatorship of the proletariat in one
country, the revolutionary movement of the proletariat in all countries. Main reserves: the semi-proletarian and small-peasant masses
in the developed countries, the liberation movement in the colonies
and dependent countries. . . ." (Stalin, *Problems of Leninism*, pp.
59, 60.).

In his famous letter to Comrade Ivanov, published in *Pravda* on
February 12, 1938, Stalin emphatically repudiated the suggestion that
the teachings found in *Problems of Leninism* were out of date. The
April 26, 1949, issue of *Izvestia* declared that Stalin's book "has bril-
liantly withstood the test of time . . . and still today preserves all its
mighty organizational and mobilizing power in the struggle for the
victory of Communism." The *Literary Gazette* of the next day stated
that "J. V. Stalin's work of genius on Leninism stands out today as
the shining, irresistible truth of our great epoch . . . and now, after
twenty-five years, it is our mighty ideological weapon, an irreplace-
able, trusty and tried guide. It arms ideologically tens of millions of
fighters for Communism throughout the world, and shows them the
only correct path to liberation from the chains of capitalist slavery."

The basic doctrine of Soviet foreign policy is the doctrine of inevitability of war, leading to the victory of Soviet power over resisting
non-Soviet states. To this effect, Stalin quotes Lenin approvingly:
"We are living not merely in a state, but in a system of states, and
the existence of the Soviet Republic side by side with imperialist
states for a long time is unthinkable. One or the other must triumph
in the end. And before that end supervenes a series of frightful
clashes between the Soviet Republic and the bourgeois states will be
inevitable. That means that if the ruling class, the proletariat, wants
to hold sway, it must prove its capacity to do so by military organization also." (Stalin, *Problems of Leninism*, Moscow, 1940, p. 156).

Soviet Communist theory, however, does recognize the necessity
of "revolutionary retreat" when called for in a period of adversity:
"To carry on a war for the overthrow of the international bourgeoisie,
a war which is a hundred more times prolonged and difficult than
the most stubborn of ordinary wars between states, and to refuse
beforehand to manoeuver, to utilize the conflict of interests (even
though temporary) among one's enemies, to refuse to temporize and
to compromise with possible (even though transient, unstable, vacillating and conditional) allies—is this not ridiculous in the extreme?

Is it not as though, in the difficult ascent of an unexplored and hitherto inaccessible mountain, we were to renounce beforehand the idea that sometimes we might have to zig-zag, sometimes retracing our steps, sometimes giving up the course once selected and trying various others?" (Stalin, *Problems of Leninism*, Moscow, 1941, pp. 69, 70). Similarly, Soviet policy admits the possibility of temporary coexistence with non-Soviet states. Indeed, it was not an uncommon trick of Soviet propaganda for Stalin to graciously grant an interview to a foreign journalist or visiting dignitary, and emphasize the possibility of peaceful coexistence. This tactic is frequently practiced to lull the opposition into a false sense of security, at a time when the opposition seems to be girding its forces in a strong defensive move. Stalin, however, made it abundantly clear that occasional Soviet statements concerning the possibility of peaceful coexistence, referred only to *temporary* coexistence: "We are, evidently, speaking of temporary agreements with the capitalist governments in the sphere of industry, trade, and perhaps, in the sphere of diplomatic relations." (Stalin, *Works*, Russian edition, vol. 10, p. 123, Moscow, 1949).

David Dallin, whose books on the Soviet Union have placed him high among the leading authorities of this field, states that "It is perfectly safe to say that not a single high ranking Communist in the Soviet Union believes in the possibility of a lasting peaceful settlement of the present world-wide contest for power. The only question in the minds of the Soviet leaders is when and where the conflict will break out." (Dallin, *The New Soviet Empire*, Yale University Press, 1951, p. 70). James Burnham, another important critic of Soviet foreign policy, holds that the Communist doctrine of "permanent wars and revolutions" means the end of any sane distinction between eras of peace and war. Burnham points out that for the Soviets, war is a permanent condition until the leading anti-Soviet states are defeated, and a world U.S.S.R. is established. (See Mr. Burnham's *Coming Defeat of Communism*, John Day, 1950.) Timothy Taracouzio, in his incisive study *War and Peace in Soviet Diplomacy* (Macmillan, 1940), shows conclusively that to the Soviets, the terms war and peace are merely two sides of the same coin. Thus for the leaders in the Kremlin, war and peace are but tactics to be employed in the relentless march towards world conquest. Stalin, and Lenin before him, distinguished between "just" wars (those conducted by the Soviet Union), and "unjust" wars (those conducted by non-Soviet states). In his *Works*, he says: "We support a liberating anti-imperialist revolutionary war despite the fact that such a war, as is well known, is not only not devoid of 'horrors of bloodshed', but even abounds in such horrors." (Stalin, *Works*, Moscow, 1949, vol. 12, pp. 175-6). Examples of such a war are the Soviet attack on Finland in 1939, and the Soviet-directed attack against Korea in 1950.

The fact that the Soviet Union is the most highly militarized state in the world, not merely in its armaments but even more so in its propaganda atmosphere and in its educational system, is not accidental. Occasional Soviet statements that Soviet aims are "peaceful" and solely defensive, are merely propagandistic tactics. Of course, Stalin several times pointed out that true "peace" can only exist under the conditions of a world U.S.S.R., and therefore, when Stalin said he wanted "peace", he in effect was saying that he wanted war—war to establish Soviet type "peace". Soviet doctrine not only teaches that war is inevitable, and that war waged by the Soviet Union or Soviet satellites is justified, but it also teaches that *aggression* as such, is legitimate. Lenin, in his *Collected Works*, points out that ". . . it is not the offensive or defensive character of the war, but rather the interests of the . . . international movements of the proletariat, that represent the only possible point of view from which the question of the attitude of Social Democracy towards a given phenomenon in international relations can be considered and solved." (Lenin, *Collected Works*, 3rd Russian Edition, 1935, vol. 12, p. 317). And this is no isolated passage. In volume 18 of the same title, Lenin states: "We Marxists have always stood, and do stand, for a revolutionary war against counter-revolutionary peoples. For example, if Socialism were to be victorious in America or in Europe in 1920 while, let us say, Japan or China were advancing their Bismarcks against us . . . then we certainly would be for an aggressive revolutionary war against them." (*Collected Works*, vol. 18, p. 250). Volume 23 of the same work declares that "The character of the war (whether reactionary or revolutionary) is not determined by who the aggressor was, or whose land the 'enemy' has occupied. It is determined by the class which is waging the war and the politics of which this war is the continuation." (vol. 23, p. 380). In another book, Lenin wrote that "If war is waged by the proletariat after it has conquered the bourgeoisie in its own country and is waged with the object of strengthening and extending Socialism, such a war is legitimate and 'holy'." (Lenin, *Left Wing Childishness and Petit-Bourgeois Mentality*, vol. 22, p. 510, Russian edition).

Communist military aggression in Korea is but another proof that war is an essential element of Soviet foreign policy. The use of war to spread Communism originated with Lenin, and continues as basic to Soviet policy since Lenin. According to Lenin, war between states and civil strife both promote revolution, and only violence can over-throw capitalism and establish "proletarian dictatorship". Soviet em-phasis on war as an instrument of policy is not merely the product of "capitalist encirclement"—as is occasionally proclaimed by Soviet apologists. Lenin enunciated the policy of war as a means of world revolution two years before the Bolshevik seizure of power, and even longer prior to the alleged "capitalist encirclement." In a revealing article on "Disarmament" (*Sbornik Sotsial-Demokratia*, 1915), Lenin attacked the "fundamental mistake of certain revolutionary socialists who are advocates of disarmament." He declared: "It would be abso-lutely wrong, theoretically, to forget that war is the continuation of politics by other means." Lenin went on to state the "inevitability, first, of revolutionary national uprisings and wars; second, wars and revolts of the proletariat against the bourgeoisie, and third, the unity of both kinds of wars. . . . Disarmament is not an international pro-gram of the revolutionary proletariat. . . . Only after we have com-pletely forced down and expropriated the bourgeoisie of the whole world and not of one country alone. . . . Only after the disarmament of the bourgeoisie by the proletariat can the latter, without betraying its world-historical task, throw armaments on the scrap heap. . . . The victory of Socialism in one country . . . implies wars." (Quoted by Lewis Corey in the *New Leader*, June 25, 1951).

Pacifism has always been emphatically rejected by the Soviet lead-ership. With sarcastic contempt, Lenin said: "Peace at any price is a silly wishful sigh. . . . Pacifism and abstract propaganda in favor of peace are one of the means of fooling the working class. Wars are inevitable under capitalism . . . The party of the working class is obliged to fight against the trends of pacifism and democraticism in general." (Quoted by David Dallin in *The New Soviet Empire*, Yale University Press, 1951, p. 71). It is a basic premise of Soviet policy that every great war engenders revolution, and that every great revolution is linked to war. Lenin wrote that inasmuch as war was inevitable, it would be preferable "rather than fight it, prepare for it. . . . Since the Russian revolution was only the first in a new series of revolutions, wars are inevitable, and have to be expected in the future." (*Ibid.*, p. 72). Not only that, but Lenin insisted "we would not only be fools but criminals if we promised never to commit an act which could be considered aggressive in a military, strategic sense". (*Ibid.*, p. 73).

Lenin's conception of war as basic Soviet policy was adopted by Stalin, when he wrote in 1922: "The object of our strategy is to gain time . . . to take advantage of conflicts in the camp of the imperialists, to demoralize the forces of the enemy, and to accumulate forces in order to later assume the offensive." (Quoted by Corey, *New Leader*, June 25, 1951, p. 16). A year later Stalin, in his book *Marxism and the National Question*, emphasized the right of revolution by military force to achieve power regardless of national rights. This was in connection with the Soviet invasion of Poland in 1920: "There are cases when the right to self-determination enters into conflict with another, a higher principle, namely, the right of the working class, of the Communist Party, to strengthen its regime once it has achieved power. In such cases, and this must be stated frankly, the right of self-determination cannot and must not serve as a barrier to the realization of the right of the working class to its dictatorship. . . . Such was, for instance, the case in 1920 when we were forced to march on Warsaw to promote the power of the working class." (*Loc. cit.*).

While the Foreign Office of the Soviet Government, both in the League of Nations and in the United Nations stresses its rejection of war as an instrument of policy, the Comintern, and after it the Cominform, give a truer indication of what Soviet policy in effect must be. In 1928 the Comintern resolved: "The Soviet Union harbors no illusions as to the possibility of a durable peace. . . . Wars between proletarian and bourgeois states will necessarily and inevitably arise." It went on to proclaim that Communists must "combat all high-sounding phrases like 'we shall never permit another war', 'no more war', etc. . . . Leninism combats all pacifist theories concerning the abolition of war. . . . Wars of proletarian dictatorship against world capitalism are inevitable and revolutionary." (Resolutions of the Sixth World Congress of the Communist International, 1928, p. 9).

Lenin made himself quite clear when he wrote: "The Communist Party emphatically rejects the reactionary illusions of petit-bourgeois democrats about achieving disarmament under capitalism. It sets against them . . . the slogan of crushing the resistance of exploiters, of a fight to victory over the bourgeoisie of the whole world, both internal civil wars and international wars." (Lenin, *Collected Works*, 3rd Russian edition, vol. 22, p. 97).

The Soviet Union has at least eight times resorted to war as an instrument of policy. The first of these was the Soviet invasion of Poland in 1920. Rejecting offers of peace and mediation from London, Paris, and Warsaw, Lenin decided to attack Warsaw, and then drive on into Germany, the long-sought Soviet prize in Europe. The original defensive war became frankly and avowedly offensive. From the Polish war arose the conception that the Soviet Union is entitled to wage offensive war, and that such a war is "just"—a war of "libera-

tion". Thus we have the "liberation" of Poland, the Baltic states, the
central and east European states, and China and Korea.

The second war waged by the Soviet state was the 1929 attack in
Manchuria. One year after the U.S.S.R. adhered to the Kellogg-
Briand pact outlawing war, Soviet military forces attacked Chinese
forces in wanton aggression, primarily to secure control of the prized
Chinese Eastern Railway. The Litvinov legend—Maxim Litvinov's
repeated assertion that the Soviet Government would never start a
war—was assiduously kept alive throughout the 'thirties, in spite of
considerable Soviet aid and encouragement to the Negrin regime in
Spain, aid extending to complete control of the "Loyalist" Department
of Defense. The Socialist Defense Minister, Indalecio Prieto, testified that Spaniards were unable to control this department—that complete control resided in Soviet General Goriev and the commanders
of the International Brigades.

In spite of the repeated assertions of peaceful intent, eagerly accepted at face value by many who simultaneously were not fooled by
similar Fascist and Nazi assertions, the Soviet government was planning another major military venture in the late 'thirties. Lev Mekhlis,
editor of *Pravda,* stated early in 1939 that in case of war, "military
operations must be transferred to the territory of the enemy; we must
fulfill our obligations and increase the number of Soviet Republics."
(Eighteenth Congress of the Communist Party of the Soviet Union,
Moscow, 1939, p. 273). A year earlier Stalin, in his famous *History
of the Communist Party,* reiterated the Soviet thesis of a "just" war.
In the fall of 1939 the Soviet Government waged the third of its wars.
By agreement with the German Government, Soviet armies attacked
Poland from the east in mid-September, and conquered the eastern
half of that unhappy country. Two months later the Soviets waged
their fourth war of aggression, this time against little Finland. Without any declaration of war, the Soviet Government, after three months
hard fighting, finally overcame the stout Finnish defense.

The fifth war in which the Soviet Union engaged was the war with
Germany, from mid-1941 to mid-1945. This war was defensive until
1944, when the Soviets "liberated" eastern and central Europe, to
transform once independent states into Soviet republics called "people's democracies". In 1947 the Soviet Government directed its satellites in Yugoslavia, Bulgaria, and Albania to attack Greece, under the
guise of "sympathy" for the Communist guerrillas in rebellion against
the Greek Government. The United Nations Commission found all
three Soviet satellites guilty of aggression. So far as is known, however, no Soviet troops were actually involved, although Soviet muni-

tions and supplies were present in considerable number. The sixth war—offensive in nature, which the U.S.S.R. took part in, was the attack on Japan on August 9, 1945. Japan had been all but defeated, and six days later Japan capitulated after four years of battle with the United States and the British Commonwealth allies in the Pacific. The war had been fought to achieve "national goals"—the acquisition of Chinese ports, the removal of industrial machinery to Russia, forced labor by Japanese, annexation of large territories with non-Russian populations. The seventh war was the Soviet-directed war of the Chinese Communist armies against the Chinese National Government, resulting in the acquisition of the greatest of all the Soviet-controlled states. The eighth war was the Soviet-directed attack against the Republic of Korea, on June 25th, 1950. In this war, so carefully pre- pared for by the Soviets, huge quantities of Soviet guns, tanks, planes, and, perhaps, Soviet military personnel in at least supervisory capaci- ties, played key roles. Without the supporting hand of the U.S.S.R., neither Communist China nor the puppet north Koreans were capa- ble of sustaining a major war effort. This aggressive war had, by mid-1952 inflicted 110,000 casualties on the United States, and well over 400,000 casualties on its Korean ally. (Dallin, *op. cit.*, pp. 70-84).

Communism has gained control of no state outside Russia other than through violence, and either military or diplomatic intervention by the Soviet Union. The failure of Communist parties at the polls, and the inability of any Communist party to achieve a monopoly of politi- cal power by itself, has increased the Soviet Union's use of war as an instrument of national policy. The states of east-central Europe with rather small Communist parties had little enthusiasm for Communism. Communism gained control in these countries because of Soviet mili- tary and diplomatic acts. On the other hand France and Italy had rather sizeable Communist factions after 1944, but the Soviet Union failed to gain control of those states because of its failure to move in directly. In Poland, Hungary, Rumania, Bulgaria, Albania, East Ger- many, and the Baltic states, the Soviet Army was employed to impose Communist regimes. While there was no Soviet Army as such in Czechoslovakia in 1948, the presence of Soviet troops in the back- ground, and probably as well in plain clothes roles, paralyzed resist- ance to the capture of power by the Communist minority. Soviet Russia supplied arms and military training for the Chinese Commu- nists, while in north Korea the Russians set up a Communist dictator- ship, trained and equipped its army, and turned it loose upon the Republic of Korea. Soviet troops of occupation in Manchuria also worked to impose Communism, unloading large supplies of captured

Japanese munitions for Mao Tse-tung's soldiers, to be used against the Chinese Government. The Chinese Communist regime has chosen the path of war not only in Korea, but also in Tibet, and perhaps Indo-China and Formosa.

Communism is basically Soviet power, and Soviet power essentially comprises Soviet economic and military strength, and superior Soviet diplomacy. It was not the attractiveness of Communism as an idea which led to Communism's success in Poland and Korea: it was the power of the Soviet state, militarily and diplomatically, that made the difference. Ireland, India, and the Latin American states have low standards of living, yet Communism has failed to make great headway in most of these countries. The German and Austrian federal republics have labored under severe economic handicaps since 1945, yet the Communist parties of these states are very small indeed. Let us assume that every south-east Asian had a full belly and a high standard of living—would that prevent a repetition of Soviet successes in Korea and eastern Europe? Czechoslovakia had a rather high standard of living, a rather healthy economy, but that did not prevent Soviet seizure of that country, and its transformation into a "people's republic". Indeed Moscow has demonstrated that for considerable periods power becomes the primary factor in history, while economic phenomena are products of and deviations from it. The well-known Marxist formula of economic determinism has been reversed: power serves as the "foundation" and economics as the "superstructure".

Power is the midwife, Marx once said, at the birth of a new society. In this respect a curious reversal of roles has occurred in the middle of the twentieth century. The Soviets stress power as the key to success in establishing Communism in a state. But the western world, trying to understand Soviet victories and the spread of Communism, digs into sociology, explaining Communist successes as the result of low living standards, land hunger in China, famine in India, poverty in eastern Europe. General Marshall, quite properly never suspected of Marxist views, elaborated a great plan to improve social conditions in Europe in order to prevent Communist victories. The essence of the so-called "Point Four" program is the belief that raised living standards and technical assistance to depressed areas will solve the Communist problem. Yet a glance at the record shows that millions in economic aid to France and Britain, far from decreasing pro-Soviet sympathies in those countries, have seen over the period 1948-1952 a rise in pro-Soviet feeling. On the other hand, countries like Spain, Sweden, Norway, Portugal, and many Latin American states, which

have received little or no aid from the United States, have little or
no Communist problem to contend with.

While we have been philosophizing about the abject poverty in the
Balkans or in China as the source of Communist successes, Moscow itself has not cared overly about the social conditions in its satellites.
Although chaos prevails in industry, trade remains disrupted, and
famine threatens, Malenkov is confident that no danger will arise
from the satellites so long as Soviet machinery dominates the "people's democracies." Nor is Malenkov in doubt as to whether, contrary to Marxian precepts, the most backward peoples of his backward realm, such as the north Koreans and the inhabitants of Sinkiang
and Tibet, are "ripe for Socialism". Police and army suffice to resolve
this problem; to Soviet Russia "political power is the creator of social
systems, not the other way around." (*Ibid.*, p. 27).

Soviet foreign policy and Communist successes abroad are, however, not solely based on Soviet military power, Soviet diplomacy, and
the effectiveness of Soviet fifth columns. Soviet policy retains the initiative, and succeeds propagandistically, because of a Soviet insistence on maintenance of prestige. The Big Three wartime conferences
had to be held on Russian soil or nearby soil. American diplomats,
citizens, and flyers are ordered out, imprisoned, and shot down, and
there is no retaliation. Communist China attacks Korea, but Korean
and American fighting men cannot retaliate against China. At every
turn the Soviet Union and its allies insist on, and increase their prestige. The "UN" negotiators at Panmunjom continually seek some "formula" which will allow the Chinese and Korean Communists an ave-
nue of escape to "save face." George Kennan, leading State Department specialist on the Soviet Union, wrote an article in *Foreign Affairs*
in 1947 which he signed "X". This article broke with all appeasement
policies, and enunciated the program of "containment". But Mr.
Kennan then went on to say: "It is a *sine qua non* of successful dealing with Russia that . . . demands on Russian policy should be put
forward in such a manner as to leave the way open for a compliance
not too detrimental to Russian prestige." ("Sources of Soviet Conduct",
Foreign Affairs, July 1947, p. 576).

To "leave the way open" means that while trying to stem the Soviet
offensive the United States must at the same time build a golden
bridge for a Soviet retreat; it must help the Kremlin to take a way
back which can be pictured as a successful offensive by Kremlin public
relations men. But, as David Dallin so aptly pointed out, policies of
this kind cannot be effective in the case of the Soviet Union because
"they leave untouched the very source of imperial power and the

cement that holds the structure together—prestige and the legend of invincibility." Neville Chamberlain, the great engineer of golden bridges for Adolf Hitler, has already shown how bankrupt is the policy of Mr. Kennan in this regard. Two years of negotiations at Panmunjom, on top of endless and fruitless talks with Russia on the German and Austrian questions—during all of which the western powers sought vainly to "compromise" in order to leave Soviet prestige and success unimpaired—all this is additional proof of the impossibility of the "golden bridge" approach. (Dallin, *op. cit.*, pp. 34-39.)

To Moscow, the cold war (which continues in Europe even though the hot war started in Asia in 1950) is largely a matter of building up Soviet prestige and aura of invincibility, and of correspondingly deflating American prestige. With calculated moves, Moscow tries to damage America's prestige all over the world by making her appear ridiculous, helpless, and weak. Every ounce of prestige lost by the United States is an ounce gained for Soviet power. This is true in the Angus Ward case, the Robert Vogeler case, the Koje Island disorders, and the shooting down of unarmed American, French, and Swedish aircraft. In the spring of 1951 Communist armies were on the run in Korea and American prestige ran high in Asia. As was the case during the Chinese civil war, when the Communists were losing, they would ask for a "truce", to stop the enemy advance and gain time to build up shattered strength. Jacob Malik of the Soviet Union hinted that the Communists might be "willing" to talk truce. Instead of pressing its advantage, the United States and the United Nations jumped through the Soviet hoop and accepted the notion of debating the enemy instead of defeating him. We lost our advantage, and the Soviets immediately posed as the champions of "peace"—the honest broker. The prestige we lost was gained by the Soviet Government.

The main weapons of Soviet foreign policy have been summarized by Stalin as follows: "(1) to utilize every contradiction and conflict among surrounding capitalist groups and governments for the purpose of disintegrating imperialism; (2) to spare no pains or means to assist the proletarian revolutions of the west; (3) to take all necessary measures to strengthen the national liberation movement in the east, and (4) to strengthen the Red Army." (Stalin, "The Party Before and After the Seizure of Power", *Works*, Moscow, 1947, vol. 5, p. 111.) There is nothing to indicate any deviation from these principles by Malenkov, who predicted in 1949 that "a third world war will mean the end of world capitalism."

2

Soviet Policies in Action

Robert Strausz-Hupé and Stefan Possony, in their work entitled *International Relations* (McGraw-Hill, 1950), accurately describe the role of diplomacy in Soviet foreign policy as follows: "Diplomacy is a major *offensive* weapon in the arsenal of world revolution." They go on to point out that "The Soviets are innately incapable of using diplomatic tactics different from those described by Machiavelli . . . unless they give up their objective of World Communism—which would be tantamount to giving up themselves." (p. 740). American diplomats are in the habit of negotiating with the Soviet Union on the assumption that diplomacy is a means of settling disputes and adjusting national conflicts by compromise; for the Soviets, however, diplomacy replaces or supports revolutionary attack.

March 1917 marked the end of the monarchy in Russia. A few months later, the provisional republican government, which tried simultaneously to bring democracy to Russia and continue the war effort against the Central Powers, was overthrown by the Bolshevik coup d'etat of November, 1917. The German General Staff had carried Lenin and other Bolshevik leaders by train from Switzerland to Russia with express instructions to overthrow the Kerensky government and conclude an armistice with the Central Powers, allowing Germany to turn her entire attention to the subjugation of France. On March 3, 1918, the Soviet leaders signed the Treaty of Brest-Litovsk, with the Central Powers. Actually, there was little else for the Soviets to do. German armies were moving on Petrograd, and had the Bolsheviks chosen to resist, their shaky regime would certainly have been toppled, and Communism would have come to an inglorious end. Lenin justified the treaty in the following words: "Having started as a spectacular success in one country, revolution may have to go through periods of trial because final victory is possible only on a world-wide scale and through the united efforts of workers in all countries. Our task is to exercise tact and caution; we must maneuver and retreat until reinforcements come to our aid." (Quoted in *Trends in Russian Foreign Policy Since World War I*, prepared by the Library of Congress for the Committee on Foreign Relations, 80th Congress, 1st session, 1947, p. 1). Lenin made this decision in the face of strong opposition from Trotsky and other hot heads who felt it was a betrayal of Marx to make a "deal" with any imperialist government. Lenin pointed out, however, that Communist revolutions throughout the world were nowhere succeeding, and that it was necessary first to build up the Soviet base of operations or "vanguard", and then to spread Communism through the use of Soviet military power, Soviet diplomacy, and Soviet fifth columns abroad—the Communist parties. For the impatient Marxists, it was a bitter pill to have to swallow, for they had confidently expected spontaneous Communist revolutions to occur throughout the world in the wake of the devastation and unrest caused by World War I.

The years 1917 to 1921 were years of civil war, war with Poland, and near war with the Allies. At times, the Soviet state was reduced to the insignificant size of early medieval Russia. But the newly created Red Army, led by Trotsky and several former Tsarist generals, was able to stave off disaster, partly because of the military and psychological blunders of the anti-Bolshevik groups, and partly because of the lukewarm support given by the Allied Powers to the anti-revolutionary White movement. Commenting on this many years later, Winston Churchill declared: "The failure to strangle Bolshevism at its birth and to bring Russia . . . by one means or another into the general democratic system lies heavy upon us today." (Speech at the Mid-Century Convocation, Massachusetts Institute of Technology, March 31, 1949).

At the same time that the new Russian government ostensibly collaborated with the Germans after Brest-Litovsk, it engaged in open and clandestine propaganda and subversive activities to further the cause of world revolution, concentrating largely on fostering revolution in Germany and Austria. During 1918 the various national minorities inside and on the peripheries of Russia revolted, and proclaimed their independence. This included the Baltic nations, the Ukraine, White Russia, and the Caucasian and Trans-Caucasian peoples. At first the Soviet regime could do little about these revolts, but later it gained sufficient strength to put many of them down, to retain most of these nations within the Russian Empire. By the end of 1918 the revolutions in Germany, Austria, and Hungary had broken out, but quickly failed, except for a few months of bloody success in Hungary, where Bela Kun established a Bolshevik dictatorship. The Bolsheviks did receive unexpected support when the western Allies forced the Germans to evacuate the occupied Russian provinces in the west. The Red Army wasted little time in re-occupying these areas, and wiped out the various autonomous, puppet, and anti-Bolshevik administrations.

On March 4, 1919, the Communist International (Comintern) was established by the Soviet Government, to support and guide revolutionary movements abroad. The International was quickly created in all important countries of the world, and was adhered to by all Communist parties. It was to remain for many years the vehicle which carried the instructions, personnel, and supplies from the Kremlin to Soviet fifth columns in every country of the world. The Second Comintern Congress, held in July 1920, in Moscow, proclaimed that the "Communist International declares the cause of Soviet Russia to be its own cause, and that the international proletariat will not lay down its arms until Soviet Russia has become a member of a World Federation of Soviet Republics."

By November, 1920, the backbone of the White (anti-Bolshevik) armies had been broken. In that month General Wrangel ordered the evacuation of remaining anti-Bolshevik forces from the Crimean peninsula. This followed the defeat of White armies in the Ukraine, White Russia, and in the Archangel-Murmansk area. These various anti-Bolshevik groups had been operating on the periphery of Russia for several years—largely out of contact with one another, poorly supplied and equipped, and plagued by internal political controversies between monarchists, republicans, Social Revolutionaries (radical peasants) and Mensheviks (evolutionary Socialists). The failure of the Whites was enhanced by the refusal of the British, French, American, and Japanese forces who temporarily occupied Archangel, Murmansk, Odessa, and Vladivostok to guard Allied supplies, to render any substantial assistance to the anti-Bolshevik cause. Of all the Allied troops in Russia, the Japanese, on the Siberian mainland, were the last to leave. Their departure in 1922 was due largely to the pressure exerted by the United States. This withdrawal coincided with the collapse of the White regime of Admiral Kolchak in Siberia.

In 1920, the Soviet Union became involved in a war with Poland. The Polish state had been reestablished in 1918 after over a century of Russian, German, and Austrian occupation. But efforts of the Polish Government to return to the eastern boundary which preceded the Russian seizure of 1772 were resisted by the Red Army, which then began to march through Poland towards Warsaw. Polish forces rallied outside the gates of the capital, however, and under the leadership of French General Maxim Weygand, repulsed the Bolshevik invasion. At this time several European governments, notably the French, considered intervening to push the Bolsheviks entirely outside the 1772 Polish-Russian frontier, but the idea died stillborn. This excellent opportunity to smash the Soviet regime was to some degree not taken

advantage of due to the propaganda activities of the Third International, as well as the natural war-tiredness of the European populations. Agents of the Comintern organized strikes in European ports,
preventing shipments of arms to the Polish Army. Systematic Communist propaganda exploited the postwar fatigue of the French and
British. The threatened rout of the Red Army turned into a stalemate,
and the Treaty of Riga (1921) established a Polish-Russian boundary
which was to remain in effect until the Hitler-Stalin pact and the Yalta
decisions—both of which gave to Soviet Russia Polish territory in
eastern Poland—half of the entire Polish state.

March of 1921 found the Soviet regime at peace, but in a seriously
weakened condition. Although it had survived the civil war and the
war with Poland, it was plagued with internal discontent and the loss
of many nations of old imperial Russia. The Baltic states, Poland,
and central Europe were now independent, and national aspirations in
the Ukraine and the Caucasus and Trans-Caucasus continued. It was
only through bitter and bloody fighting that the Red Army and its
local allies crushed the popular uprisings in Georgia, Azerbaijan,
Armenia, Bokhara, and the Ukraine. Elaborate treaties of federation
were concluded with the new Communist regimes of these territories,
and while the world looked on in a state of paralysis, the principle of
national self-determination was violated repeatedly, while the Soviet
Government extended its centralized control over these areas. These
Soviet repressions of national aspirations coincided with a new Soviet
ridicule of pacifism, and an emphasis on the necessity of Soviet military strength to achieve Communist control where "spontaneous"
Communist revolutions had everywhere failed.

The economic situation in Russia worsened steadily, as a result of
the war and unrest, and the failure of Marxist principles as applied
rigidly and ruthlessly to the Russian scene. In 1922 a great famine
spread throughout the countryside. The United States, while temporarily spurning diplomatic relations with the Soviet Union, supplied
the funds which enabled Herbert Hoover to set up an organization
for feeding the hungry population of Russia. The Soviets accepted
that help grudgingly, and put numerous obstacles in the way of a
humanitarian venture which profited only themselves. In order to
stabilize the internal economic situation, the Soviet regime made considerable concessions to the peasants in the New Economic Plan which
brought a limited type of private enterprise to Russia from the beginning of 1922 to 1928.

By the end of the civil war, Soviet diplomacy faced a dismal pros-
pect. Only a few countries had extended diplomatic recognition, and

foreign trade lagged badly. In 1922, however, the Soviet Union was
admitted to the Genoa Conference, which was to consider the economic and financial reconstruction of Europe. This conference made
little headway, in part because the Soviets were unwilling to make
restitution for confiscated property owned in Russia by foreigners. The
Genoa Conference was followed by an act of great international importance, however. Germany and the Soviet Union, both looked upon
with suspicion and distrust by the western world, concluded the Treaty
of Rapallo, on April 16, 1922. The Russo-German rapprochement was
the first major achievement of the young Soviet diplomatic corps. The
treaty remained the pivot of Soviet foreign policy during the following decade, and enabled the Soviet diplomats to play on the dissen-
sions between the countries of the western world. Rapallo began the
military cooperation between the Soviet leaders and the German generals which helped to circumvent the disarmament provisions of the
Versailles treaty. Having obtained diplomatic recognition from Germany, the Soviet regime was now approached by increasing numbers
of other states, with the result that the Soviet Union's position in the
international community was normalized. The culmination to this
development came in 1933 when the last of the great powers, the
United States, extended diplomatic recognition to the U.S.S.R. At the
same time trade agreements were concluded between the Communist
regime and neighboring states, with a resultant strengthening of
Russia's internal economic situation. This was accompanied by assistance from western technicians who travelled to Russia to help
industrialize the country.

While consolidating her position externally, in order to gain breathing space and build up at home, the Soviet Union continued agitation
in behalf of world revolution. The Third International supported a
Communist uprising in Germany, in spite of the Rapallo agreement.
The Constitution of 1922 declared that: "The instability of the international situation renders inevitable the creation of a common front
by the Soviet republics against capitalist encirclement. . . . The new
United State (the U.S.S.R.) shall stand as a firm bulwark against
world capitalism and form a decisive step toward the union of all the
workers of all countries into one World Socialist Soviet Republic."

Lenin's death in 1924 led to a struggle for power between Stalin
and Trotsky. Stalin's triumph in this struggle was followed by the
enunciation of his doctrine of "Socialism in one country." This doctrine, so much misunderstood by the non-Soviet world, implied abso-
lutely no abandonment of the long-term Soviet goal of world conquest. It merely established as a fact that the strengthening of the

Soviet base of operations, or "vanguard" must precede world revolution. After establishing Soviet type Socialism in Russia, there could ensue outside diplomatic, military, and fifth column activity leading to the extension of Communism to non-Soviet areas. Stalin declared: ". . . could the Russian Communists confine their work within the narrow bounds of the Russian revolution? Of course not." The Soviets must "go beyond these bounds in their work . . . to overthrow Capitalism in their own country and to forge a new fighting weapon for the proletariat . . . in order to facilitate the task of overthrowing capitalism for the proletarians of all countries." (*Problems of Leninism*, p. 6).

Soviet policy operated then, and continues to operate, on two fronts. One is the formal diplomatic front, and the other is the actual politico-military front, which may see a quite different behavior on the part of Soviet fifth columns as directed by the Comintern (now Cominform), or Communist armed units. Thus the 'twenties saw a Soviet diplomatic front which concluded non-aggression treaties with many states (to lull them into a false sense of security), while maintaining unimpaired revolutionary activity—especially in China. Indeed, Soviet revolutionary activity in Great Britain led to Comintern assistance to British Communists involved in the general strike of 1926, an action which caused suspension of British-Soviet relations until 1929. During the crisis in Anglo-Russian relations, the Soviets held fast to their pro-German policy. In 1926 the Treaty of Rapallo was reaffirmed by the Treaty of Berlin. The Soviet Government continued to support secret German armaments. Major Fritz Tschunke, an officer in charge of liaison between the Russian regime and German industry, testified: "It is no secret that, during the depression years Germany was kept afloat largely because it received substantial orders from the Russians. . . . these orders made it possible for our industry to maintain and enlarge its factories and workshops, to keep up with technological progress, to retain its force of skilled laborers and to educate young specialists. It is doubtful whether, under these conditions, so gigantic a rearmament program (as that of the Nazis) could have been accomplished as rapidly and effectively." (Memorandum to the German Government, September 22, 1939, as quoted by Strausz-Hupé and Possony, *op. cit.*, p. 745). Even after Hitler came to power, and Soviet Russia had an ostensible anti-Fascist tendency, Russia continued to maintain close economic relations with Germany, and German-Soviet commerce continued to facilitate German rearmament.

Soviet reaction to the League of Nations was, initially, to call it a capitalist plot; as time wore on, however, the Soviets saw in it excellent possibilities to spread Soviet psychological warfare, and to keep the non-Soviet world confused and divided when confronted with Soviet power. Litvinov, the Soviet Foreign Minister, called for disarmament in the League of Nations, but in fact was only interested in disarmament of the non-Soviet powers. He steadily opposed effective powers of inspection for disarmament teams, and used the League as a platform to increase the prestige and influence of the Soviet Government. The real attitude of the Soviet Government was far better revealed by the following 1928 Comintern resolution: "The aim of the Soviet proposals was not to spread pacifist illusions, but to destroy them; not to support capitalism . . . but to propagate the fundamental Marxian postulate that disarmament and the abolition of war are possible only with the fall of capitalism. . . . It goes without saying that not a single Communist thought for a minute that the imperialists would accept the Soviet disarmament proposals." (*International Press Correspondence*, English edition, Vienna, November 28, 1928, p. 1596).

As Germany and Japan posed an ever greater threat to Soviet spheres of interest, Communist policy attempted, in the middle 'thirties, to swerve away from the tie with Germany and the anti-Versailles line, and towards at least a temporary rapprochement with Great Britain, France, the United States, and China. The U.S.S.R. entered the League of Nations in 1934, and concluded rather vague sounding military agreements with France and Czechoslovakia in 1935. The same year saw the signing of a quite meaningless non-aggression pact between the Soviet Union and China. The years 1929 to 1934 had seen a return to active Soviet revolutionary activity, all the way from China to Spain. Stalin made every effort to undermine the non-Soviet areas during the depression years, while maintaining the German friendship policy. After 1935, however, Stalin saw that it was to his advantage to employ as a tactical maneuver an approach to the anti-Nazi and anti-Fascist coalition. This tactical change also had its manifestation in Comintern and foreign Communist activity. Prior to 1933, foreign Communist parties had made no efforts to camouflage their revolutionary doctrine. The common caricature of the Communist with disshevelled hair, a wild look in his eye, and a bomb in his pocket, was not too far from the truth. But by the middle 'thirties, the foreign Communist combed his hair, put on a tie, put the bomb away in safe-keeping, wore a blue serge suit, and appeared as an honest "liberal" who wanted to improve living standards, correct abuses, and fight Fascism. Whereas formerly Socialists and other reformist groups had been looked upon as "social Fascists" (this included Franklin Roosevelt and the "New Deal"), Communists now were instructed to join together with these reformist groups, to form a "popular front" of Communists, Socialists, and "liberals". The purpose was to ride into political power as part of a "liberal" or anti-Fascist coalition, and then increase Communist strength and influence inside the coalition with the intent of achieving ultimately a monopoly of power. This actually happened in Spain, when the Popular Front of 1936 was transformed into a tool of the Communists and Soviet foreign policy. The Spanish Communist leader Andres Nin proclaimed in the fall of 1936: "The Government no longer exists, we are the Government." The Socialist Minister of Defense soon discovered that Soviet General Goriev was running the "Loyalist" armies and International Brigades. The Communists enjoyed some successes in France, China, and the United States during the tactical period known as the "popular front" or "united front". It was during the five years before World War II that Soviet espionage and infiltration rings made their way into American government—among them the Harold Ware group, which included Alger Hiss.

As members of the League of Nations from 1934-1939, the Soviets not only proclaimed their undying allegiance to the principle of disarmament, but to collective security as well. The first real test of Soviet sincerity came with the Italo-Abyssinian conflict. In 1936, when the moment came to act collective security as well as preach it, the Russians stood quietly aside. They maintained commercial relations with Italy and increased their sale of oil to that country (see especially Max Beloff, *The Foreign Policy of Soviet Russia*, New York, Oxford, vol. I, p. 202). It is of course true, that Soviet behavior was no worse than that of the democratic states. The point is, however, that they not only acted in the same manner, but that they also benefitted from the fact that "capitalistic" oil firms indeed had reduced their sales to Italy. Inasmuch as the Russian Government owned and operated its petroleum industry, it was clear that if the Russians sold and carried oil to Italy, it was governmental policy—a policy that contradicted the principle of collective security so ardently professed by Soviet diplomats at Geneva.

Soviet behavior during the Czech crisis in 1938 was another example of the Kremlin professing one thing, while simultaneously doing the reverse. The Russian military agreement with Czechoslovakia stipulated that Soviet aid would be extended to the Czechs if France also supported them. Neither country did, in fact, extend any aid to Czechoslovakia. Soviet propaganda nevertheless disseminated the

impression that Russia was ready to stand by Czechoslovakia. However, the official *History of Diplomacy*, edited by Vladimir Potem-
kiene, former Soviet Deputy Foreign Commissar, states that the
U.S.S.R. did not think the pact had lost its effectiveness because the
French did not act. Indeed this history claims the Soviet Union
was still willing to help if the Czech Government asked for assistance.
But the fact is that whereas the Soviets talked very tough to the Polish
Government about having troops on the Czech frontier, it never addressed any complaints to the Nazi regime. Furthermore, if the Russians had contemplated any moves to aid Czechoslovakia, they would
have had to march through Poland or Rumania. Yet there is no evidence that the Soviet Union ever approached either the Poles or the
Rumanians to obtain rights of transit and offer guarantees that Russian troops would get out at the end of the operation. The Soviet
Government was, at this time, also rather loud in its demands that
the League of Nations take action under Article XI of the Covenant
(calling for League sanctions to safeguard peace when war threatened). Again there was no Soviet action in this regard. If Russia had
invoked either Article XI or X she might have strengthened the cause
of collective security, and could have forced a vote at Geneva which
England and France would have had to act upon. It was clearly
within Russia's power to observe the procedures of collective security
which she advocated. Instead, the Soviet Union suggested through
private channels that *other* governments take action (see Strausz-
Hupé and Possony, *op. cit.*, pp. 749, 750). Not only that, but at the
height of the Czech crisis, President Benes tried to reach Stalin by
phone. Stalin was nowhere to be found. Clearly enough, Stalin
would have been available if the Soviet Union had any intention of
standing by Czechoslovakia. It has been charged by some that the
Munich pact was an attempt on the part of France and Britain to iso-
late Russia—a charge nowhere supported, not even by Soviet documents themselves. The purpose of the Anglo-French policy was prevention or delay of war (very much like U.S.-U.N. policy in Korea in
1951 and 1952). It was the result of appeasement and not of any anti-
Russian policy. The Soviets, far from taking action themselves, were
just as guilty of appeasement as the western powers.

The spring of 1939 saw Soviet foreign policy swing back to a pro-
German orientation. The Soviet Ambassador in Berlin, Merekalov,
was instructed to open up negotiations with the Nazis with a view
to establishing a complete Russo-German solidarity with which to con-
front the "decadent democracies." In May, 1939, Litvinov was replaced as Foreign Commissar by Molotov, to indicate to the Nazis

that no Jewish citizen of the U.S.S.R. would stand in the way of Russo-German friendship. The talks became increasingly friendly, culminating in Von Ribbentrop's visit to Moscow, and the conclusion of the secret protocol of August 23rd, 1939. The existence of this protocol was unknown to the outside world for nine years. All that was made public by the two dictators was an innocuous nonaggression pact, which made it appear that the Soviet Union was merely going to remain neutral during the period of German aggression. In fact, the secret protocol makes it clear that Stalin and Hitler must *jointly* share the guilt of starting World War II. The protocol planned the joint Nazi-Soviet aggression of the first year and one-half of the second world war. By its terms Russia achieved spheres of interest in eastern Poland, the Baltic states, Bessarabia, and northern Bucovina (the latter two being Rumanian territories). Molotov boasted: "One swift blow to Poland, first by the German Army and then by the Red Army, and nothing was left of this ugly offspring of the Versailles treaty . . ." (U.S. Department of State, *Nazi-Soviet Relations, 1939-1941*, Washington, Government Printing Office, 1948, p. 78). The Soviet Government concluded its successful negotiations for war at precisely the same time that it pretended to negotiate with British and French political and military representatives in Moscow for peace.

The Hitler-Stalin pact also saw a rapprochement between Russia and Italy, and Russia and Japan. Thus *de facto*, the Soviet Union became a member of the Axis. The alliance with Japan, formally concluded in the early spring of 1941, coincided with successful efforts of the Soviet spy ring in Tokyo, led by Richard Sorge, to deflect Japanese aggression away from the north, and turn it instead southwards—towards American and British and Dutch interests in the Pacific. The Soviet Union in fact knew of the Pearl Harbor attack months before it occurred, but never bothered to inform the United States Government, even after the Germans attacked Russia in the summer of 1941, and the United States and Britain gave Russia all-out support. (For the Pearl Harbor aspect of Soviet policy and the Sorge spy ring, see Ralph de Toledano, *Spies, Dupes, and Diplomats*, New York, Duell, Sloan, and Pearce, 1952, pp. 102-121.)

Not only did Soviet military forces conquer eastern Poland, portions of Rumania, and the Baltic states, but they started a major war in Finland—a war which they badly bungled. Had Finland received any aid from the western powers the entire course of World War II might have been changed. The best the League of Nations could do was to expel Russia from its membership. Meantime, after initial reverses, Soviet armies finally overwhelmed the gallant and undermanned

Finns in the early spring of 1940. Simultaneously, the Soviet Union
was living up to Stalin's pledge to Germany: "The Soviet Union would
never stand for Germany's getting into a difficult position". Russia
supplied Germany's military machine with badly needed raw materials—especially oil, iron ore, scrap iron, chromium, manganese, plati-
num, phosphates, foodstuffs, cotton, and lumber. Telegrams of con-
gratulations were sent by Stalin to Hitler following German military
moves into Poland, the Low Countries, and France. Communist parties in foreign lands were directed by the Comintern to facilitate Germany's program. In France, the Communists did their utmost to
undermine national morale and to delay armaments. In the United
States they paralyzed several key industries to sabotage the lend-
lease effort; they also picketed the White House with Frederick V.
Field leading the American Peace Mobilization with chants: "The
Yanks Aren't Coming." Needless to say this attitude of the American
Communists ended abruptly with the German attack on Russia on
June 22nd, 1941. In addition to these actions, the Soviet Union supported German naval operations, facilitated German communications
with Japan, and lent diplomatic support to Germany's attack on Norway and Denmark.

At the end of 1940, the Nazi-Soviet coalition began a series of negotiations to more effectively seal off influence of the "decadent democracies" from Europe, Africa and Asia. Molotov was invited to Berlin,
where a map of the world was spread before him, and large blocks
of territory were provisionally given to Germany, Russia, Italy, and
Japan. Prior to this meeting, however, frictions had begun to develop
between the aggressor nations. This friction largely centered over
differing interpretations of the original secret protocol as it related
to the Balkans—especially Bulgaria. Molotov wanted precise German guarantees for Soviet hegemony in Bulgaria. Hitler countered
by offering Russia carte blanche south to the Indian Ocean, but ex-
cluding the Balkans. Negotiations ended in a stalemate, and in January, 1941, Hitler secretly decided upon Operation Barbarossa—the attack on the Soviet Union. The Nazi-Soviet agreement continued in
effect, however, until the day of the attack, with Russia ridiculing
American and British warnings that Hitler had decided to end the
honeymoon. Indeed Russian raw material shipments continued to
reach the German Army until the very day of the attack.

Soviet policy after June 22, 1941, was a desperate effort to survive.
The German armies sliced deep into Russia, like a hot knife through
butter. Russia's pleas for help were immediately answered by Britain
and the United States, with promises of unconditional all-out aid. The

wonder is that Germany was able to penetrate so deeply into Russian territory, while simultaneously garrisoning Fortress Europe and fighting in North Africa. The Soviet Government, on the other hand, was able to concentrate entirely on the western front, for its pact with Japan insured peace for Russia in the Far East.

From the beginning of the war with Germany until the battle of Stalingrad, at the end of 1942, the Soviet Union, by force of circumstances, was conciliatory to the West in the extreme. It re-established relations with the exiled Polish Government, and signed the Atlantic Charter on January 1, 1942 (Declaration of the United Nations). By the end of 1942, however, when it became clear that the German onslaught had been broken, the Russians regained their freedom of action, and became increasingly uncooperative. From 1943 to 1945 their policy was one of extracting major concessions from the western powers—who were still under the spell of the honeymoon with Russia. Despite promises to the contrary, the Russians kept their military operations completely secret. Allied personnel in Russia found their freedom of movement severely curtailed. American flyers from the Doolittle raid on Tokyo who were forced to land at Vladivostok were interned. The granting of air bases for shuttle bombing was delayed over and over again; the United States Air Force suffered very heavy losses due to Russian refusal to admit American fighter aircraft. (See John R. Deane, *The Strange Alliance*, New York, Viking, 1947, pp. 122-125). The Soviet Government broke its pledges on the return of lend-lease equipment, and concealed from the Russian people the almost superhuman American efforts to save Russia from destruction.

To force Great Britain and the United States into compliance, the Soviets repeatedly contrived to give the impression that they would conclude a separate agreement with Germany unless their demands were met. Indeed considerable evidence indicates that this is precisely what they did. Lest their brothers-in-arms grow sluggish, the Soviets accused the Unitd States and Britain several times of wanting to negotiate a separate peace with Germany—usually with the result that the western powers fell all over each other to make concessions and show their "good faith." After Stalingrad, the Soviets rigged their requests with a view not to defense against Germany, but rather with the intent of aggression and expansion into central Europe and the Far East. The conferences of Teheran, Yalta, and Potsdam served the purpose of furthering the new Soviet program of building a gigantic Empire both in the East and in the West.

James Burnham, in his incisive *The Struggle for the World* (John Day, 1947), holds that the "cold war"—a new war—World War III—

began in April, 1944, when Soviet agents aided an anti-Greek Government mutiny in Cairo. Whatever be the exact date, it is clear that Soviet policy, even during World War II, was oriented in the direction of achieving Soviet hegemony on the Eurasian continent by the mid-century, and whereas Anglo-American policy continued to be effusively pro-Soviet at least until 1946, the Soviets did not reciprocate. For them Germany was no longer the enemy. The enemy was the Anglo-American bloc. For this was potentially the only power group capable of offering any resistance to Soviet imperial designs. But from 1943 to 1946, maximum concessions were extracted from the western powers at the Teheran, Yalta, and Potsdam conferences, and at the Paris "peace" conference of 1946. The result of these conferences was the establishment of a new power situation which obliterated the once-free nations of central Europe and several in Asia, and made the Atlantic Charter look like a scrap of paper.

Poland was the first victim of the new Soviet policy. At the Teheran conference in 1943, Stalin was promised undetermined Polish territories in eastern Poland. This promise, made by President Roosevelt, was never communicated to the Polish Government. Then in August, 1944, the Soviet Army stood by quietly while the Polish Underground Army of General Bor-Komorowski was destroyed by the Germans in Warsaw. After having demanded that the Poles rise against the Nazis, the Russians refused to render any assistance, even after strong pleas from the Polish Government in London and President Roosevelt. The destruction of the Polish Home Army by the Germans was followed by Soviet invasion ("liberation") of eastern Poland. Soviet policy was crowned with success at the Yalta conference (1945) when the United States and Great Britain abandoned the Polish exile Government, and agreed to recognize the Soviet-sponsored Lublin Committee once that group "broadened" itself to include non-Communists, and held free elections. There were no free elections, and after allowing the non-Communist Mikolajczyk to assume an unimportant post in the government, the Soviet puppets forced him to flee for his life in 1947. In addition to this, Roosevelt and Churchill agreed to give Stalin eastern Poland up to the "Curzon line." This was a ruse to return to Russia those Polish territories assigned the U.S.S.R. by Hitler in the form of the Molotov-Ribbentrop line. The Curzon line had never been an agreed political boundary between Russia and Poland, and never included the province of Galicia—which was assigned to the Soviets at Yalta. The only agreed boundary between Poland and Russia had been the Riga line of 1921—reaffirmed several times in non-aggression pacts between Poland and the Soviet Union.

(For commentaries on the Polish question see the following: Jan Cie-chenowski, *Defeat in Victory*, Doubleday, 1947; Stanislaus Mikolajczyk, *The Rape of Poland*, Whittlesey House, 1948; Arthur Bliss Lane, *I Saw Poland Betrayed*, Bobbs Merrill, 1948).

Simultaneously with the conquest of Poland, the Soviet Government also acquired temporary control of Yugoslavia. At the time of Teheran, the western powers agreed to abandon the Yugoslav Government in exile, and throw their support to the Communist Tito-Broz. The result was a gradual weakening of the Chetnik forces of Mihailovich, culminating in the political murder by Tito of a man who had supported the Allies from the very start of World War II. Tito won control of Yugoslavia with U.S. and British military and economic assistance and proceeded to establish an absolute Communist dictatorship. (See David Martin, *Ally Betrayed*, Prentice-Hall, 1946; Leigh White, *Balkan Caesar*, Scribners, 1950; Hal Lehrman, *Russia's Europe*, Appleton, 1947.)

Soviet military action, together with diplomatic cooperation or diplomatic acquiescence, resulted in Soviet victories in Czechoslovakia, Bulgaria, Rumania, Hungary, and Albania. Most amazing of all these was the Bulgarian operation. The Soviet Union was not at war with Bulgaria. When, in 1944, the Bulgarians overthrew their pro-German Government and installed a government friendly to the Allies, it appeared that Russia would naturally accept Bulgaria's offer of aid against the retreating Germans. When the Red Army arrived at the Bulgarian frontier, there was no reason why the Soviets should have moved into a friendly country. Nevertheless Russia declared war on Bulgaria, invaded the country, and installed a Soviet regime. Albania was seized with Tito's aid, and has remained under Soviet control even after Tito's defection from the Soviet Empire. Hungary and Rumania were taken by the Soviet armies, and Communist regimes installed while the United States and Britain sent feeble notes of protest. It was said that there should be no interference "for the sake of Allied unity." The result was the negation of a semi-free election in Hungary which favored the anti-Communist Smallholder Party. In Czechoslovakia, the Soviets achieved supremacy in a coalition government after outlawing the largest pre-war Czech party, and then established a monopoly of political power in the coup d'etat of 1948.

In June, 1945, the Soviet policy-makers scored another great victory at the Potsdam conference. Here Stalin secured control of north East Prussia, eastern Germany, eastern Austria, and German external assets along the Danube. Berlin, the former German capital, was placed inside the Soviet zone, although provided with Four Power (the United States, Great Britain, France and the U.S.S.R.) Administration. The ineptitude of John G. Winant, American representative on the European Advisory Commission, in addition to a refusal on the part of the U.S. Department of State to make an issue of it, resulted in the western powers not having any legal path of entry into Berlin from their zones in western Germany.

With victory in Europe assured, the Soviet Union no longer needed the alliance with Japan. Soviet expansion in the Far East was presaged at Yalta when Russia promised to enter the Pacific war within a specified time limit after the defeat of Germany. Soviet expansion in the area was assured when the United States and Great Britain, without consulting the Chinese Government, gave to Russia effective control of the Manchurian railways, the ports of Dairen and Port Arthur, and de facto control of Mongolia and Sinkiang. This changed the balance of power in the Far East decisively in favor of the Soviet Union at the expense of our Chinese ally. Additionally, the Soviet Union was given southern Sakhalin, and the Kurile Islands, thus effectively outflanking Japan, as well as thrusting Russian power right into the lap of the war-weary Chinese Government. The western powers had, at the Cairo conference (1943) promised China the return of all Chinese territories seized by Japan. This agreement was expressly violated by the Yalta concessions to the Soviet Union. At the same time, the United States agreed to allow Soviet troops into Korea, as far as the 38th parallel, to accept Japanese surrenders in that area. This resulted in Soviet control of north Korea, and, in conjunction with the Manchurian and Liaotung peninsula concessions, paved the way for aggression into south Korea in June, 1950.

The Soviet Union did not enter the Pacific war until the last week of the fighting. As it turned out, Soviet entrance into the Pacific war was not only not needed by the United States and the British Commonwealth contingents, but it was undesirable. The leaders of the Kremlin realized, however, that Soviet participation in the war, however slight, would give Russia an excuse for having a hand in the Far Eastern political settlements, including Japan. Soviet activity in the Far East included Communist uprisings in Indo-China, Indonesia, Burma, Thailand, and Malaya. In many cases these Communists had collaborated with the Japanese during World War II. Indeed, the Japanese stimulated a nationalistic fever which the Communists used as a club against the British, the French, and the Dutch.

The diplomatic achievements of Soviet representatives at the United Nations Conference in San Francisco in mid-1945, were the capstone to the new Soviet policy. There the Soviet veto in the UN Security

Council was approved, Communist Poland was admitted to the UN, and anti-Communist Spain was excluded. With the aid of presiding officer Alger Hiss, a wave of pro-Soviet emotionalism spread to insure compliance with all Soviet requests. The very essence of the spirit at San Francisco was to bring the Soviet Union into the UN organization, no matter what the cost.

By the end of World War II the Soviet Union had greatly increased its territorial extent, and achieved de facto control over still other numerous territories. It had established a zone of domination between the Sea of Japan in the east and central Germany in the west. Stalin had succeeded where Hitler and Tojo had failed. Russia was the only true victor of the second world war. (For an excellent and comprehensive discussion of the political repercussions of World War II see William Henry Chamberlin, *America's Second Crusade*, Chicago, Regnery, 1951).

3

Soviet Peace Policies

Soviet foreign policy, in its activities against the Free World, has taken over many words and concepts associated with a free society—e.g., "freedom", "democracy", and "peace"—and perverted them in meaning to serve the Communist cause. A study of the word "peace" as used by the Soviets provides a clear case in point of this subversion. To be for "peace" in the Soviet Empire means that one must harvest the crops on time, fulfill the plan of deliveries to the State, support the Five or Six Year Plan in one's respective country, protect state property, "volunteer" for extra work or work more intensively, make all economies in the interest of the State, and support government loans. "Peace" means support for the conclusion of a Five Power Pact (including Red China), the "unification" of Germany (under Soviet aegis), the support of the Oder-Neisse line as the definitive border between Poland and Germany, and other Soviet projects. To be for "peace" one must support the government slate of candidates at "elections", and one must hate the western democracies and the non-Soviet realm generally. "Peace" means friendship for the U.S.S.R. and unqualified support of Stalin's policies throughout the world. In these and other ways the word "peace" is performing yeoman service in the cause of Communism and Soviet policy.

Even the most casual perusal of Communist literature will convince the reader that "peace" and hatred for the non-Soviet realm are synonymous terms. To be for "peace" one must hate especially the United States—the strongest of all non-Soviet countries. Within the Soviet Empire, the "peace" campaign incites hatred among all classes of people. Instruction for school children is based on the principle that: "Soviet patriotism is indissolubly connected with hatred toward the enemies of the Socialist Fatherland. 'It is impossible to conquer the enemy without having learned to hate him with all the might of one's soul . . .' Hatred fosters vigilance and irreconcilability toward the enemy and leads to the destruction of everything that prevents Soviet peoples from building a happy life. The teaching of hatred toward the enemies of the toilers enriches the conception of Socialistic humanism by distinguishing it from sugary and hypocritical 'philanthropy'". (*Small Soviet Encyclopedia*, Moscow, 1947, vol. 2, 1045).

The terms "war" and "peace" are interchangeable terms which the

Communists use to fit the mood and the propaganda line of the moment. The millions of words expended by Soviet writers and speakers against war, the numerous petitions circulated by "partisans of peace", the various "peace congresses", "peace protection laws", and the campaign against warmongering and praise for the blessings of peace, would naturally lead one to believe that pacificism would be extolled by all official Communist publications. A closer examination of the Soviet attitude, however, shows that all these fair words about peace and pacifism are mere words employed to delude non-Communists into being peaceful while the Communists do them in. Official Communist publications have never made any pretense about this; they condemn quite consistently both pacifism and pacifists. A fair example of the official Soviet view is found in the Soviet Dictionary of Foreign Words, edited by Professors Liekhin and Petrov, and published in 1949 by Gosizdat, Moscow. It defines pacifism in the following terms: "Pacifism—a bourgeois movement opposing all wars. Mendaciously masking themselves with the slogan of pacifism, the reactionaries oppose national-liberative, revolutionary, civil, and other just wars, the aim of which is the defense of the people against attacks from the outside, the liberation of people from capitalist slavery, the liberation of colonial and dependent countries from imperialist oppression. . . . The policy of the pacifists promotes imperialist, aggressive, and unjust wars." (p. 484).

The complete absurdity of the Soviet stand on disarmament, and evidence that for the Soviets "peace" means "war", is found in the following: "It goes without saying that not a single Communist thought for a moment that the imperialists would accept the Soviet disarmament proposals. . . . the disarmament policy of the Soviet Government must be utilized for purposes of agitation. . . . However, they must not be utilized as a pretext for advancing similar demands in capitalist countries, but as a means: (1) for recruiting sympathizers for the Soviet Union—the champion of peace and Socialism, (2) for utilizing the *results* of the Soviet disarmament policy and its exposure of the imperialists in the effort to eradicate all pacifist illusions and to carry on propaganda among the masses in support of the only way toward disarmament and abolition of war, viz., arming of the proletariat, overthrowing the bourgeoisie and establishing the proletarian dictatorship." (*International Press Correspondence*, No. 84, Nov. 28, 1928, vol. 8, pp. 1596-7).

For the Soviets, war and peace are interchangeable words, to be used as policy dictates. War may mean peace, and peace may mean war, the criterion being whether a particular movement or action is or is not beneficial to the Communist cause. Although soft-pedalled at times, the previously mentioned Communist distinction between "just" (pro-Communist) and "unjust" (anti-Communist) war is a vital part of the Communist philosophy. The October 1, 1950 issue of *Krasnaya Zvesda*, official Soviet War Ministry newspaper, gave as an example of a "just" war, that in which the "Great Fatherland of the Soviet people" fought the "fascist aggressors" in World War II. The paper omitted to mention the role played in this war by the United States and Great Britain, and failed to list territories seized by the Soviet Union during that war which were independent or non-Soviet prior to 1941. The "armed intervention of the American imperialists in Korea" is given as an example of an "unjust" war. This same newspaper described a "just" war as being one fought "for the liberation of colonies and dependent countries from the oppression of imperialists." This definition leaves to the Soviet Union, professed big brother and protector of small nations, the right to determine which nations are dependent on the imperialists. It is on the basis of this definition that the Communists have called the civil war of the Chinese Communists against the National Government as a move towards "peace". On September 27, 1950, Radio Prague reported: "Speaking about the peace campaign, the Premier said it was not enough to wish for peace but it was necessary to maintain it and often to fight for its maintenance. Recently Popular Democratic China had to fight for her peace which was disturbed by the reactionary Army of Chiang Kai-shek, armed and paid by the American capitalists."

Upon reading Clausewitz' dictum "a conqueror is a lover of peace", Lenin is said to have remarked: "Ah, very witty." The Warsaw "Partisans of Peace" declared in November, 1950 that "you have to attain peace through fighting." "Peace" postal stamps issued by the East German Communist regime in January, 1951 had printed on them: "Achieve peace by fighting." Stalin several times made it completely clear that real peace cannot exist until the Soviet Empire eliminates all non-Soviet states and establishes a world Soviet Empire. Obviously, then, a Soviet "peace" (i.e., a Soviet world), can only be achieved through war—wars to destroy non-Soviet states. The Russians, furthermore, enjoy a very convenient ambiguity of the Russian word *mir* (peace). For when they are parading under the banner "We demand peace" (*Trebuyem mira*), the same words proclaim "We demand the world."

According to the Soviets, the Viet Minh forces similarly were acting for "peace" when they attacked native anti-Communist and French forces in Indo-China. Radio Moscow asserted on August 29, 1951:

"The just war on the part of the Vietnamese enjoys the warmest support of democratic and peace-loving fighters of the entire world." In the same vein, Radio Moscow, had, on the previous day characterized the tasks of the Moroccan Communists in the following terms: "The plenary session of the Central Committee of the Moroccan Communist Party, held on March 20, 1949, pointed out in its summation: 'The best way to fight for peace in Morocco is . . . striking blows at the imperialist forces and consolidating the Moroccan national movement. Striking blows at the imperialist forces means weakening their military potential; strengthening the national movement means making the rear lines of the warmongers untenable."

Thus the Viet Minh and the Chinese Communists make peace by waging war; thus peace will come to French Morocco through war against the French; peace will come to Korea through war by the Communists against the United States, the Republic of Korea, and United Nations members present there. Black is white and white is black.

The Soviet Union not only is capable of justifying a war against the "capitalists" and "imperialists", but even against a Communist country if that country happens to be unfriendly to the Soviet Union. The suppression of Tito is regarded as the only event which will avert "war". Radio Sofia broadcast the following on October 28, 1950: ". . . The place of the Yugoslav peoples is in the first ranks of the fighters for peace against the Anglo-American warmongers and their henchman, Tito. That is why the fight for peace is indivisible from the fight against Tito's gang . . ." In addition to this, certain *bona fide* national wars of liberation are, in Soviet terminology "unjust" if they are contrary to the best interests of World Communism. Thus the national liberation wars in the Baltic states and in the trans-Caucasus after 1919 were "unjust wars" to be suppressed by the Soviet Union.

In order to qualify as a "peaceful country", a state must acknowledge the infallibility of the Soviet Union. A Moscow Tass Agency dispatch of October 17, 1950, characterized the situation in the following words: "In the mighty army of the Partisans of Peace the workers of the People's Democracies march shoulder to shoulder with the Soviet people. The people who have become the masters of their fate recognize that the greatest guarantee for peace and work is the further strengthening of the national economy and unbreakable friendship and fraternal union with the great Socialist Power—the U.S.S.R.—as well as the establishment of still closer ties between the countries of the people's democracies."

To be for "peace" one must not only glorify the Soviet Union, but also the name of Stalin. Reporting a speech delivered by Vice-Premier Poptomov, Radio Sofia declared, on September 22, 1950: "The term 'peace' is today inseparable from the name of Stalin and the name of Stalin is inseparable from the conception of peace and friendship among all peoples."

"Peace" to the Soviet Government quite clearly implies warlike acts by the Soviet Government and its satellites. The people are urged to "struggle for peace" or to "fight for peace". Radio Budapest (June 3, 1950) spoke of the "consolidation of the Hungarian sector of the peace front." The U.S.S.R. and its satellites are in the forefront to guard the "peace sector" while the "Partisans of Peace" are the soldiers in the fight. On February 22, 1950 Radio Budapest reported: "Hungary wishes to be a bastion—not a bridge in the international peace front." On June 10, 1950, Radio Sofia carried the address of the third national conference of the Bulgarian Communist Party: "Stand in the front ranks of the defense of peace. Raise the flag even higher in the battle against the warmongers." Not even decorations are overlooked in the "peace campaign". The Polish newspaper *Glos Pracy* reported on July 27, 1951 that "President Boleslaw Beirut bestowed high state decorations on many prominent fighters in the peace defense movement." This militant, belligerent spirit runs through all Communist literature mentioning "peace". In giving his impressions of the 1950 Warsaw "Peace" Congress, John Rogge, former American leader in the Progressive Party, stated: "Because of the way in which the congress was led, and because of the speeches and discussions there, I received the impression that the congress intended to establish peace through force." (Radio Belgrade, November 25, 1950).

The Communist authorities in the Soviet Empire have utilized the natural desire of Soviet subjects for peace as a device to squeeze even more work and money from them. The people are told that they must make contributions, sacrifices, and "voluntary" work on Sundays and holidays a part of their daily life. Similarly, all those who fail to comply are "warmongers". In industry the fight for "peace" impresses on the workers the need of "voluntary" labor to increase production. Radio Warsaw reported on August 14, 1950, that "the workers of the transportation equipment factory in Rzeszow, resolved to prolong their peace shifts which they started on August 9 until September 2. . . . The struggle for peace is increasing steadily . . . staffs of twenty collieries resolved to reply to warmongers by increased coal extraction . . . reports of new production commitments are pouring in in ever increasing numbers." Aid to Communists in north Korea and Communist China is part and parcel of the same "peace" struggle.

In Hungary even the lowly dog is called on to make a contribution towards peace. In addition to the collection for glass and scrap iron as part of the "peace" effort in all satellite states, the Communists of Hungary have announced a need for dog hair. They offer four forints (about thirty-five cents) for freshly clipped dog hair, and have set up special collection points for this commodity. Clippings of dog hair are used to line soldiers' great coats and for cartridge wadding. The lot of the dog in Hungary had been difficult enough prior to the dog hair drive. Ever since the Communist cold war began, bones have been declared a strategic material, essential to the Communist glue industry. A friendly restaurant waiter who saves a bone or two for a neighborhood dog can easily be denounced for sabotage.

Earnings of Soviet satellite peasants, meager as they are, must be cut into as part of the "peace drive." An article in the Hungarian *Szabad Nep* (September 30, 1950) entitled "Whole Country Backs Peace Loan Drive" says that "the whole country is agog with enthusiasm to ensure the triumph of the peace plan. In this the workers of the big factories are leading the way, having subscribed the first day as much as they did in a whole week to the peace loan a year ago."

In April 1916, Lenin told a Marxist meeting that "Every 'peace' program is a deception of the people and a piece of hypocrisy unless its principal object is to explain to the masses the need for a revolution, and to support, aid, and develop the revolutionary struggle of the masses that is starting everywhere." (Lenin, *Selected Works*, International Publishers, New York, 1943, vol. 5, p. 237). Thus the word peace has been used ever since by the Soviet regime and its supporters to justify any and all sorts of projects whose relation to peace is tenuous to say the least. Accordingly, to be for "peace" means to support Communist candidates at elections, while to vote against them is to vote for war. As Radio Tirana announced on April 11, 1950: "By voting for the candidates of the Democratic Front we condemn the warmongers and inflict yet heavier blows on the internal and external enemies of the Republic." The warmongering nature of those who fail to support the Communist slate of candidates may be seen from the following quotation from the Hungarian newspaper *Vilagossag* (November 22, 1950): ". . . here in the thirteenth district about a thousand votes were cast against the People's Front at the local council elections. These votes were cast by . . . partisans of war. We must not forget this, and must be vigilant so as to be able to unmask all evil-doers and all enemies of peace."

"Peace laws" have been enacted in the Soviet satellites to be used as an excuse to suppress every free expression of opinion and to punish opponents of the sweatshop industry programs. An article in the Hungarian *Szabad Nep* (December 17, 1950) stated: "Whoever incites today against the consolidation of labor discipline in the factories trying to prevent backward workers from fulfilling the norms, is an enemy of peace. . . . The same applies to those who endeavor to persuade the working peasants to violate their obligations towards the state."

The Communists also invoke the word "peace" to justify a wide variety of other activities and causes. On September 12, 1950, Radio Tirana carried the following item: "A climbing expedition was held recently on the northern regions of the country under the slogan 'for the defense of peace'. The expedition consisted of 110 persons, divided into nine teams. Iron Peak was renamed 'Peace Peak'." Radio Prague described on October 28, 1950 the holding of "peace" relay races. On June 10, 1950, the Polish newspaper *Trybuna Ludu* described a "peace cruise" to Leningrad by four Polish vessels. The fight for peace in Rumania went all out in the spring of 1950, as evidenced by the following announcement of the *Romania Libera*, regarding the intensification of the fight for peace between March 26-April 2, 1950: "The Fight for Peace Committee of Bucharest has drawn up an activity plan for this week, which includes editing of blitz newspapers dedicated to the fight for peace, special reading sessions and literary meetings, organization of peace corners and show windows with peace literature."

At the end of July, 1951, Soviet policy brought into being a new English language publication, *News*, in which the "peace" policy is given full play specifically for English language audiences. The theme was, from the beginning, that peaceful coexistence between the Soviet Empire and the Free World was possible if only the United States would abandon its warmongering, get out of Korea, and recognize Communist China. A very strenuous effort was made to play up to the peace-at-any-price advocates in the Free World and to the timid, building pressure against the United States Government to make every necessary concession to the Soviet Union and Communist China to "keep the peace."

The succession to power of Malenkov in March, 1953, saw an intensification of the Soviet "peace" campaign—a campaign which coincided, appropriately enough, with Soviet fighter attacks on American and British aircraft near the Iron Curtain.

4

Communism in China

Shortly after the October revolution of 1917, the Bolsheviks, at that time barely able to hold onto their Russian conquest, assured the Chinese Government that Russia renounced all imperial Tsarist ambitions in China, and sought a policy of friendship and conciliation with China. This was embodied in a declaration of Acting Commissar for Foreign Affairs L. M. Karakhan, published July 25, 1919, (For text see *China Handbook*, Taipeh, Taiwan, 1951, p. 356). In actuality, however, this Russian declaration meant little. At that time there were in the Far East large groups of White Russians operating in various parts of Asiatic Russia. The Allies were occupying Vladivostok, and Japanese troops were in parts of Siberia. As to the Chinese Eastern Railway, which the Russian declaration sought to return to China —it had been already returned to China by the Allies, even though Japan was making free use of the road in its post-war activity in the Far East. Under these circumstances, the "concessions" made by Russia to China amounted to renouncing something she did not have. Nevertheless, the Soviet note of July 25, 1919 was of considerable propaganda value not only in China but throughout Asia.

A year later Karakhan published a second declaration (see *China Year Book*, 1924, pp. 870-972), which was considerably less expansive than the first. This second note demanded that China refrain from aiding anti-Bolshevik activity, and also demanded China recognize "with due regard the needs" of the Soviet Union in the Chinese Eastern Railway. Russia had meantime established a puppet "Far Eastern Republic" in Outer Mongolia, and was in a better position generally than the year before.

In 1921 the Soviet Government sent two different emissaries to China, who engaged in pro-Communist propaganda activities, but did little else. In the summer of 1922 Moscow sent Mr. Joffe to China. One of the first things Joffe did was to claim that no previous notes published by the Soviet Foreign Office renounced Russian rights in China. He specifically made reference to the Chinese Eastern Railway, which, he said, could not be restored to China without compensation. Under such demands, negotiations for the resumption of diplomatic relations could hardly proceed. Joffe did, however, make good use of his stay in Peiping by carrying on propaganda and furthering

Communist activities in the capital. Failing to make headway in Pei-ping, Joffe proceeded to Shanghai, where he met Dr. Sun Yat-sen. In January, 1923, the two issued a joint statement, which said in part: "Dr. Sun Yat-sen holds that the Communistic order . . . cannot actu-ally be introduced into China, because there do not exist here the conditions for the successful establishment of . . . Sovietism. This view is shared by Mr. Joffe, who . . . has assured Dr. Sun that China has the warmest sympathy of the Russian people, and can count on support from Russia." (*China Handbook*, 1951, p. 359).

In March, 1923, Karakhan himself came to take the place of Joffe, and after protracted negotiations he finally succeeded in concluding a treaty with the Chinese Government on May 21st, 1924. This treaty recognized Chinese sovereignty in Outer Mongolia, promised the withdrawal of Soviet troops from Outer Mongolia, but insisted on a Soviet interest in the Chinese Eastern Railway. No sooner had the relations between the two countries been resumed than the Russians increased their propaganda activities and their assistance to the Chi-nese Communists (in direct violation of the May 31, 1924 treaty). The Soviet Embassy became the center of subversive activities and Communist plots. A raid, carried out on April 5th, 1927, uncovered large quantities of Communist literature, and documents were found implicating the Soviet Government and its agents engaged in foment-ing insurrections in various parts of China. A group of Chinese Com-munists hiding in the Embassy building were arrested and executed for treason. All this was a far cry from Mr. Joffe's solemn promise to Dr. Sun that there was nothing to fear from the Soviet Union. This activity was also a direct violation of the 1924 treaty.

Following the Sun-Joffe agreement, a group of Russian political and military advisers arrived, ostensibly to work under Dr. Sun, who had established his Revolutionary Government in Canton in February, 1923. The group was headed by Michael Borodin and General Galen (alias Bluecher). Through their influence in the reorganization of the Kuomintang, an understanding was reached in January, 1924 al-lowing Communists to join the Kuomintang. Li Ta-chao, then an important Communist leader, assured the Kuomintang in solemn terms that the Communists ". . . have not the slightest intention of turning the Kuomintang into a Communist party." (*China Handbook*, 1951, p. 361). However, Communist action proved to be contrary to Com-munist words. Early in 1927, when the Kuomintang-Nationalists were crossing the Yangtze in their effort to unify China, the Communists sabotaged the expedition by creating a reign of terror behind the lines in Hunan, Hupeh, and Kiangsi. Nationalist leader Chiang Kai-shek took the expedition to Nanking, and in April, 1927 this city was declared the national capital of China. Simultaneously an anti-Communist purge was carried out in the Kuomintang. In July of the same year the Communists started their armed rebellion against the Nanking Government.

Soviet policy showed its true colors in China during the short-lived war of October, 1929, when the Soviet Government seized the Chinese Eastern Railway. The attack came at an inopportune time for the National Government, which had not yet been able to extend its control to Manchuria. The forces of Chang Tso-lin, loyal to Chiang Kai-shek, sought to check the Soviet advance, but they were too disorganized, and plagued by Japanese obstruction in southern Manchuria. The Russians were thus able to achieve an easy victory over Chang's forces. Soviet conquest of the Railway, however, was short-lived, for in 1935 the road was sold by the Soviet Union to the puppet Japanese state of Manchukuo. This act in itself was also a violation of the 1924 treaty with China.

In 1936, after the Japanese had completed their occupation of Manchuria, Russia dealt another blow to the National Government of China by creating a Soviet satellite in Outer Mongolia. The 1924 treaty had stated: "The Government of the U.S.S.R. recognizes that Outer Mongolia is an integral part of the Republic of China and respects China's sovereignty therein." Soviet Russia extended recognition to this puppet state, which it called the Mongolian People's Republic. The process of detaching Outer Mongolia from China was concluded by the action of the Yalta concessions, and a Soviet-sponsored "plebiscite" on October 20th, 1945.

The next step in Soviet interference in China began in 1945. At the Yalta Conference (February, 1945) Stalin secured, as the price of his participation of seven days in the war against Japan, a pledge from President Roosevelt and Prime Minister Churchill to use their influence in persuading China (1) to recognize the status quo in Outer Mongolia, and (2) to restore to the Soviet Union the rights the Tsars obtained from China before 1905, which included the leasing of Port Arthur to the U.S.S.R. as a naval base, internationalization of the port of Dairen, and joint operation of the Chinese Eastern Railway and the South Manchuria Railway. These demands, which included also recognition of "Soviet preeminent interests" throughout, were thrust upon the Chinese Government by the Russo-Chinese Treaty of August 14th, 1945. China had not been consulted about these concessions to the Soviet Government, and had, in fact, been promised the return of these territories at the Cairo conference, in addition to

the return of the island of Formosa to "the Republic of China"—the
legal term for the National Government of Chiang Kai-shek. The
language of the August 14th treaty makes it very evident that the
Chinese Government was *forced* to accept the Yalta concessions. China
had fought the Japanese for fourteen years, and Russia fought for
seven days—yet Russia received *Chinese* territory as thanks from the
United States and Great Britain.

On November 25, 1949, Dr. T. F. Tsiang, head of the Chinese
delegation to the United Nations, charged Soviet violation of the 1945
treaty, as well as Soviet complicity in the Communist rebellion, and
Soviet violations of the UN Charter. Characteristically, the United
Nations, when faced with aggressive acts by the Soviet Union, did nothing. It was not until early 1952 that the UN declared Soviet Russia
to have violated the 1945 treaty—and that was the end of UN action.
The Soviet Union specifically violated the 1945 treaty in the following
manner: (1) by refusing to give "moral support as well as aid in military supplies" solely to the National Government, (2) by refusing to
respect Chinese sovereignty over Manchuria, Port Arthur, and Dairen,
(3) by continuing to interfere in Sinkiang. Dr. Tsiang also produced,
in his speech of November 25, 1949, detailed evidence of Soviet aid
to the Communists, and Soviet interference in Manchuria and China.
(See *China Handbook*, 1951, pp. 365-388).

The Chinese Communist military chief Chu Teh acknowledged
Soviet aid in a speech at Peiping, July 16, 1949: "It can be easily seen
that the victory of the Chinese people's democratic revolution is inseparable from the friendly aid of the Soviet Union." He concluded
that had the Soviet Government not come to Communism's aid in
China the "victory of the Chinese revolution would have been impossible." On July 1, 1949, Mao Tse-tung had made it clear exactly
where he stood: "To sit on the fence is impossible. A third road does
not exist. . . . We oppose the illusion of a third road. Not only in
China but also throughout the world . . . one neither leans to the side
of imperialism or to the side of socialism. Neutrality is a camouflage,
and a third road does not exist. . . . Internationally we belong to the
anti-imperialist front, headed by the Soviet Union . . ." (*China Handbook*, 1951, p. 382).

With Manchuria as a base of operation, and with huge stores of
Japanese arms supplied to them by the Russians, the Chinese Communist armies moved down into north China. Russian-trained Korean
and Chinese troops were able to push the military forces of the Chinese National Government off the mainland, onto the islands of Hainan
and Formosa. After the inauguration of the "People's Republic of

China" by the Communists at Peiping, the Soviet Union lost no time in tightening its control over the regime it had created. This took the form of a series of treaties between Soviet Russia and the Chinese Communist regime, beginning with the agreement of February 14, 1950.

The most significant fact of Far Eastern developments since World War II is the establishment of Soviet power in China, and the rise of Communism as a politico-military movement which threatens all Asia. Chinese Communism, under Soviet tutelage, and armed and supplied by the Soviet Union, expanded militarily into Tibet and north Korea during 1950, and under the guise of "truce" talks starting in July, 1951, gained time to build up a gigantic air striking power. Communist air and land power in Asia has as its long-term objective the conquest of Japan. Indo-China, Burma, Nepal, India, Formosa, are also in danger of attack. The Soviet decision to attack the Republic of Korea on June 25th, 1950 was an indication that Communism in Asia was willing to risk all-out hot war to attain its objectives.

The importance of the establishment of Soviet power in China cannot be underestimated, inasmuch as it changes the entire balance of power in the Far East. Soviet foreign policy achieved perhaps its greatest triumph in seizing for Soviet purposes the vast territorial extent and teeming population of mainland China. The consequences of this triumph were deep-seated for the people of Korea, and the American and other fighting men who came to Korea to try to save that Republic from the Communist onslaught.

Dmitri Manuilsky, a leading Soviet diplomat from the Ukraine, wrote in his pamphlet "China in Revolt" (1926), the following: "The Chinese revolution will exert a revolutionizing influence on the movement of all Asia. . . . China will become the major power of the Pacific; it will become a menacing threat for the capitalist world. . . . China must inevitably clash with American Imperialism. . . . Revolutionary China, which has become an active factor in Far Eastern politics, can become, in alliance with the U.S.S.R., the greatest world factor in the Far East." (pp. 32, 46, 55, as quoted by Alice Widener in the *Freeman*, July 2, 1952). Nikolai Bukharin, writing in the same pamphlet, declared: ". . . we must not underestimate the immense importance of the movement in China, for it is one of the most important movements in the history of the world, and will strike a mighty blow at all capitalist stabilization." (p. 64). Stalin, in his *Marxism and the Nationalist and Colonial Questions*, (New York, International Publishers, 1928, p. 235) discusses the Chinese situation in the following words: "Now as to the stages of the Chinese Revolution . . . In my opinion they should be three: The first stage was the revolution of the general national united front, the second stage is the bourgeois-democratic revolution. . . . The third stage is the Soviet revolution, which has yet to come."

Soviet policy in China was successful during the years 1945-1949 not only due to the actions and efforts of the Soviet Government and the Chinese Communists, but also because of the actions of the United States Government. The Yalta concessions to the Soviet Union set the stage. Soviet control of Manchuria meant that the Chinese Communists had a base of operations from which to drive southward. As Japan was surrendering, the Soviet Army poured into Manchuria ahead of the forces of the Chinese National Army. As a condition of allowing the latter to enter Manchuria, Moscow tried to get the Chinese Government to agree to joint ownership of all Manchurian resources and industries. Failing this, Russia looted the area of eight hundred million dollars worth of industrial equipment and handed over huge supplies of captured Japanese arms to the Chinese Communists, whom they had meanwhile allowed to enter Manchuria. By the time the Soviet Army withdrew, the Communists were in possession of Manchuria and the captured arms.

On November 2, 1945, Soviet pressures prevented American Admiral Barbey from landing Nationalist troops at the port of Yingkow. These troops were authorized to accept Japanese surrenders in Manchuria and restore Chinese sovereignty to Manchuria as provided for in the August 14, 1945, Russo-Chinese treaty. Admiral Barbey was also prevented from landing at the Manchurian port of Hulutao, after Communist troops fired at his launch. The Manchurian ports of Dairen and Port Arthur were also denied the National Government by the Soviet Government, even though the former was supposed to be an "international" port with Chinese sovereignty recognized.

Since Chinese Nationalist troops were unable to reach Manchuria by sea, they had to try to reach it by the overland route. Denied the use of certain railways in north China by the Russians, these troops were confronted by Chinese Communists, armed by Russia, at the time they reached the Manchurian frontier. The United States Government, instead of protesting, and giving assistance to the Chinese Government, sent General George C. Marshall to China to try to settle the impending conflict; but in so doing, the United States treated the robber and the robbed as equals: the Chinese National Government and the Communist rebels were accorded equal status—as though they were two quarreling factions. The instructions which President Truman handed to General Marshall (instructions drawn up by John

Carter Vincent, Secretary of State Byrnes, and Marshall himself), in effect barred American aid to the National Government until after it had made peace with the Communists and brought the Communists into the Chinese Government. The President specifically stated: "The United States . . . believes that peace, unity, and democratic reform in China will be furthered if the basis of this Government is broadened to include other political elements in the country." Secretary Byrnes, in his statement of December 9, 1945, referred to the Communists as the "so-called Communists". This was the result of State Department feeling that the Chinese Communists were not really Communists, but "agrarian democrats" or "agrarian reformers". President Truman's statement of December 15th demanded "fair and effective representation" for the Communists in the Chinese Government. The Department of State's White Paper on China relates that General Marshall was supposed to treat "each side impartially". United States policy in China, as enunciated by President Truman and implemented by General Marshall, was based on the assumption that the civil war in China was strictly an internal matter, having no connection with Soviet Russia's policy of expansion by revolution.

The United States had no means of exerting pressure on the Chinese Communists to come to terms with the National Government, or to honor their pledges if an agreement were worked out. Only Stalin was in a position to do this. America's compulsions could and were exerted only against the National Government. By withholding both economic and military aid from the National Government until it came to terms with the Communist rebel forces, the United States Government put the Communists in a position in which they could blackmail the National Government.

The Chinese Communists were fortunate that their cause was presented to General Marshall by Chou En-lai, the handsome, intelligent, and charming man who was later to direct the foreign affairs of the Chinese Communist regime. According to Freda Utley, "Chou En-lai has for years shown a singular capacity for converting American journalists to the belief that the Chinese Communist Party was composed of liberal 'agrarian reformers' who should be backed against the . . . 'reactionary' government of Chiang Kai-shek." (*The China Story*, Chicago, Regnery, 1951, pp. 10, 11). Considerable evidence is present to indicate that the fascinating Chou En-lai confirmed what General Marshall had been told by John Carter Vincent and General Joseph Stilwell—i. e., that Chinese Communists were not "real Communists", and that they could be "detached" from their apparent Russian affiliation provided only they were helped by America to bring "democracy" to China.

General Marshall sponsored tentative political and military agreements in January and February, but these agreements were broken almost immediately, primarily because of the refusal of the Communists to honor their pledge to allow the Nationalists to enter Manchuria. A captured document obtained by George Weller, *Chicago Daily News* correspondent, revealed a secret agreement between the Soviet Army and the Chinese Communists pledging 5,000 Russian officers and men to help the Communists against the Chinese Government, and obligating the Communists to subordinate their command to that of the Russians'. The date on this document was January 19, 1946, just nine days after the Communists had signed a truce agreement in Chungking advising General Marshall of their sincere desire to help establish a united "democratic" China. (See Weller dispatch in *Chicago Daily News*, May 6, 1946).

In spite of Russian military aid and advice to the Communists, well-equipped and trained Nationalist armies won important victories in the spring and early summer of 1946. As was their habit, the Communists, upon being thrown back, demanded that General Marshall re-impose a truce. This he did in May, thus halting the offensive of the Nationalist armies. At the end of July, 1946, General Marshall clamped an embargo on the sale of arms and ammunition to Nationalist China. For almost a year thereafter, the Chinese Government, far from being *given* any Amercian aid, was unable to *buy* a single round of ammunition from the United States. On August 18, 1946, President Truman issued an executive order stating that China was not to be allowed to acquire any "surplus" American weapons "which could be used in fighting a civil war." It was in this way that the anti-Communist forces of China were thrown back on their reserves, and the limited supply of their own arsenals. These were soon to prove wholly inadequate to match the vast quantities of Japanese munitions handed over to the Chinese Communists by the Soviet Army in Manchuria.

During World War II, the United States agreed to train and equip thirty-nine Chinese divisions. That promise was broken by General Marshall after he arrived in China. The few divisions that had already been trained and equipped were not permitted to acquire ammunition from the United States. Strangest of all, the summer of 1946 saw General Marshall accede to a Communist request to assign American officers to train the Communist armies. American Under-Secretary of State Acheson told the House Committee on Foreign Affairs on June

19, 1946: "The Communist leaders have asked, and General Marshall
has agreed, that integration with other forces be preceded by a brief
period of United States training and by the supply of minimum quantities of equipment." As it developed, these officers and the American
equipment never got to the Communists because of the battle situation. The projected aid to the Communists was strange indeed, since
Chinese Communist hostility to America was by this date being openly
proclaimed. Communist radio stations were blaring forth that "the
only difference between American and Japanese imperialism is that
American imperialism is stronger, and its aggressive methods appear
civilized and legal on the surface." During this period, there were
numerous incidents in which the Communists shot, killed, wounded,
and imprisoned American Marines stationed in north China.

Secretary Acheson restated American policy on June 28, 1946, when
he declared: "Too much stress cannot be laid on the hope that our
economic assistance be carried out in China through the medium of
a government fully and fairly representative of all important Chinese
political elements, including the Chinese Communists."

The summer and fall of 1946 saw continued Nationalist military
victories, interspersed with truces imposed by General Marshall.
The Nationalists still had some ammunition, and the Communists had
not yet had time to train enough men in the use of arms supplied them
by the Russians. Indeed contingents of Chinese and Korean Communists were still undergoing training in Russia. The Nationalists
pushed the Communists to Harbin, and then captured Kalgan and
other strategic points in north China. By November, 1946, the White
Paper on China states: ". . . the Government's forces . . . reached what
turned out to be the highest point of its military position." Continued
American pressure forced Chiang to cease fire again on November 8,
1946. The Communists were offered positions in the Chinese Government, but refused. Meanwhile they harassed communications,
waged guerrilla warfare, and perpetuated ruin and chaos throughout
the countryside, while preparing their biggest military operations of
the war.

In December, 1946, General Marshall told Chiang Kai-shek that
the Communists were too strong to overcome militarily, and that therefore "it was imperative that efforts be made to bring them into the
Government." Chiang Kai-shek replied: "I am firmly convinced that
the Communists never intended to cooperate with the National Government, and that, acting under Russian influence, their purpose was
to disrupt the National Government."

General Marshall's efforts to mediate the war, bring the Communists into the government, and reform China under war conditions were a failure. On January 7, 1947, Marshall made the following statement as he left China: ". . . the National Assembly has adopted a democratic constitution. . . . it was unfortunate that the Communists did not see fit to participate in the Assembly, since the constitution . . . seems to include every major point they wanted." He castigated the Communists who "do not hesitate at the most drastic measures to gain their ends, as for instance, the destruction of communications in order to wreck the economy of China and produce a situation that would facilitate the overthrow or collapse of the Government, without any regard to the immediate suffering of the people involved." However, Marshall went on to criticize "reactionary" leaders of the National Government, and said of the Communists: "On the side of the Chinese Communist Party are, I believe, liberals as well as radicals. . . . it has appeared to me that there is a definite liberal group among the Communists, especially of young men who have turned to the Communists in disgust at the corruption evident in the local governments —men who would put the interest of the Chinese people above ruthless measures to establish a Communist ideology in the immediate future."

General Marshall's refusal to aid Nationalist China unless and until it came to terms with the Communists was quite inconsistent with his policy toward Greece as Secretary of State. As Freda Utley points out in her interesting study: 'Soon after taking office he recommended that 400 millions be given Greece to keep the Communists out, while he continued to deny any help to the Chinese National Government unless it would take the Communists in." (*The China Story*, p. 24).

Marshall withdrew the Marines from China in the spring of 1947, assuring Molotov that American forces were being removed from China "as quickly as shipping becomes available." Thus was the last vestige of American support and prestige withdrawn from China. By the end of the year the tide of battle had changed, as the year's embargo began to make itself felt on the ammunition-short Nationalist armies. Well-equipped Communist armies began to move south, and the fall of China was at hand.

Colonel L. B. Moody, United States Ordnance expert in China, commented as follows on our aid to China: ". . . military aid means to the Chinese infantry weapons and ammunition above all else, and it is precisely these items which the United States action has consistently denied, delayed, or limited. Only passing reference will be made to the billions of moldy cigarettes, blown-up guns, junk bombs, and disabled vehicles from the Pacific Islands, which have been totalled up

. . . in various State Department, Communist, and leftist statements to create the impression that we have furnished the Nationalist Government with hundreds of millions or even billions of dollars worth of fighting equipment." (Speech in Washington, D. C., April 11, 1950). Congress did appropriate funds to render military assistance to China in 1948, but this proved to be too late. As Vice Admiral Russell S. Berkey testified on May 15, 1950: "The Chinese Reds would still be north of the Great Wall if specific items of arms authorized by Congress two years ago had reached the Nationalist forces in time. For some reason or other it took nine months to get specific items to China. Somewhere in the United States somebody slipped up, bogged down, or was interfered with. It has never been made plain why this material did not arrive in time."

Thus it was that Soviet policy in the Far East was enabled to achieve the conquest of China. American policy toward the Soviet Union and the Chinese Communists bore a striking resemblance to Neville Chamberlain's attitude toward Germany in 1938. The interesting part of the American China policy was that, whereas it had extended all-out aid to Nationalist China with no questions asked against Japan, it was unwilling to extend the same unqualified aid against Communism. Appeasement in China was to be paid off—by the blood investment in Korea.

THE CHINESE SOVIETS

Following the overthrow of the old Manchu dynasty in 1911, Sun Yat-sen became the intellectual leader of the movement for modernism in general, and for nationalism and democracy in particular in China. Under his leadership a republican form of government was established in Canton, with the dominant party being the Kuomintang (National People's Party). Sun and the Kuomintang announced three basic principles of action: (1) racial nationalism, (2) people's democracy, and (3) people's livelihood. While Sun explicitly rejected Marxist Communism, his principles and those of the Kuomintang were easily twisted to fit Communist purposes.

The Communist organization in China dates from the formation of the Institute of Marxism by Chen Tu-hsiu in Shanghai in 1920. A professor at the National Peking University, Chen joined the Third International while on a visit to Moscow in 1921. Upon his return to China he convened the First National Congress of the Chinese Communist Party in Shanghai on July 1st, 1921. Among those present was Mao Tse-tung. In 1922 the Chinese Communists affiliated with the Comintern. Michael Borodin was sent to Canton from Moscow in September, 1923. He advised Moscow that the Kuomintang Party of Dr. Sun was the most promising vehicle of the Communist revolution in China, and Moscow decided to order the Chinese Communists "under the guidance and with the aid of the Comintern" to adopt a political and tactical line of national united front with the Kuomintang. (Mao Tse-tung, *China, the March Toward Unity*, New York, The Worker's Library, 1937, p. 92). Members of the Communist Party holding important posts in the Kuomintang by 1924 were Mao Tse-tung and Li Ta-chao.

Soon after the death of Dr. Sun (March 12, 1925) friction developed between Communists and anti-Communists in the Kuomintang. The Communists opposed the Northern expedition of 1925 for fear that success would strengthen the Kuomintang nationally, and make more difficult a Communist seizure of power. Meantime Sun's successor, Chiang Kai-shek, increasingly aware of Communist activities, began to strengthen the anti-Communist wing of the Kuomintang. However, a precarious "united front" was maintained between 1924 and mid-1927 between the Communists and the anti-Communists. Neither side felt the time to be ripe to make a major move. In the summer of 1927, when Kuomintang armies had captured Nanking as part of their effort to unify China under one central government, Communist elements rioted, thus leading to the first break in the united front. Chiang Kai-shek established a non-Communist Kuomintang Government in Nanking, while a pro-Communist regime was established at Wuhan. Chiang struck out energetically against the Communists in Shanghai and elsewhere, but was unable to achieve complete victory.

An internal split in the Communist party became evident after the rise of a non-Communist Kuomintang. Chu Teh, Li Li San, Chou En-lai and others organized a revolutionary committee on August 1, 1927, and started a series of abortive uprisings in Canton, Changsha, and Nanchang. On the 7th of August Chen Tu-hsui resigned as secretary-general of the Communist Party after being attacked by Mao Tse-tung and Chu Chiu-po. Shortly thereafter Chu fell from favor, leaving the field to Mao. In 1929 Chen was expelled from the party as a Trotskyite. Li Li San sought to take power in the Chinese Communist Party in 1930, but failed; his program was deemed too premature by the Comintern.

Upon the orders of the Comintern, the "Soviet Republic of China" was established in Juikin, Kiangsi province, in November, 1931, with Mao Tse-tung as chairman. His military chief was Chu Teh, whose Communist army was patterned on the Soviet model. This Communist rebellion had to be put down by the National (Kuomintang) Government. After several years hostilities, Government forces succeeded in tightening the ring around Juikin. Faced by total destruction in November, 1935, the Communists, led by Mao, Chu, and Chou En-lai, started their "long march" across several provinces, finally settling in a small area around Yenan in the northwest of China.

The following year saw a change in Communist tactics, dictated by the Moscow popular front (united front) tactics, as well as by Japanese aggression. Additionally, the Soviet Government, at this time active in Spain and Europe generally, was not anxious to become involved in a war in China, or against Japan. Therefore a united front policy, which would set up a strong China as a buffer between the Soviet Union and Japan, was desirable. The kidnapping and al-most immediate release of Chiang Kai-shek by a pro-Communist group in Sian (December 1936) signalized that Moscow believed it more advantageous to support a united front, temporarily led by Chiang, in China, than to seize him, thus winning a momentary ad-vantage, but with the end result that China would be split, become an easy prey to Japanese aggression, and be wiped out as a buffer in front of Russia.

The Chinese Soviet Government was abolished in 1937, and the Communist armies were reorganized into the Eighth Route Army (later the 18th Group Army). But the new tactic of the united front —of apparent conciliation—was only a tactical maneuver, not a change of policy. Mao Tse-tung told his comrades in 1937: "The war between China and Japan is an excellent opportunity for the development of our party. Our determined policy is 70 percent expansion, 20 percent dealing with the Kuomintang, and 10 percent fighting Japan." He outlined a three-stage program as follows: "The first stage is to com-promise with the Kuomintang, with the view of maintaining our exist-ence. The second stage is to fight for a balance of power *vis a vis* the Kuomintang to achieve equilibruim. The third stage is to infil-trate deeply into central China, to establish bases there, in order to launch counter-offensives against the Kuomintang, with the view of taking away from the Kuomintang its leading position." (Committee on Foreign Affairs, *The Strategy and Tactics of World Communism*, Supplement III, *Communism in China*, U. S. Government Printing Office, Washington, 1949, p. 24). An October, 1937 resolution of the Chinese Communist Politburo made clear that the long-range program envisaged conquest of the Kuomintang and China: "In Chinese poli-tics, armed force is the determining factor; we must, therefore, during the war, do our very best to expand our armed might so that we may lay the foundation upon which we could seize revolutionary leadership." (*Loc. cit.*) Under the banner of nationalism, the Communists intensified their mass propaganda penetration, and sought to rally patriotic feeling in support of the Red Army under its new name of Eighth Route Army. This coincided with increasingly successful foreign Communist propaganda to the effect that the Chinese Communists were not real Communists, but merely "agrarian reformers" interested in China for the Chinese.

Throughout the war with Japan the publicity from Communist China was excellent. The Communists were almost entirely remote from direct observation by the foreign press, and made the most of the opportunity to issue a stream of accounts of heroic exploits—many of them accepted without reservations by certain "liberal" publications in America and elsewhere. Actually, the Communists avoided battle with the diligence they had learned in years of guerrilla warfare. The Japanese, according to their own account suffered nearly a million casualties in the entire war with China, and less than ten percent of these occurred in fighting the Communists. The art of playing two opponents against each other, subjecting them both to serious losses while building one's own strength, was practiced more effectively by Chinese Communism than by any other country or group in the second world war.

With powerful support not only from the Soviet Union, but from the Yalta concessions and numerous high-placed American officials and writers, Chinese Communism finally gained complete control over the mainland of China. On October 1, 1949, the "Central People's Government of the People's Republic of China" was proclaimed. Political power over Communist China was placed in the hands of a small group of about twelve men clustered around Mao Tse-tung. The Politburo included: Mao Tse-tung, leader; Chou En-lai, premier and foreign minister; Gen. Chu Teh, commander-in-chief of military forces; Chen Yun, chairman of the financial and economic commissions; Lin Po-chu (formerly Lin Tzu-han), secretary general of the Central Government Council; and Peng Chen, mayor of Peiping. In February, 1952, Peng Chen introduced the drastic decree that brought the purge of the "counterrevolutionaries". This campaign involved mass arrests and wholesale executions throughout the country. The Communists admitted killing 14 million Chinese, exclusive of the civil war, between 1947-1952 (See *New Leader*, January 12, 1953, p. 18).

Top Chinese Communists appointed to key positions were Kao Kang, chairman of the Manchurian Regional Government; Gen. Lin Piao, nominally head of the Central-South Administrative Zone; Kang Sheng, secret police; Tung Pi-wu, chairman of the Political and Legal

Affairs Commission; and Chang Wen-tien, ambassador to the Soviet Union.

The Politburo, which acts for a larger Central Committee, presides over a power structure that enables a small group of men to dominate an elite party, and an elite party (less than 1.5% of the population) to dominate a country. By means of a system the Communists call "democratic centralism", orders are issued at the top and penetrate down through party-controlled agencies to party-controlled mass organizations at the bottom. Communists control every vital aspect of the state: the Government, schools, press, army, police, courts, and the economy. The army and police provide the real teeth of authority. Virtually everybody has been organized either into some kind of "mass organization" or as an automatic member of a closely supervised "street government" grouping. It is difficult to be a silent member of any of these organizations. The accent is on reindoctrination ("brain-washing") of the nation by *Hsueh Hsi* (study) and on endless agitation. The schools and universities are particularly active in the "brain-washing" process.

Communist China has not only achieved its internal goal of establishing a monopoly of political power, purging the dissidents, expelling all western influences (including the missionaries), but it has acted as a junior partner-in-aggression with the Soviet Union. Given supplies and equipment from the U.S.S.R., Communist Chinese manpower is capable of serving Soviet purposes in Korea, Tibet, Viet Nam, and against Formosa, Burma, Malaya, Siam, India, and ultimately Japan. This frees the bulk of the Russian manpower for action in the Middle East or Europe.

5

Communism in Southeast Asia

Ever since the Japanese surrender in 1945, the Soviet program for the conquest of southeast Asia has followed a carefully developed route. Initially the Communists built a trade union and political base in Indo-China and surrounding areas through the World Federation of Trade Unions. They attempted general strikes and terror tactics in capturing political power. Failing in this, Soviet policy switched to the "get tough" tactic of Cominform chief Zhdanov, and guerrilla warfare mounted on an ever increasing scale in southeast Asia. The Soviet victory in China in 1949 was the prelude not only to Communist military activity in Korea, but to a stepped-up military program to the south. The path initially blazed by Hideki Tojo was again overrun.

Pouring down from the mountain passes on the south China border, Communist guerrilla troops swept downwards into the heart of southeast Asia—producer of two-thirds of the world's exportable rice, and rich in natural rubber, tin, manganese, and other vital strategic materials. The offensive was designed to drive the French from Indo-China, leading to the collapse of Burma, Thailand (Siam), and Malaya, and outflanking India. Indonesia, the Philippines, and Japan would be isolated, as would Australia and New Zealand. Japan would lose her source of rice, her raw materials, and her trade area. With Korea, the Kuriles, and Sakhalin in Soviet hands, three hundred million people—more than twice the whole population of the United States, would fall into Stalin's lap.

INDO-CHINA

The Soviet policy-executor in Indo-China is Ho Chi-minh. He has been a Communist all his life, yet many naive Americans and others have hailed him as a patriot fighting for the freedom of his country. As far back as 1916 he was active in Communist circles in Paris; in 1923 the Communist Party in France sent him as a delegate to the *Krestintern* (Red Peasant) Congress in Moscow, where he served two years as a colonial problems expert. In 1925 he became advisor to the Soviet agent Borodin at the Russian consulate in Canton, and subsequently he travelled throughout southeast Asia organizing Communist associations. In 1931 he founded the Communist Party of Indo-

52

China, while serving as head of the Far Eastern Bureau of the Comintern in Hong Kong. In 1941 he founded the Viet Minh Communist front in south China and has headed the same organization in Indo-China since that time.

The French have occupied Indo-China for most of the past century. Starting from Saigon, they gradually extended their rule through Cochin China in the south, Annam in the central area, up the coast to the Tonkin delta, and finally into the adjoining kingdoms of Cambodia and Laos. Despite, however, the many French contributions to Indo-China, the native nationalist movement continued to grow and flourish. Nationalist revolts against French rule were put down with considerable severity. The Communists, who had originally come from China, were quick to see in this situation an opportunity to use nationalism as a lever for higher Soviet purposes. Here was a "national war of liberation" which should be supported because it would rebound to the ultimate benefit of Communism in Asia. Accordingly, the Communists made common cause with the nationalists, who were blinded as to the nature of their new companions in the common anti-French struggle. Although the Communists were a small minority, it was soon apparent that they were the elite or the vanguard, which was leading the largely non-Communist nationalist movement.

The quick defeat of France in World War II, together with five years of Japanese occupation of Indo-China did great damage to French prestige among the natives. In addition, five years of anti-western Japanese propaganda, and Japanese use of native personnel to man the puppet government, did much to stir up the "Asia for the Asiatics" feeling. Ho Chi-minh had been out of the country during most of the occupation, until he returned secretly some months before the Japanese surrender to work underground as leader of the popular front coalition known as the Viet Minh—nationalist groups under strong Communist influence. Following the Japanese surrender in the north, Ho Chi-minh's organization gained control of a large area; it also received a large supply of arms from outside Indo-China to supplement the military aid received from the United States during the war—aid given indiscriminately to "anti-Japanese" guerrillas. In the south the French resumed control, and Indo-China found itself in a situation not too different from that of Korea.

On March 6, 1946, Ho Chi-minh won his biggest political victory: he and his Communist-dominated Viet Minh were recognized by the French as head of the newly constituted Viet Nam government. The new nation was to include Annam in the central section and Tonkin

to the north. Several factors must be taken into account to explain
the French action. First, it seems that the French were not yet
fully aware of the degree of Communist influence in the Viet Minh
movement; secondly, the French Government of this period included
Communists, who, in conjunction with parallel Soviet pressure, insisted on recognition of Ho Chi-minh; thirdly, France, together with
Britain and the United States, was still living in the honeymoon
atmosphere of wartime coalition with Communism, and perhaps was
thus unable to discern the impending Communist danger in Indo-
China.

Following French recognition, Ho Chi-minh continued to consolidate his gains, wiping out pockets of native anti-Communist strength,
and making it appear that the entire nationalist movement was his
own. One of the first to observe the Communist danger was the
Emperor Bao Dai. After being "used" briefly by Ho Chi-minh, Bao
Dai abdicated, to await a new turn in developments. In June, 1946
Ho Chi-minh went to France to demand inclusion of Cochin China
in the Viet Nam state, as well as to urge a more extensive autonomy
for his new regime. It was during these negotiations, from June to
September, that the French became aware of the exact nature and
intentions of Ho Chi-minh. The latter kept increasing his demands,
hoping that the French wanted peace at any price. Failing to achieve
his goal, Ho Chi-minh returned to Hanoi, where he secretly prepared
one of the most savage massacres in modern history. Six days after
Christmas, 1946, the grounds around the homes of European residents
in Hanoi were infiltrated by Viet Minh assassins. At a signal throughout the city, the invaders pulled out their knives and attacked whole
families, slaughtering thousands of innocent men, women, and children. Other Communist terror tactics occurred elsewhere in Viet
Nam. The best estimate is that some eight hundred thousand were
killed and several hundred kidnapped and carried off to the hills of
the hinterland, as Ho Chi-minh brought events to a showdown with
the French. (See Thomas E. Dewey, *Journey to the Far Pacific*,
Doubleday, 1952, pp. 214-216).

The surprise of the attack and its impact were so great that the
French were almost driven from the northern part of the country.
Heavy reinforcements were rushed from France to Viet Nam, and the
French immediately made plans to build up an anti-Communist move-
ment with as much native participation as was feasible under a war
situation. This was to be the Viet Nam Government led by Emperor
Bao Dai. Soon near-independent states were also established in Laos
and Cambodia.

In January, 1950, Communist China, which had extended steady aid and support to the Viet Minh regime to the south, formalized its relationship by recognizing the "Viet Nam Democratic Republic" as the legal government of Viet Nam. The Peiping newspaper Jen Min Jih-pao proclaimed (As reproduced in *Izvestia* January 21, 1950): "The Chinese people extend a warm welcome to the Viet Nam Democratic Republic as their friendly neighbor, and are confident that the establishment of diplomatic relations between China and Viet Nam will mark a great event in the struggle for national liberation in the Orient. . . . The liberation of the greater part of the territory of Viet Nam . . . is driving a sharp wedge into the imperialist front in southeast Asia . . ." The Soviet Union followed suit on January 30th, with the bland statement: "The Government of the U.S.S.R. hereby acknowledges the receipt of President Ho Chi-minh's message of January 14th. . . . After examining the proposal of the Government of the Democratic Republic of Viet Nam and further taking into consideration the fact that the Democratic Republic represents an overwhelming majority of the country's population, the Soviet Government has decided to establish diplomatic relations . . ."

At the end of November, 1950, the Communist Chinese General Wu Hsiu-chuan told the United Nations Security Council: "The United States' armed aggression against Taiwan is inseparable from its interference in the internal affairs of the Viet Nam Republic, its support of the French aggressors and their Bao Dai puppet regime, and its armed attack on the Viet Nam people. . . . The Chinese people cannot but be deeply concerned with the unfolding of the aggressive plot of the United States against Viet Nam." (As quoted by Richard Deverall in *America*, January 20, 1951, p. 453). General Wu Hsiu-chuan then threatened: "Yielding neither to the enticements nor to the threats of American imperialism, they (the Asian Communists) will fight dauntlessly on to win the final victory in their struggle for national independence." Shortly thereafter Viet General Vo Nguyen Giap launched a major offensive against French forces.

The Burmese newspaper *Nation* declared on June 4, 1951 that Chinese, Burmese, and Indo-Chinese Communists had established an overall command for southeast Asia at Kunming, China. This command had the task of directing southeast Asian Communist activities, and is known as the Central Committee of the People's Liberation Armies of southeast Asia. During November, 1951, a series of top flight conferences were held in Peiping to plan future Communist strategy for southeast Asia.

Simultaneously with the entrance of Communist China into the

Korean war in November, 1950, Soviet experts began to work with Communist Chinese military and naval leaders to create a naval and submarine base at Yulin, southernmost city on the island of Hainan. Hainan is just off the China coast west of Hong Kong, and outflanks all the northern sector of Indo-China. In February, 1950, roads and railways from central China to the Indo-China border were improved and expanded, and the major part of the program was completed at the beginning of 1952. During 1951 Communist China established a military training post for Indo-Chinese Communist troops, and by the end of the year five divisions had received complete training and were back in action in Viet Nam. Red China built a series of air bases on the Indo-China frontier, capable of offensive action against the French and native anti-Communist troops in Viet Nam. By June, 1951, there were in action 125 regular Viet Minh battalions totalling 138,000 men. (*New York Times*, June 29 and August 24, 1951.)

The Indo-Chinese arm of Soviet policy is organized in a manner quite similar to that of Communist China. The Communist-dominated parts of Viet Nam have a controlling Communist Party, called the Labor Party (Lao Dong), and a new coalition front—the Lienviet or National Union League, which includes all satellite non-Communist groups. The Lienviet was the result of a merger of an older Lienviet group of the Viet Minh (League for National Independence). Leaders of the Labor (Communist) Party, besides Ho Chi-minh, include Truong Chinh, Ton Duc Thang, and Prince Savanavong (son of the King of Laos). Among the puppet groups which merged into the Lienviet organization were the Democratic Party, the Socialist Party, the Viet Nam-Soviet Friendship Association, the China-Viet Nam Friendship Association, and the National Union Front of Cambodia. The Lienviet, under the leadership of the Labor Party (Communist) is the political organization behind the Viet Minh regime of Ho Chi-minh. Strongest in Viet Nam, it has branches also in Laos and Cambodia. The relationship is precisely the same as that of the Communist Party in Russia to the Government of the U.S.S.R.

Chinese Communist assistance to the Viet Minh forces includes economic and technical aid, as well as military assistance. Textile, and rice-milling machinery, equipment for the manufacture of tele-communications materials, items for the establishment of motor repair shops, as well as lathes and other tools for enlarging and improving Viet Minh arsenals—all these have come from Communist China. During 1951, more than 1,000 skilled Chinese workers and technicians went to Viet Nam Communist areas to help install materials supplied by Red China. A high proportion of the tonnage shipped overland from China to Viet Nam consists of food for the forces of Ho Chi-minh. The mountainous regions of north Viet Nam, held by Communist forces, do not produce enough foor for the Viet Minh, and Communist China makes up the deficit.

The Viet Minh regime has regluar training centers for civil administrators on the Communist China pattern, and the recruiting and training of the military forces has been established under Chinese Communist aegis. The training of key Viet Minh army personnel in south China began in 1950. One difficulty in Chinese Communist aid getting to Ho Chi-minh is the limited transportation facilities. In addition to the sea route from Hainan to Communist ports in Viet Nam, the best overland route is the railway from Kwangsi to the border. Truck routes exist, but Communist China, as of mid-1952, was using most of its trucks in Manchuria and Korea. (*New York Times,* January 5, 1952).

The French have granted what amounts to independence to Viet Nam, Cambodia, and Laos, where anti-Communist governments have, since 1949, slowly built up military forces to work with the French against the Communist insurgents. Viet Nam is the scene of the greatest military activity, followed by Cambodia, and Laos. On June 3, 1952, Emperor Bao Dai designated Nguyen Van Tam to succeed Tran Van Huu as Premier of Viet Nam. Van Tam, the former Defense Minister, declared his intention of placing the entire economy of Viet Nam on a war footing under a "true government of national union." He planned to build up Viet Nam's army from four to eight divisions by the end of 1952, and stated that ". . . to combat Communism I am going to practice socialism with agrarian reform to win the population to our national cause." He said that he would cut the interest on farm loans and give farmers in recovered areas a valid title to land promised them. (*New York Times,* June 4, 1952.)

On June 15, 1952, the King of Cambodia dismissed the dictatorial government of the pro-Communist Democratic Party, and formed a new government of "national union." The King and the Opposition parties had repeatedly asked the government of Huy Kanthoul to take strong action against the rebels led by Son Ngoc Thanh, who sought to oust the French from Cambodia with the aid of Viet Minh forces.

American military aid to the states of Viet Nam, Cambodia, and Laos, and to their French protectors, helped stem the Communist tide in 1951 and 1952. The French commander, General Lattre de Tassigny, led a series of brilliant military actions against the Viet Minh forces, until his untimely death in the spring of 1952. At that time the French appointed Jean Letourneau to take over the political superintendency, and General Salan to assume military command of the anti-Communist forces. Tran Van Kha, first Vietnamese ambassador to the United States, declared on June 14th, 1952: "We in the Far East are fully aware that the battle against Communist aggression in our part of the world is being fought on two fronts. One is Korea. . . . The other is Viet Nam. . . . As Vietnamese, we feel deeply our responsibility to accept our share . . . to keep the free world free. That is why we are expanding every effort to build a national army, capable of doing its part alongside free forces guaranteeing our own common security today." (*New York Times*, June 16, 1952).

THAILAND

James Michener said of Thailand (Siam) as he left it in 1951: "Siam is the joyous land. Never in my life have I left a land with more regret. In many ways Siam is a foretaste of what all Asia may some day become. . . . the land has prospered under its own haphazard guidance for some 2,000 years. It is a gentle and wonderful place." (*The Voice of Asia*, Random House, 1951, p. 190). Soviet policy for Thailand, however, seems intent on ending "the gentle and wonderful" situation.

A Siamese doctor told Michener: "America has the atom bomb. Why don't you use it? If China is not stopped soon they will surely overrun us. What can Thailand do against China? Many thousands of Chinese live in Bangkok already and would create great trouble if war started." A cab driver told him: "We don't complain against the Chinese who are here now. Most of them are good people. But the Communists who control China now will never let our Chinese alone. The doctor is right. If you have the atomic bomb, why don't you use it? Now, when there is some chance of doing good with it." The doctor concluded: "All America does is threaten. You say you are going to get mad pretty soon. Pretty soon nobody will worry about your threats anymore . . ." (*ibid.*, pp. 196, 197).

Hemmed in by Communist China, Indo-China, Burma, and Malaya, with strong Communist rebel groups in all three latter states, Thailand has nevertheless declared herself unequivocally in favor of the Free World. The foreign policy of Thailand's Prime Minister Phibun Songgram, is one of open anti-Communism and close cooperation with the United States, and the anti-Communist forces of Indo-China, Malaya, and Korea. Thailand was one of the first states to offer military assistance to the American and Korean troops in the summer of 1950. In addition, Thailand has refused to recognize the regime of Mao Tse-tung in Communist China.

In December, 1946, the weak and pro-Soviet regime of Pridi Phanomyang entered into an agreement with the Soviet Union for the exchange of ambassadors. The Soviet Minister arrived in Bangkok in March 1948. The Russian legation with a staff of twenty members, with twenty additional guards, messengers, and miscellaneous helpers, attracted considerable attention because its large size contrasted sharply with the very small number of Soviet citizens in Thailand. It is generally believed that this Bangkok legation directs much of the Communist activity in southeast Asia.

Phibun Songgram took over the reins of government from Pridi Phanomyang in November, 1947, in a bloodless coup. His first move was to offer cooperation to the British by closing the Thai-Malayan frontier to Communist guerrillas operating in Malay. He also proceeded to take firm measures against Communism at home, as well as abroad. Phibun's chief problem is guarding Thailand from Communist encroachment, and dealing with Thailand's powerful Chinese minority. If Indo-China were to fall to the Communists, Thailand, with its strategic geographic location and valuable rice supplies might find itself next in line. As to the Chinese minority, many of them might try to accommodate themselves to the Communist groups, and some have, since 1949, played the game of the Communists in southeast Asia. This has resulted in occasional action by Phibun against the Chinese in Thailand suspected of aiding and abetting Communist activity.

At the beginning of March, 1951, the Communist Viet Minh radio predicted an early "civil war" in Thailand (see dispatch of Tillman Durdin, *New York Times*, March 8, 1951). The broadcast implied that the rebellion would be led by the Thai Communist Party. Referring to the "Front of National and Democratic Union", promoted by the Thai Communists, it asserted that Thailand's exiled leader Pridi Phanomyang was a key figure of the Front. The broadcast demanded that the Front "get rid of the dictatorship of Marshall Phibun, the valet of American imperialists."

On June 30th, there was a navy-led revolt against the government of Phibun. The latter was kidnapped, and there ensued a series of battles between loyal and insurgent forces, with the Phibun Government forces finally regaining control. Phibun escaped from his captors during the battle and resumed his position as chief of state. Considerable evidence pointed to Pridi Phanomyang being the instigator of the revolt. Some observers believed that Pridi, a so-called "liberal" with Marxist leanings (he was much in favor with American officials during World War II) chose to work with the Communists in order to gain control of the Thai government. The Communists, on the other hand, have used Pridi as a "front" behind which they hope to win the final victory. Pridi has visited Communist China, and was reported several times as being at Ho Chi-minh's headquarters in Communist Viet Nam. Also in the picture is the Soviet Embassy, which by 1950 had 200 persons working in its Bangkok building—far more than necessary to handle normal diplomatic relations with Thailand.

Another internal Thai upheaval took place on November 29, 1951, when military leaders staged a coup d'etat, which greeted young King Phuniphol Adulet upon his return from Switzerland. Leaders of the coup included General Phin Chunavan and General Pao Suriyanond. They persuaded Phibun to remain as Prime Minister of the new regime, which apparently was established to strengthen the hold of the military in Thail politics. Actually the change in regime seemed to affect things very little, although adoption of the 1932 Constiution indicated a slight increase of power for the executive branch of government in dealing with inflation, corruption, and Communism.

Soviet policy for Thailand, regardless of superficial internal changes in the country, seemed faced with unrelenting opposition from the Thai government. On August 27, 1951, Prince Nakkhatra Mangala, father-in-law of the King and member of the Privy Council declared: "We are firmly on the side of the United States." A month before, Phibun told foreign newsmen that a cease-fire in Korea would not bring lasting peace. He said that "the next phase of the Communist program in Asia after a Korean cease-fire will be to infiltrate all countries of southeast Asia; Communist tactics of world war, infiltration, and 'volunteer' invasions will be used against Thailand, Indo-China, Burma, and then Indonesia." (*New York Times*, July 8, 1951).

BURMA

Burma, along with Thailand, produces enough extra rice to help feed the people of India, Japan, the Philippines, Malaya, Singapore, Hong Kong, Ceylon, and Java. Soviet control of these sources of rice in southeast Asia would have important repercussions. The Soviet Union could hold back rice from those who opposed its will, or sell this basic food to people who bowed to its demands. Oil and tin in these areas could also be used as economic weapons. Burma is rich in all three commodities. In the hands of International Communism the 5,000 miles of mainland and islands from Burma to New Guinea would become a mighty barrier cutting off the Indian Ocean from the western Pacific. The riches of southeast Asia, plus its strategic position, could give Soviet policy-makers a big club to hold over most of the mainland of Asia including India, and the power to affect the future of Japan, the Philippines, Australia, India, and Pakistan.

Less than three months after Burma received its independence from Great Britain in 1948, a Communist-led insurrection broke out in the country. Later in the year other dissatisfied groups, including some army mutineers and most of the Peoples Volunteer Organization (PVO) also went into revolt. The PVO was a semi-military group of ex-soldiers who took part in the World War II resistance movement. At about the same time, Burma's largest minority group, the Karens, renewed their demands for a separate Karen state. They wanted to remain a distinct social entity, with their own language and customs. They believe that as a minority they are subject to unfair treatment and are at a disadvantage both politically and economically. In January, 1949, a militant Karen organization began an armed revolt against the Government. In some places Karen and Communist forces worked together, and in March, 1949 the PVO and the army mutineers also began to cooperate with the Communists. Soviet policy achieved the establishment of the "Peoples Democratic Front". With headquarters in Prome (150 miles north of Rangoon), the Communist front attempted to govern a large part of central Burma.

During the first half of 1950, the Burmese Government was able to regain some of the territory it had lost to the rebel groups. In March, 1950, the PVO broke with the Communists, and many party members, including several leaders, surrendered to the Government. The Karen insurgents also suffered losses, including their leader, and capital city of Toungoo.

Most of the Communist forces are located in central Burma, and can be supplied with military equipment by the Chinese Communists. Burma recognized Communist China in 1949, and the Embassy of the "People's Republic of China" soon established effective liaison with the Communist rebel groups in the capital city. Burma also established diplomatic relations with the Soviet Union in 1949, and in April of 1950 a large Soviet delegation moved into a huge mansion in Rangoon. The fifty Russians in the legation were obviously not all at work on strictly diplomatic activity. On top of this, Rangoon also is the seat of a large unofficial mission from Communist Indo-China,

which is active in propaganda work, and devotes considerable time
to aiding the clandestine Communist movement in nearby Thailand.
It appeared that Soviet policy for southeast Asia was in the act of
moving its headquarters from Bangkok to Rangoon—where the political climate was somewhat more desirable from the Communist point
of view. (*New York Times,* April 13, 1950).

The Burmese Government has, since its inception, been dominated
by the Anti-Fascist People's Freedom League, which is largely Socialist in composition, and with Marxist leanings. Headed by Thakin Nu
(later U Nu), the Government party is actually faced with two Communist groups—the White Flag Communists (Soviet), and the Red
Flag Communists (independent Marxist). Of these, the Soviet White
Flag Communists present, of course, the greater threat. Fortunately
for the Government, however, the Red Flag Communists seem just as
antagonistic to the White Flag group as they are to the Government,
and vice-versa.

On August 9, 1950, the Soviet Communist cause was strengthened
by the action of the pro-Communist Workers and Peasants Party joining hands with the White Flag (Soviet) Communists. It appeared
that Soviet policy aimed at a build-up of forces in northeast Burma
for an eventual merger with the Chinese Communists in bordering
Yunnan province. The Workers and Peasants Party was a dissident
element of the dominant Socialist Party of Thakin Nu, led by former
Labor Minister Thakin Lwin. The latter, together with another pro-
Soviet Socialist, Thakin Hla Kyway, were expelled from executive
positions in the Government coalition on September 21, 1950, for
speeches and activity in support of the Communist aggressors in
Korea and of Soviet policies generally. These men headed up the
Trade Union Congress, which at the same time was also cast out of
the Government coalition. Both pro-Soviets had repeatedly praised
the Soviet-controlled World Federation of Trade Unions. Other dissident Socialists who joined the Soviet cause at this time included
Thakin Chit Maung, peasant organizer, and Myo Nyunt, student organizer. These defections were timed to increase Communist prestige in Asia—on top of the Chinese Communist offensive in Korea at
the time. (See dispatches of Tillman Durdin in *New York Times,* September 22 and December 15, 1950).

The spring of 1952 saw Soviet policy in Burma swing to the "peace
offensive". Defense Minister U Ba Swe confirmed reports that peace
feelers had been put out by the Communists, demanding a "united
front" to combat "American imperialism, and its stooges, the Kuomintang and the Karen insurgent group." U Ba Swe said that the Com-

munists hoped by talking peace to gain a breathing spell which would enable them to reorganize and consolidate their forces. The Minister recalled that in the past Burma's Communists had profited by such maneuvers. He also offered proof that Communist leaders Thakin Tan Tun and Thakin Soe were at that time meeting in central Burma with Karen leaders to form a united front against the Government. (Durdin, *New York Times*, March 25, 1952). On June 16, 1952, the Government Minister Bo Khin Maung Gale revealed that Communist leader Thakin Tun Tan had written a letter to his deputy Bo Sein Tin, which explained that the Communist "peace" move was merely a temporary expedient whereby the Communists hoped to get into the Government in order to bore from within and ultimately gain a monopoly of political power. Three weeks later, Government sources revealed that Burmese Communists were being trained for future military activity in Burma by Chinese Communist Army training centers on the Burmese frontier.

One of the most fantastic aspects of the Burmese situation is that the Burmese Government is not only fighting the two Communist groups, the Karens, and assorted other dissident elements, but that it is using American military aid to fight American Chinese allies located in eastern Burma (Kengtung province). These Chinese, numbering about 10,000, sought refuge in Burma following the Communist conquest of China. Loyal to the Republic of China (located on Formosa after 1949), these troops are constantly harassed by Burmese Government forces, who fear the presence of these Chinese Government troops might antagonize Mao Tse-tung, and give him some sort of pretext for attacking Burma as he did Korea and Tibet. It was also charged that Thailand was aiding these Chinese soldiers, as part of the general anti-Communist struggle, a struggle which Burma is only interested in as it affects internal Burmese problems.

Burmese appeasement of Communist China extended not only to diplomatic recognition, but also to countenancing Mao Tse-tung's demands for a large slice of northern Burmese territory traversed by the Stillwell Road. On February 7, 1952, the Burmese Ambassador to Peiping, U Myint Thein, recommended to his government that Mao be given the northern triangle of Burma, involving hundreds of square miles.

Burma's foreign policy is officially "neutral", as was India's during World War II, and during the Korean war. India, Burma, and Indonesia profess to see little to choose from between the Soviet Union and the United States, and their "peace-at-any-price" attitude toward Soviet expansion in Asia plays directly into Soviet policy execution.

James Michener relates his conversation with a typical Burmese Government spokesman: ". . . as between Communism and another war, they'll take Communism." (*The Voice of Asia*, Random House, 1951, p. 221). This same Burmese told Michener: "We side with India in international affairs, and Nehru says India will not be overrun by the Chinese." When he was asked: "You agree with Nehru when he says there is no danger from Red China?" the reply was "Yes."

MALAYA

Moscow's policy in Malaya is executed by the Communist Malayan Races Liberation Army, which, in mid-1952 numbered about 4,000 men, divided into regiments of 400 men apiece. They are supported by the Min Yuen, the underground Communist Party in Malaya. Operating under rigid Communist discipline in small bands in the jungle their numbers appear to be limited only by the amount of guns and ammunition available. Striking out from their mobile camps in the jungle and then quickly disappearing, these 4,000 bandits have, since 1948, harried and baffled a force of nearly 150,000 British and Commonwealth troops. In Malaya the Communists discovered a terrain where, by their threat to vital dollar-earning rubber and tin resources, a small force can hold down infinitely larger numbers of troops and police, and where a Communist underground can intimidate or cajole a population already split by racial resentments. Malaya, and the great base of Singapore form the hard core—on land, at sea, and in the air—of the defensive system in southeast Asia. If Indo-China should fall to Soviet expansion, Siam and Burma would soon follow, and Malaya would be exposed and indefensible.

Originally, the Malayan Communist Party had its origins as an offshoot of the Chinese Communist Party, and at the mid-century 95% of the Malayan Communists are Chinese (there are almost as many Chinese in Malaya as there are Malayans). Soviet policy is directed from Peiping, which is the Cominform's Far East headquarters. Here the activities of all Far Eastern Communists are controlled. Communist China has specific Soviet instructions to achieve in Malaya a "Malayan People's Republic" by armed insurrection. (See Henry Lieberman's article, *New York Times*, August 20, 1951). Insurrections in Burma and Malaya broke out in 1948, following a communist conference in Calcutta on the "situation in the colonial and semi-colonial areas" of Asia. According to a former political commissar in the Malayan Races Liberation Army, Malayan Communist leader Ching Peng

(P'ing) visited Communist China just prior to the Communist rebellion, to receive instructions on how to proceed.

In its early stages, the Malayan Communist Party operated under the Comintern's Far Eastern Bureau in Shanghai, which had a Pan-Pacific Trade Union Secretariat to organize the workers of south Asia. The Malayan Communists, mainly Chinese, were periodically visited by Comintern agent Joseph Ducroux, alias Serge Lefranc, a French Communist arrested by the Singapore police in 1931. A meeting reminiscent of the early Pan-Pacific Trade Union Secretariat was held in Peiping in the fall of 1949, when Asian and Australian representatives of the Soviet-controlled World Federation of Trade Unions met to discuss "area problems". Among those attending were Chinese, Korean, Indo-Chinese, Burmese, Siamese, Indonesian, Australian, and Malayan Communists. It is generally believed that it was at this conference that Soviet intentions for Korea were transmitted to Far Eastern Communists. (See article by Richard Deverall, *America*, January 20, 1951). This conference also saw Malayan Communists receive new instructions for operations against the British.

Ching Peng, the little publicized secretary-general of the Malayan Communist Party, is a Malayan born Chinese (date of birth believed to be 1919). He led the guerrillas of Perak state during World War II, and seized control of the party machinery in 1948 after the former party chieftan Loi Teck (alias Wright) fled under party charges of "gradualism, misappropriation of party funds, and collaboration with the Japanese." Unfortunately for Ching Peng, Malaya has no common border with Communist China, and hence contact with Peiping can only be made via Thailand, which is the strongest anti-Communist state of southeast Asia. Even at that, Malayan Communist military units have a number of training and rest camps in Betong, a salient that juts down from Thailand into Malaya.

The number one Communist target in Malaya is the second largest state of the Malayan Federation, Perak—premier producer of tin and rubber, and wealthiest of all Malayan states. The 500,000 Chinese of Perak outnumber the 400,000 Malays, immigrant Indians, and Pakistanis. Perak's tens of thousands of tin, mine, and rubber estate workers have been particularly vulnerable to Communist pressures, both terrorist and political. The state's tin industry, with its large-scale Chinese ownership management, has been a major cause of Communist penetration in Perak, and the tribute (financial) which the Communists exact *sub rosa* from the owners, managers, and workers of the industry—enforced through ruthless terrorist killings—has brought more funds into Communist coffers than any other single source of revenue in the Malay peninsula.

Communist activities in Perak are typical of the overall Malayan operation. Operating from jungle hideouts, the Reds raid the mines, estates, and villages, stage road ambushes, burn property, harass military posts, and, in individual acts of terrorism, murder persons who fail to cooperate with them or perform key functions in the Government or the country's economy. Armed Communist bands are assisted by a network of agents within the civilian population who collect money, supply food, and serve as spies and agents of intimidation (Tillman Durdin, New York Times, July 28, 1952).

Communist propaganda in Malaya is directed at ejecting the British, and also at extolling the Soviet Union. The distribution of Russian and Chinese Communist films in Malaya and southeast Asia generally has resulted in influencing thousands of Asians who know little or nothing of Great Britain and the United States. About sixty Russian films are available in southeast Asia and south China, some of them in Mandarin, the official Chinese language. Many of these films are 16 mm., for showing from mobile projectors in the villages. Their audience is probably the world's largest. Among Russian films shown in the area since 1950 is one of the fall of Berlin, which dramatically shows the strength of the Soviet Army and the "benignity" of Josef Stalin. Care is taken to identify the Russian leaders; Mongolian troops are prominent in this picture, and their relationship with European Russians must impress race-conscious Asians as much as the scenes of Russian military might. Chinese newsreels about Korea are also widely shown. They include scenes showing American dead and prisoners of war, with Chinese "volunteers" tending to the wounds of the "aggressive troops of the Wall Street bosses." These films cannot legally be shown in Malaya, and therefore their effectiveness is greater in the neighboring states. However, the American and British films shown in Malaya and southeast Asia generally often unwittingly serve Communist purposes. Their pre-occupation with sex, crime, and indifferent public morals is used by Communist leaders to support the Soviet line about western moral decadence. Most Asians are not amused by drinking scenes and public displays of affection. The Russians and the Chinese Communists are more careful, and there is little in their films to offend Asian modesty. Soviet policy is deliberately based on an effort to win over the Asians through carefully conceived propaganda. (Richard Deverall, "Hollywood's Betrayal in Asia", America, June 21, 1952).

Two weapons which the British authorities have employed in dealing with the Communist problem are resettlement of rural inhabitants to areas where the Communists cannot infiltrate and influence them, and special catering to the political and social aspirations of the huge Chinese groups of Malaya. Unfortunately the resettlement program has caused considerable economic disruption, and the Communists in some cases have gone in with the resettled groups to continue to harass and cajole them. The British effort to bring the largely loyal Chinese Malayans into the anti-Communist fight seems more promising of satisfactory results. Sir Gerald Templer, British High Commissioner for Malaya, has sought since the beginning of 1952 to give Malaya's economically powerful Chinese (2,500,000) some kind of political voice without stirring up the peninsula's 2,500,000 indigenous Malays. He found an ally in Cheng-lock Tan, a stalwart anti-Communist whom the Reds once tried to assassinate. Tan founded the Malayan-Chinese Association in 1949 to provide Malaya's Chinese with a spiritual alternative to Marxism. At first, the association helped resettle Chinese squatters from bandit-infested areas. But Tan wished to do far more. In mid-July, 1952, the Association was transformed into the first Malayan-wide Chinese political party devoted to assisting the British authorities against the Communist bandits. It also champions the political claims of the Chinese in Malaya. Many of the Chinese in this new party are strongly inclined toward the Chinese Republic on Formosa, and their anti-Communist sentiments do not stem from any short-sighted internal situation, but rather do they regard the problem as world-wide, and transcending national boundaries.

On July 28, 1952, the British announced the formation of a special 1500-man Chinese military unit to help protect the tin rich Kinta Valley from Communist terrorism and extortion. Americans, Britishers, and Frenchmen are the big producers of tin in the Kinta Valley, but the most numerous of the tin mine operators are the Chinese. This predominantly Chinese character of the Kinta tin industry made it especially vulnerable to political terrorists and pressures from the Chinese Communists and their Malayan allies. Practically every mine laborer is believed to be paying a monthly tribute to the Communists. Their take from the Kinta mines was estimated in mid-1952 to be 500,-000 Straits dollars annually. The British and Tan strongly feel that only Chinese can effectively deal with the peculiar problems of the Kinta area.

The British are not only faced with the Communist problem in Malaya, but also in British Borneo and Sarawak. On August 7th, 1952, Communist military bands raided the village of Kuching, Sarawak. Here again, the large Chinese groups are constant prey to Communist pressures.

It is interesting to note that whereas Great Britain has recognized Communist China and hinders anti-Communist activities in Hong Kong and even Singapore, it is dependent on the aid of pro-Nationalist Chinese in Malaya and other British territories to curtail Communist encroachments in southeast Asia. A leading British colonial administrator, Sir Franklin Gimson, declared upon his retirement in 1952: "It is imperative that the Free Chinese forces be strengthened to prevent the Reds from moving into Indo-China, after which they would have Burma and Thailand. We can defend Malaya, but the loss of those countries would be very serious to the world." (Thomas E. Dewey, *Journey to the Far Pacific*, Doubleday, 1952, p. 285).

INDONESIA

Soviet policy in Indonesia made its supreme effort on September 18, 1948, when the Soviet agent Muso established a Communist regime in Madiun, Java. The Indonesian Communists were joined by the Socialists of former premier Amir Sjarifudin and the Labor Party of former premier Setiadjit, and a Soviet Government was proclaimed. After several days' fighting, Republic of Indonesia troops put down the rebellion and Soviet leaders Muso, Sjarifudin, and Alimin were executed.

Travelling under a false name, Muso arrived from Moscow (via Bangkok) in Java, on August 12, 1948. He posed as private secretary to Dr. Suripno, Indonesian Minister to Prague. Muso's first public appearance was at a meeting of the Indonesian Communist Party at Jogjakarta on August 20th. The meeting adopted resolutions demanding that the Indonesian Government of Premier Hatta break off negotiations with the Dutch, establish diplomatic relations with Soviet Russia, form a "national front" government giving Communist key cabinet posts, and stand firmly against the Dutch. Nine days afterwards, Muso persuaded Sjarifudin's Socialists and Setiadjit's Labor Party to join the Communists; he also had the support of the recalled Prague Minister Suripno, and the Trade Union Federation (SOBSI). The subsequent uprising did much to sober the Indonesian regime into a realization that Dutch warnings of Communist machinations were substantially correct.

In 1945 Mohammed Yusuf revived the *Partai Kommunis Indonesia* (PKI), claiming it to be the legitimate successor of the original PKI formed in 1920 and declared illegal after uprisings on Java and Sumatra in 1926. Yusuf's frontal assault tactics against the policies of Indonesian leaders Hatta and Sukarno led to his arrest in March, 1946. Following this development, leading Communists in Indonesia established a new Communist Party, led by Sardjono, who had previously been active in Communist work both in Java and Australia (where he headed the Free Indonesia group in Brisbane). At first Sardjono adopted a policy of nominal collaboration with the Indonesian Government, and ostensibly supported the Linggadjati and Renville agreements made with the Dutch.

Meanwhile another Communist, Tan Malakka, a Moscow-trained revolutionary, organized the "People's Front," which originally included Sjarifudin's Socialist Youth Movement (*Pesindo*). However, Tan Malakka's highly critical attitude toward Indonesian President Soekarno led to defection from the Front, and finally, to the arrest of Tan Malakka by the Government. While under police custody, in June, 1946, Tan Malakka somehow managed to kidnap Premier Sjahrir, but prompt action by President Soekarno resulted in the seizure and imprisonment of Tan Malakka, who was finally executed on April 16, 1949. This was not, however, until after he had formed a new extremist political faction known as the *Partai Murba*.

The collapse of Tan Malakka's People's Front opened the way to formation of a new Communist-dominated coalition, the *Sajap Kiri*, an organization including the Indonesian Communist Party (PKI), the *Pesindo*, the Socialist Party, also led by Sjarifudin, and the *Partai Buruh Indonesia* (PBI—Indonesian Workers Front). The *Sajap Kiri* gave nominal support to the cabinet of Sjahrir, but frustrated his actual efforts to seek agreement with the Dutch. Its representative in the government, Defense Minister Sjarifudin (who later admitted secret Communist membership) refused to ask Indonesian Republican troops to carry out cease-fire orders, thus dooming the Linggadjati agreement with the Dutch. Sjarifudin succeeded Sjahrir as premier, and among his cabinet appointees was Minister of State Maruto Darusman, Vice President of the PKI. Sjarifudin represented Indonesia during the negotiations with the Dutch aboard the U.S.S. Renville; the American representative Mr. Frank Graham, who described the Dutch as "Totalitarian" and the Indonesians as the "forces of freedom," apparently never realized who Sjarifudin really was.

The Communist-controlled *Sjap Kiri* was succeeded in early 1948 by the *Front Demokrasi Rakjat* (Democratic Peoples Front), which gave nominal support to the Hatta Government. Muso's arrival in August, 1948 resulted in a further Communist consolidation and increase of strength, which encouraged the Soviet insurrection of September.

The usual tactic of infiltrating the labor movement had an early success for Indonesia's Communists. The largest union of the country, the Federation of Industrial Workers—SOBSI, *Sentral Organisai Buruh Seluruh Indonesia,* claims 1,300,000 in 28 unions. Formed on November 29, 1946, it merged with the PKI in September, 1948. Indeed the PKI takes credit for organizing SOBSI, and its two leaders, Setiadjit and Bujung Soleh are party members. SOBSI was government-financed from the start, and uses the hammer and sickle insignia. Other PKI affiliates include the *Barisan Tani* (Peasant Union), headed by PKI President Sardjono, and the *Sarbupri* (Plantation Workers Union), led by PkI Vice-President Maruto Darusman. The latter group was given the task by the Republican Army in the summer of 1947 to carry out the "scorched earth" program against the Dutch. The Peasant Union has its own para-military organization, known as the *Laskpar Tani.*

The Indonesian Communists have had a particularly close tie with the Malayan Stalinites. The General Labor Union (GLU) of Singapore, largely Communist-dominated, has worked closely with the Malayan Nationalist Party and the *Pembantu Merdeka Indonesia,* both Communist-oriented organizations, affiliated with the PKI. The Malay Communists have been at all times in closest possible contact with their allies in Indonesia. A letter captured by the Dutch, dated May 5, 1948, written by a leading Indonesian Communist, shows how Communist leader Djamaludin was sent to Singapore with a considerable sum to establish better working relationships with the Malay Communists, and to open up an Indonesian Communist center in the city. For a time, the Indonesian Republic even gave direct support to Communist operations in Singapore. This is shown in a letter dated June 14, 1948, in which the Republican Governor of West Sumatra asked a Mr. Utoyo, Republican representative in Singapore, to establish an organization to do espionage work against the Dutch. Mr. Utoyo was specifically told: "You are allowed to get members of the PKI for this especially strategic organization to work together with other organizations established in Singapore and Malaya." (*Communism in the Republic of Indonesia,* Netherlands Information Bureau, New York, September, 1948, p. 7). All expenses for this operation were to be borne by the Indonesian regime.

The relationship between the PKI and the headquarters of the international Communist movement in Moscow has been a close one. Most top PKI leaders have been trained in Moscow. Muso first went there in 1925, seeking Stalin's support for a revolution in Java. Following the unsuccessful revolt of 1926, Muso, who was in Singapore,

made his way back to Moscow, where he remained until his return to
Java in August, 1948. Indeed, during his twenty-two years in Russia,
Muso received a more intensive training than any other Moscow
foreign agent. Highly regarded by Stalin, Muso was groomed to become the chief Communist leader of south-east Asia, having attended
the Lenin Institute and other schools to study military tactics, political
organization, propaganda, economics, and foreign languages.

One of PKI's most influential leaders, Mas Alimin Prawirodirdjo,
sometimes known as Pak Alimin, went directly to Moscow after his exile
from Indonesia by the Dutch in 1925. For many years he studied at
the Lenin University, where he came into contact with such prominent
Communists as China's Chou En-lai, Britain's Harry Pollitt, Australia's
Sharkey, France's Thorez, and America's Browder. During the years
1933-1941 Alimin was an active propagandist of the Comintern in
Europe, the Middle East, and China. In 1936 he took part in organized riots in Palestine. At the time of the Japanese push on Malaya,
Alimin was the official Soviet representative in Kuala Limpur (Malaya) and had taken on Soviet citizenship. On V-J day he was in China
with his friend Chou En-lai. Upon receipt of new instructions from
Moscow, Almin proceeded to Java, "to arrive amongst his own people
as a messenger from Moscow: Javanese by birth, Russian by citizenship, and Communist by faith," as the Batavia correspondent of the
Indian *Hindustan Times* so aptly put it.

Another leading PKI officer, Sardjono, was active for some time
in Australia, where he headed the Central Committee for a Free Indonesia. While there he maintained close ties with Australia's Communists in Brisbane.

Communist machinations in Indonesia, made evident to the
Indonesian Government by the rebellion of 1948, continued to be more
or less ignored by government officials. The party remained legal, had
a few representatives in the non-elected "Parliament," and retained its
stranglehold over the economy. In addition to controlling over half a
million plantation workers, the Communists held key positions among
railway and dock workers, and in the oil, tin, and textile industries.
Communists, operating not only legally, but illegally as well, continued
guerrilla activities against the Government. The Communist conquest
of China led to an upsurge of Communist activities in Indonesia, especially in efforts to influence two million Chinese of Indonesia. On
August 16, 1951, the Indonesian Government arrested 100 persons,
including sixteen members of Parliament, on charges of working with
Mao Tse-tung to overthrow the Indonesian regime. Among those
seized was Ang Yang-coan, editor of the Chinese daily *Sin Po*, and

Rustam Effendy, former Communist member of the Dutch Parliament.

Oddly enough, however, Indonesia recognized Communist China, which operates a sixty-man legation in Jakarta, headed by Wang Jen-hsu, who was associated with the Communist coup at Madiun. This Embassy has become the center of Communist operations in Indonesia, encouraging the Indonesian regime to be at least "neutral" as between Communist expansion in Asia, and efforts by the United Nations to contain this expansion.

On February 23, 1952, the anti-Communist cabinet headed by Dr. Sukiman (who had led the Communist round-ups of August, 1951) resigned as a result of pressures brought to bear opposing Indonesian acceptance of American economic aid as a threat to the "neutral" policy. A new Government was formed by Dr. Wilopo, who took over the Foreign Ministry from Achmad Subardjo, the man responsible for negotiating with the United States.

Indonesia, which follows the Nehru line in foreign affairs, continues to be plagued by a Communist threat which it would rather pretend did not exist. Communist armed bands roam the country, at times working with the fanatical Moslem Darul Islam guerrillas. Communists continue to control most of the economy, and are free to operate as a legal party. Communist activity in nearby British Borneo has been on the increase since August, 1951. Communists are in the vanguard of the popular demand for Dutch Western New Guinea. Soviet policy, if it could succeed in gaining control of Indonesia, would then establish a bridge to Australian Communism, and imperil the security of the south Pacific.

6

Communism in Japan and the Pacific

In the Yoyogi section of Tokyo, on a rutted road called Meiji street, stands a two-story grayish cement building near the famed Meiji shrine. Over the door a sign proclaims *Kyosanto Hombu*—Communist Party headquarters. This Red Meiji shrine is flanked on one side by a wooden building housing a Communist newspaper office, and on the other by a bookstore overflowing with Communist literature.

In central Tokyo near the Correspondents' Club stands a rambling five story building. A sign identifies it as Mitsubishi 21—the 21st building constructed on the extensive lands in the region owned by the Mitsubishi interests. It housed a high proportion of the 218 members of the Soviet mission to Japan. To Mitsubishi 21 came the Japanese Reds for guidance and advice. The Japanese Communist leaders were released from jail and personally escorted to their homes by United States Foreign Service Officers in 1945. Japanese Communists in Japan were allowed to return, and were given full freedom of action. These actions were taken in accordance with the Potsdam Declaration and in obedience to directives from Washington at a time when the after-glow of the European alliance between the democracies and the U.S.S.R. during the latter portion of World War II had not yet entirely faded.

In January, 1947 Communist-dominated unions in Japan were able to plan an effective strike in defiance of General MacArthur's authority because they were assured by Russian and other elements inside the Far Eastern Commission that "political strikes" would be sanctioned.

Soviet policy in Japan was designed, after 1945, to weaken American influence, form an alliance with Japanese nationalism, particularly as it was aimed against the United States, move into the key areas of Japanese political life vacated by the Occupation purges, and draw a "neutral" Japan to ever closer association with Communist China and the Soviet Union. With a hard core of 55,000 party members, and ringed dupes, sympathizers, and many Japanese Socialists, considerable success was achieved. Jap Communists infiltrated their own people as well as fellow travelers into the school system as replacements for 120,000 purged Japanese school teachers.

The chief Communist method of exerting power, however, was by gaining control of existing mass organizations, particularly unions.

In Japan where unionism is new and confusing, the usual trick of in-
flitrating unions with Communist "fractions" was quite successful. The
Communists were frequently able to win over the new and unsoph-
isticated heads of certain unions.

Some Communist influence in the trade unions has been lost to the
Socialists since the Korean war. In 1947, and for some time thereafter, the two Communist strongholds were the Government Railway
Workers with 540,000 members, and the Communications Ministry Em-
ployees Union, with 380,000 members. In January, 1947 the Communists moved in to support union demands for higher wages to meet the
inflated cost of living. Communists organized the All-Japan Labor
Unions Joint Struggle Committee, a third of whose 46 members were
Communists, and whose three leaders and active directors were Communist-controlled. The Joint Committee was led by the Communists
to precipitate a general strike by the nearly two million who followed
its directives. The strategy was partly aimed at overthrowing the
Yoshida Government. The demands made by the committee were set
so high that they could not possibly be acceptable to the Government.
The strike was thus frankly political, as was admitted by Yoshio Shiga,
one of the leading Communists involved. Soviet strategy actually went
far beyond the overthrow of the Yoshida Cabinet. It aimed primarily
at wrecking the American occupation by creating conditions of chaos
in Japan. The strike would rapidly have produced starvation and civil
disorders plus industrial paralysis.

The Communist strike action had not fully taken into account
the measure of General MacArthur, however. He stepped in with a
written order forbidding the strike and promising drastic penalties for
violation of the order. The Russians on the Far Eastern Commission
were unable to carry out their pledges of support. For the first time
since 1945 the Communists in Japan lost face, and Japanese non-Communist union leaders began to realize just who it was that their bed-
fellows were serving.

Following the establishment of the Occupation in 1945, the Japanese
Communists established a three man dictatorship of the party. These
three men were Kyuichi Tokuda, Sanzo Nosaka, and Yoshio Shiga.
Tokuda was born in Okinawa in 1894, and became a criminal lawyer.
He helped found the Communist Party in Japan, and visited Moscow
three times, in 1922, 1926 and 1927. Arrested by the Japanese in 1928,
he remained in jail until released by the Americans in 1945. Immediately he became secretary-general of the Jap Communist Party, and
was elected to the Diet (Parliament) in 1946. Violently anti-American,
Tokuda is an expert rabble-rousing speaker, dynamic, arrogant, and

uncompromising. He opposes coalitions with "liberals," and strongly favors "direct action."

Nosaka was born in 1892, studied at Keio University, became an economist, and joined the Communists when a young man. He fled to Russia in 1931, and has more Soviet background than other leading Japanese Communists. He once served on the executive committee of the Comintern. In 1943 Nosaka went to Chinese Communist headquarters in Yenan, and in January 1946 was allowed to return to Japan. A so-called "intellectual", Nosaka has considerable appeal to Japanese of similar classification. He is the best informed Japanese Communist concerning the outside world, and for some time was the closest to the Russians. Nosaka is at his best when the Jap Communists are told to carry out a "united front" policy of rapprochement with Socialists and "liberals."

Yoshio Shiga stands between the Tokuda and Nosaka factions. A fine lecturer and propagandist, he has much the same background as his compatriots in regard to arrests and imprisonment.

As late as 1949, the Communists polled nearly three million votes (9.6% of the total), but the April, 1951 elections saw them drop to 336,000 votes (less than one percent). This was the result of joining with the Socialists to oppose any peace treaty that did not include Soviet Russia and Communist China. A change in Soviet tactics for Japan occurred in 1950, when the "soft" policy of Nosaka was changed to the "hard" policy of Tokuda. The result was at least a temporary shock to many "liberals" who had played the Communist game, thinking the Communist to be merely more to the "Left" than they. The "hard" policy also saw a relaxation of the Communist grip on the unions, and the rise of moderate Socialist influence in many unions formerly oriented toward Moscow. The Soviet attack on the Korean Republic was a major contribution to strengthening the anti-Communist forces in Japan, for ever since June 25, 1950, those Japanese who consistently played the Communist game could no longer be passed as innocents who did not know what was going on.

The signing of the Japanese peace treaty in the spring of 1952, provided that all Japanese property must be returned to Japan within 90 days of the effective date of the treaty. This posed quite a problem to the Soviet Government which maintained a large delegation of Soviet clerks, military men, intelligence officers, and propaganda experts. Either Soviet Russia had to withdraw its mission from Tokyo, or else it would have to regularize its relations with the new Japan, and sign the peace treaty. The decision was to withdraw.

In November, 1951, the Soviet Union sought through devious means to lure Japan into an economic rapprochement with Asian Communism. The Soviet mission in Tokyo invited top Japanese businessmen, government officials, industrialists and ex-military men to a cocktail party celebrating the anniversary of the Russian revolution. On November 26th, Soviet economic experts conferred with leading Japanese commercial groups to explore the possibilities of Japanese Soviet trade, as well as Japanese-Chinese Communist trade. In April, 1952, several Japanese traveled to Moscow to attend the Economic Conference, designed to break up the impending anti-Soviet coalition, and bring especially Britain and Japan into commerical and economic relationships with the Communist world.

The signing of the peace treaty, and the expected withdrawal of the Soviet mission in Tokyo was not only offset by Soviet economic pressures on Japan, but also by the continued presence of Soviet military units, a few miles from the northernmost island of Hokkaido. This island contains only four million Japanese, is mountainous, has long, difficult-to-defend coastlines which front Soviet islands (Given Russia at Yalta), and maintains communications with Nippon only by air and ferry. Communications on Hokkaido during the winter months are extremely poor. In the summer, a few sabotage teams could tie the rail network into knots. Beginning in 1950, Soviet patrol boats have been seizing Japanese fishing craft and their crews, returning them months after capture. In the spring of 1952 Soviet-made mines appeared in considerable numbers in the Tsugaru Straits, which divide Hokkaido from the main Japanese island of Honshu. Noboru Saito, Director-General of the Japanese Rural Police, has said that between 1946 and 1952 no less than 10,400 illegal "immigrants" were apprehended on Hokkaido. During October, 1951, the Japanese residents on the island were increasingly disturbed by the noise of Soviet offshore gunfire, and the display of Soviet searchlights at night from Soviet submarines and patrol boats. On October 23, 1951, it was revealed that the Soviets were strongly fortifying Kunashiri Island, only twenty miles from Hokkaido. Soviet steamers loaded with tanks and trucks were seen passing through the straits, and Soviet air activity increased.

In the immediate post-World War II period, Communist "people's courts" operated on Hokkaido, and were used by the Communists to establish control in the rich coal mining areas of Hokkaido's Bibai and Sunagawa areas. During 1948 Communist leader Nosaka toured the entire island and told well-guarded, secret Communist meetings of the strategic importance of the Communist cadres in Hokkaido for the years ahead. Communist interest in Hokkaido is based on the obvious fact that Russian territory is less than three miles away; additionally, disruption of Hokkaido could bring serious dislocation to the Japanese economy as a whole. In Hokkaido is found 25% of Japan's coal, 40% of the manganese ore production, 32% of the fisheries output, 25% of the milk cows, 80% of the asbestos, 80% of all newsprint production, and almost 100% of the mercury production. Guerrilla activity supported from Soviet-held territory in Sakhalin and the Kuriles (formerly Japanese but now Russian thanks to Yalta) is a distinct possibility for Hokkaido, particularly if the Soviets consolidate their Korean position, as a result of the United Nations failure to drive the aggressor out of Korea. (Richard Deverall, "Red Star Over Japan," *America*, March 1, 1952).

Soviet policy in Japan was dealt severe blows not only by the unfavorable reaction which Soviet aggression in Korea had on the Japanese people, but also by the retention of thousands of Japanese soldiers by the Soviet Union—captured by Russia in its week-long participation in the second World War's Asian theatre. Increasingly, Communist policy-makers realized that their only remaining effective weapon was Japanese nationalism, especially as directed against the United States occupation. Stalin issued a statement on December 31, 1951, expressing "the profound sympathy of the peoples of the Soviet Union for the Japanese people who are in difficult straits because of foreign occupation." This statement was followed by Communist riots in February and April, building up for a huge anti-American demonstration on May Day, 1952. Para-military groups were prepared for action by the issuance by the Communist High Command on January 23, 1952 of a pamphlet entitled "How to Raise Flower Bulbs." This pamphlet dealt with the organization of guerrilla units, and how to operate against the police in large cities. It went on to assert that "the struggle is advancing in a military direction. . . . we must commence preparation for armament and action." The Japanese people, it stated, "have been developing a resistance to, and struggle in defense against American imperialism." So-called "nuclear defense teams," consisting of five to ten persons each, were organized by Communist workers in factories, rural communities, and schools, and included those "who have the determination, will, and ability to fight against American imperialists and traitors." (Quoted by Takeo Naoi in the *New Leader*, May 12, 1952). This secret Communist pamphlet goes far to explain the extraordinary magnitude and violence of the May Day riots, which caused two deaths and hundreds of injured throughout Japan. Norman Thomas, who was present in Tokyo at the time, described the riots as a "minor dress rehearsal for revolution." It was clear that the signing of the peace treaty and the end of the occupation would bring no peace to Japan. The Japanese Government was now faced with the problem of what to do with the Pandora's box on Meiji street, which had been opened by the Americans in 1945.

Soviet policy in Japan has been executed not only by the local Communist Party, but also by activities of Soviet agents and their foreign allies. The most outstanding known example of this type of operation was the spy ring organized by Soviet agent Richard Sorge, with its center in Japan, and with outlets on the entire Asian continent. Agnes Smedley, reputedly a newspaper correspondent, but actually a veteran in Soviet espionage, was chief recruiter of the ring in China.

Richard Sorge was a secret German Communist, assigned by the Soviet Government to the Far East. He was directly connected with the Intelligence section of the Soviet Army with the rank of Colonel. By getting himself named as press attache of the German Embassy in Tokyo, he gained entree into official Japanese circles. Through Agnes Smedley he was introduced to Hotsumi Ozaki, who became his right hand man. Miss Smedley was also instrumental in securing the services for his ring of one Teikishi Kawai, whose affidavit aided the American authorities in their investigation. The events described took place in 1941, but the investigation occurred after the American occupation of Japan.

Ozaki, Sorge's right-hand man, was an old college friend of two prominent members of the international Institute of Pacific Relations, who had been recommended to IPR office by Edward C. Carter, American IPR leader. These two were Ushiba and Saionji, influential in the Japanese cabinet. It was in this way that Sorge was able to obtain valuable information from many sources in Tokyo, and even to guide Japanese policy along directions desired by Soviet Russia. The Soviet Government was most eager that Japan should attack the United States through the Philippines, rather than the Soviet Union via Manchuria. It was Sorge's job to have his Japanese friends close to the cabinet inform him of probable Japanese action, and to influence that decision so that it would go against the United States, and in favor of Soviet Russia. By October 15, 1941, Sorge was able to advise the Soviet Government that Japan had decide to strike south rather than north. He transmitted this information to Moscow according to his usual custom, through radio messages sent by Max Klausen, whose disappearance from Japan by way of the Soviet Embassy first put American Intelligence on his trail. At least thirty of these messages were sent to Moscow from the home of Guenther Stein, a British newspaper correspondent, and China correspondent for an IPR publication edited by Owen Lattimore. Stein's IPR articles—all favorable to Asian Communism—were distributed through the U. S. Office of War Information at precisely the same time that Stein was engaged in his activites as a member of the Sorge spy ring.

It was in this way that the Soviet Government had information on the Pearl Harbor attack, well in advance of the event. Even though Russia was our ally in Europe at this, she did not see fit to pass on this important information to the United States. Three days after the final accomplishment of his two year mission, Sorge was discovered, tried, and executed in 1944 (Institute of Pacific Relations, Hearings Before the Senate Internal Security Subcommittee, 82nd Congress, Part 2, pp. 353 ff., 449 ff.).

The Philippines

In the summer of 1950, the Communists in the Philippines believed that the islands would be theirs by 1952. Many outside observers believed this to be true. Soviet policy appeared about to repeat the China story. Communist-led *Hukbalahaps* were running wild in central Luzon, and the Philippine Government seemed powerless to do much about them. In some places they levied taxes, ran their own "Stalin" schools and newspapers, and maintained a string of "production centers." They had the passive help, at least, of thousands of villagers who were either frightened or deceived. Their Politburo met under the nose of the government in Manila and boldly drew up a "strategic plan for the seizure of national power." (See *Time*, November 26, 1951, pp. 36, 37).

The Huk leaders, from Luis Taruc on down, were trained in Moscow, and although they fooled many observers with their claim to being "agrarian reformers," it was soon evident that they were *bona fide* Stalinites bent on seizing a monopoly of political power in the Philippines to create another "Soviet Republic." Indeed Taruc admitted precisely that in 1950. World War II gave these Communist Huks their chance. During the years of Japanese occupation of the Philippines (1942-1944) the anti-Jap resistance was carried on by guerrilla forces, some of which were heavily infiltrated by the Communists. These guerrillas received military aid from the United States, which was used to good advantage later on. When the war ended, the Huks held out in the hills, looting, pillaging, attacking and defying the governmental authority in Manila. They terrorized whole villages, exacting tribute and enforcing their authority. It was said that they received supplies from Soviet submarines, and from junks out of Communist China.

A change in the situation occurred in the fall of 1950, when the

Philippines Government appointed Ramon Magsaysay Minister of Defense. When he took office there were 13,000 full time Communist Huk fighters in the hills of central Luzon, with perhaps 30,000 supporters in the cities and hinterland. By the spring of 1952 their hard core had been reduced to fewer than 8,000, and their former allies were turning against them. In Luzon villages where the hammer and sickle flew in 1950, villagers now went out of their way to help the government constabulary apprehend the Huks. Within less than two years about 2,000 Huk militants had surrendered to the government forces, while messages to army headquarters attested to the eagerness of many civilians to get out of Huk-held territory and live a free life under government protection.

Until Magsaysay took over, the whole campaign against the Huks had been marked by lethargy. Indeed the United States Government forbade the Filipinos to fight the Huks until the final apron strings to Washington were cut on July 4, 1946. During these post-war years money from Red Chinese in Malaya poured into the jungle in the form of military aid. Mimeograph machines and typewriters were reaching the Huks from American Communists such as William Pomeroy. Propaganda leaflets were smuggled in from the China coast. The Huks were riding high. It was then that Magsaysay took over personal direction of the military effort against the enemy, and supplemented it by social and economic policies of his own. Government forces moved against a rebel army deployed over an area four times as large as New York state, where many of the 20 million residents, contaminated by Communist propaganda, regarded the Huks as genial Robin Hoods. Magsaysay's forces moved against war-hardened men who knew the terrain, and who had mastered the art of the night ambush. This enemy, paradoxically enough, had been armed by United States taxpayers, and well armed. After the liberation of the Philippines, the United States Army made the fantastic error of paying 300,-000 guerrillas for services against the Japanese, without disarming one of them. The half million weapons thus left behind were increased when surplus American military supplies were dumped on the Manila market without inventory. The predicament of the Philippines was very much like that of the Chinese Government in 1946 when the Chinese Communists obtained an arsenal of Japanese weapons in Manchuria.

Side by side with the military campaign against the rebel Huks, Secretary Magsaysay offered an alternative to the Marxist promise of Utopia. He proposed a program of social rehabilitation, psychological warfare, and philosophical warfare. This approach to the problem was different from the economic determinist approach of many Anglo-

Saxon democrats who felt the entire solution lay in more food and better living conditions.

When Huk soldiers kidnap a youngster from a village and take him with them to the hills, they give him a prolonged "brain-washing" to wipe out his belief in democracy and/or religion. Magsaysay decided that the "intellectual approach" was worthwhile also as a counter-weapon. Accordingly, when in 1951 he captured twenty-two leading Huks, part of their jail time was spent in lectures by an expert on Communist philosophy pointing out to them the logical errors of Marxist thought. This head-on attack on basic Communist philosophy was a startling one to the Huks, and an effective one, as compared with the casual "current events" broadcasts of the Voice of America. However, such philosophical warfare is waged only after the Huks have been captured or surrender. Prior to that time, psychological warfare is practiced by Magsaysay; this includes air drops of surrender leaflets, and promises of amnesty and free farms for those not guilty of treason against the state.

In April, 1952, the Philippines Government launched an intensive hunt for the two Huk leaders—Luis Taruc and Jesus Lava. In the process they captured a top propagandist and educational leader of the Communist movement—American born William Pomeroy. Pomeroy came to the Philippines in 1945 with the Leyte Landings. At the time he was already an American Communist, being active in the Young Communist League. He later studied at the University of the Philippines under the G. I. Bill of Rights, and then began to work for the Huks. He taught in various Huk schools known as "Stalin universities."

At the end of 1952 a large Chinese Communist fifth column was exposed. Chin Sang, alias Chi Sen, leader of the Chinese Communist overseas organization was arrested, together with his chief lieutenants. This fifth column was charged with coordinating Huk activity with Moscow directives.

AUSTRALIA AND NEW ZEALAND

Outside of New Zealand and Australia, few people have heard of big, burly Jim Healy, product of Manchester, England, and one of Australia's top Communists. Nor have they heard of diminutive, bespectacled Toby Hill, a cockney by birth and New Zealander by upbringing, or of Jock Barnes, tall brawny mob orator. All the world, however, has heard of Harry Bridges, pro-Soviet chief of the Pacific longshoremen; what Bridges is to American longshoremen, Healy, Barnes, and Hill are to the longshoremen of Australia and New Zealand.

In the days immediately following World War II, Jim Healy, leader
of the Australian Communist-dominated longshoremen, headed a
delegation from the Australian Waterside Worker's Federation to New
Zealand. At the conclusion of the conference with their New Zealand
counter-parts, a Trans-Tasman organization had been formed, and the
two Waterside Worker's Federations, through this new body, agreed to
keep in close touch with one another to support Soviet foreign policy
and aggravate industrial and commercial troubles in the Pacific. It is
significant to note that at this time New Zealand was governed by a
Labor Administration which had given many benefits to the workers,
and was disposed to approach all problems from their viewpoint. That
this approach did little if nothing to cut the ground out from under
Anzac Communism is obvious enough.

In addition to the Anzac Communist merger, plans were made to
form a confederation of longshoremen's organizations around the
Pacific basin. In this move Harry Bridges, California Longshore and
Stalinite chief, was to play an important role. His Honolulu headquarters was to be the venue of the first conference of this proposed
confederation. Invitations went out to interested unions (i.e. Communist-dominated or influenced) in central and south America, Canada, China, India, Indonesia, etc.

Meantime the Anzac group, in close consultation with Harry Bridges,
worked hard to strengthen Soviet influence in the Pacific. Its first opportunity for international action came during the post-war difficulties
between the Dutch and the Indonesians. Playing the Communist line
"Hands off Indonesia," Dutch ships in Australian ports were declared
"hot." The New Zealand union joined the fray, and Soviet policy in the
Pacific was in high gear. There is little question as to the great influence which both Australian and New Zealand Communism had in
driving the Dutch out of Java, and strengthening the Communist
elements of the Republican movement.

Communist influence in the New Zealand longshoremen's union did
not become clearly apparent, however, until 1950 when the New
Zealand Federation of Labor expelled the Waterside Worker's Federation because it refused to sever its ties with the Soviet-controlled World
Federation of Trade Unions. Further proof of the New Zealand waterfront affiliation came when the New Zealand Waterside Worker's
Union accredited leading Australian Communists as delegates to Communist conferences in Milan and Peiping.

It was in February, 1951, that Soviet policy made its show of strength
in New Zealand. Longshoremen on the waterfront stopped work, and
ships stopped moving. The first effects of the strike were felt when

supplies of meat ceased. The slaughterhouses had to shut down. Then flour became scarce and bread supplies in the cities were endangered. It quickly became clear that unless supplies could be kept flowing, the people in the cities would soon be starving. New Zealand Prime Minister Sidney George Holland immediately organized squads of volunteer truck drivers, boat-operators, planes and pilots, to move the stationary supplies. Army personnel were pressed into longshore duty, and naval crews manned the ships. The drafting of servicemen to work the ports and coastal vessels broke the back of the strike. It also prevented another major Communist plan from succeeding. This plan was to halt the flow of food to Britain and western Europe, and to block further supplies for Korea.

Prime Minister Holland declared after winning the 142 day-old battle: "We accepted the challenge of the Communists and those who were foolish enough to heed them and become involved in the strike. We knew that the watersiders here were working with the watersiders in Australia and the longshoremen on the Pacific shore of the United States. We knew that the watersiders in Australia were openly commanded by Communists and that on the Pacific coast of America they were also under Communist domination. We knew that . . . the leadership had been planning to establish a joint secretariat in Honolulu with the object of controlling shipping throughout the Pacific. We had before us the statement of Ernest Thornton, one of the top-line executives of the Australian Communist Party, who is now a member of the Cominform staff in Peiping, that the policy of the Waterside Worker's Federation is decided in conjunction with the leaders of the Communist Party. . . . Here was a conspiracy aimed at preventing the flow of supplies to Americans in Korea, at stopping food from reaching Britain, at stalling the efforts of the western world to prepare against a possible Communist onslaught." (Quoted by William Green in USA, April, 1952, pp. 18, 19).

Holland's action was upheld by the voters of New Zealand in an election held immediately after the strike on the very issue of whether or not the Government had acted properly. The Government Party won four seats in the Parliament, and the Laborites lost four seats.

In the fall of 1951 Australian Prime Minister R. G. Menzies sought a constitutional amendment which would empower the government to dissolve the Communist Party and its auxiliaries as unlawful associations, and to eliminate Communists from trade unions, the civil service, and elsewhere. Four Australian states supported the amendment and four states opposed, but the overall popular vote resulted in a rejection by less than 100,000 votes out of five million total votes cast. Labor leader Herbert Evatt, ignoring the Korean war and the Communist control of the waterside warned the people that "Fascist, totalitarian conspirators intended to destroy the civil liberties of Australians," and his counsel prevailed. The Menzies Government was thus prevented from acting against an internal enemy whose directors were killing Australian fighting men in Korea.

Action to hold the line against further Communist encroachments in the Pacific basin was suggested in 1949 by Philippines President Quirino, who urged that the Republic of China(Formosa), the Philippines, the Korean Republic, Japan, Indo-China and Thailand form a sort of Pacific Pact, in conjunction with the United States and any other Pacific power that wished to join, to work in common against Soviet aggression in the Far East. Warmly seconded by President Rhee of Korea and Chiang Kai-shek of China, the suggestion fell on deaf ears in Washington. It was not until the Soviet attack in Korea that anything like common action was taken in the Far East to parallel the defense of Europe. The United States bolstered bilateral pacts with Japan and the Philippines with an Anzac alliance, to achieve the beginning of a better system of consultation and mutual security for parts of the Far East.

7

Communism in Korea

On Christmas Eve of 1950, Chinese Soviet Army Commander Chu Teh spoke at Peiping to a delegation that had just returned from the Warsaw "peace" conference. Ventilating China's "peaceful" intentions in Korea, General Chu Teh declared: "We will drive them (UN and Korean) forces back by our might if the United States will not withdraw from Korea and Taiwan (Formosa)." Chu Teh predicted that the "anti-imperialist feelings of the various Asiatic nations" would be built up to "a new record height." As Richard Deverall says in his article in *America* (January 20, 1951) "Anyone who, has read the published proceedings of the so-called 'labor conference staged by the World Federation of Trade Unions at Peiping during November and December of 1949 knows full well that Korean aggression was planned months before the north Koreans plunged southwards toward Seoul." At this "labor conference" Soviet policy determined on Korea as being the first of several thrusts; the others were Japan, southeast Asia, and India. Visitors in Asia during 1949 and 1950 noticed that Communist bookstores featured pamphlets on Korea and Korean "white papers" months before the actual aggression took place.

The attack on Korea directly follows the imperialist drive of the Soviet Union to Communize Asia, and to realize the prophecy of Lenin that "the road to Paris is through Peiping." When Mao Tse-tung met with Stalin in the Kremlin in February, 1950, to conclude the Chinese-Soviet military assistance pact, it was clear that the Kremlin aimed at expansion of Red China's military role in Asia, while at the same time forestalling any rearmament of Japan. The Korean attack was the logical outgrowth of the Soviet success in China, and proof to the world that Soviet military strength in Asia was considered strong enough by Stalin to risk direct military conflict.

During World War II, the United States, Britain, and China pledged their determination, in the Cairo conference declaration of December, 1943, that Korea would in due course become free and independent. This pledge was reaffirmed in the Potsdam conference declaration of July 26, 1945, and was subscribed to by the Soviet Union when it finally entered the war against Japan for the last two days. Korea was never formally divided into zones of occupation by agreement between the Big Powers involved. All that was agreed was that Russia could accept the surrender of Japanese troops north of the 38th parallel, and the United States could accept similar surrenders south of that line. As a result, Soviet forces first entered Korea on August 12, 1945, and proceeded to occupy the northern half of the country. American troops did not land in Korea until September 12th, to accept Japanese surrenders south of the 38th. But it soon became apparent that the division of Korea for surrender purposes was to be arbitrarily transformed by the Soviets into permanent political and military control of north Korea by the Soviet Empire.

At Moscow, in December, 1945, the Foreign Ministers of the United States, Britain, and Soviet Union, agreed that a provisional Korean democratic government should be set up for all Korea. An American-Russian Joint Commission was to carry out this desired end. However, every effort along these lines by the United States was blocked by the Soviet Union. The United States, unwilling to permit this situation to delay further the realization of Korean independence, then laid the question of Korea before the United Nations. In November, 1947, the General Assembly of the United Nations called for a free election in Korea to be observed by a United Nations Commission—an election which would result in a constituent asembly to draw up a constitution for a free, independent, and united Korea. The Soviet Union, however, refused to allow the United Nations Commission into north Korea and also refused to cooperate with it in any way. Consequently, the right of the Korean people to participate in a free election and to establish a free government was confined to south Korea. The election was held on May 10, 1948, under the supervision of the United Nations Korean Commission, and the Government of the Republic of Korea was established on August 15, 1948. This Government of the Republic of Korea was accepted by the United Nations in December, 1948, as the validly elected, lawful Government—the only valid Korean government. A new Commission was established to continue to try to bring north Korea into the area of the new and free Republic. The Republic of Korea was recognized by the United States on January 1, 1949, and 31 other nations followed suit. Admission of Korea to the United Nations was blocked by the Soviet Union, however.

Meanwhile, north of the 38th parallel, which had become a part of the Iron Curtain, the Soviet Empire established a Soviet colony on patterns similar to east-central Europe. A so-called Democratic People's Republic of Korea was set up as a Soviet puppet in September, 1948, in defiance of the United Nations. In North Korea, Russia brought back some 300,000 Koreans who had fled from the Japanese during the period of Japanese occupation 1905-1945; these Koreans had been screened and selected by the Soviets for Communization. The Soviets also brought back another two million who had fled into Manchuria and north China, and who there had allied themselves, after proper inducements, with the Chinese Communists. With this large nucleus, Russia established a Soviet satellite regime, based on an army of 20,000 men equipped with Soviet tanks, artillery, and planes. About 100,000 of these troops had seen service in the period 1945-1950 with the Chinese Communists against the Chinese Nationalist Government. For five years, the Soviet Union subjected the north Korean people to an unbroken barrage of propaganda, along the lines that "American imperialism was preventing the reunification of Korea, for the purpose of maintaining a military base in south Korea." The Soviets slowly but surely developed in north Korea a totalitarian puppet regime—an integral part of the Soviet Empire, with a strong and politically indoctrinated army which believed that it was going to fight for the reunification of the country.

In contrast, United States policy in south Korea consisted in trying to show both the USSR and Asia in general that the United States had no colonial or military designs on Korea. We announced and carried out a policy of withdrawing our forces as soon as possible, while simultaneously promising not to rearm the south Koreans. This policy is known as the policy of unilateral disarmament. It has never succeeded at any time in history. For the side that does not disarm, far from being edified by your exemplary behavior, is all the more tempted to strike you down, knowing in advance that you have deprived yourself of your only means of defense. The American policy was to keep the Republic of Korea so weak that nobody could charge that we were building a military base from which to attack Russia. The Republic of Korea was told that any movement north of the 38th, even to repel attacks or pursue attackers, would cause the United States to immediately cut off all aid to it. The only weapons supplied to the army of the Republic were light arms sufficient to put down small-scale guerrilla actions within the country. Repeated pleas of President Syngman Rhee for tanks, artillery, and fighting planes were brushed aside.

In pursuance of a United Nations resolution of December, 1948, to the effect that America and Russia withdraw their troops as soon as possible, the United States withdrew all its troops except for a token 500 man advisory force by June 29, 1949. The Soviets announced that they also had withdrawn but refused to allow the UN Commission in to verify the withdrawal. Thus, by mid-1949, the formidable fighting machine of north Korea was faced only by an ill-armed force in south Korea. The weakness of the position of the Republic of Korea was accentuated by official and unofficial indications from the United States that it had no intention of defending Korea. For instance, on July 17, 1949, Owen Lattimore, FDR's personal emissary to China, OWI Chief for Asia in World War II, and consultant to the Department of State on Far Eastern Affairs, made this statement: "The thing to do therefore, is to let south Korea fall, but not let it look as though we pushed it." In January and February of 1950, Secretary of State Dean Acheson declared that he did not consider Korea as within the United States security line. In this he was supported by President Truman, who overruled Defense Secretary Johnson and General Omar Bradley in order to support Acheson, who threatened to resign if his views were not adopted. Secretary Acheson also rejected General MacArthur's military recommendation that Korea was strategically important to the United States's defense of the Far East from Soviet attack. Acheson claimed MacArthur was too much concerned with military matters. He declared: "It is a mistake to become obsessed with military considerations." To the Kremlin, it was becoming increasingly clear that not only was the Republic of Korea hopelessly weak militarily, but that it had been abandoned by its supposed allies diplomatically. It is true that ten millions in military aid had been approved by the United States Government by the end of October, 1949, but unexplained delays resulted in only $200 worth of signal wire being delivered to Korea by the time the Soviets attacked on June 2, 1950.

Another factor in the weakness of Korea, was the American liberal conviction that Communism thrives on poverty, bad living conditions and standards, and that if economies and social conditions were strengthened, the problem is solved. This overlooks that fact that Communism is Soviet power, and Communism has only been established through Soviet power. It has correspondingly been stopped only by superior military might. After all, one cannot throw food packages and living standards at an advancing armed Soviet.

Politically, south Korea became healthy, as it did economically, in spite of the fact that the division of the country left most of Korean industry in the northern part of the country. Communism never gained much headway in south Korea, and thousands of refugees poured down from north to south Korea. But the decisive point here was that north Korea was stronger militarily. In summation, the Communist armies invaded the Republic of Korea for the following reasons: (1) Korea is of great strategic military value on north Asia, providing a good base from which to launch an attack on Japan and south-east Asia; (2) Russian foreign policy has long had aggressive aims against Korea; (3) the puppet regime in north Korea was militarily strong and well-propagandized; (4) the Republic of Korea was too weak militarily; (5) American policy indicated that it would not defend Korea if it was attacked; (6) the success of political and economic democracy in south Korea constituted an intolerable refutation of the Communist propaganda line in Asia.

Soviet expansion into Korea and all the Far East has been considerably facilitated through direct cooperation from fifth columns in America, and by indirect cooperation, as in the cases of John Carter Vincent, John S. Service, and Owen Lattimore. Symptomatic of our high level misunderstanding of Soviet power is the following statement from the top ranking State Department representative in Korea in mid-1946: "Naturally we shall have to stand against Russian expansion at some time and in some place but . . . Korea is not the place." He declared that the Soviets were justified in their expansion to some degree—that they were entitled to the fruits of victory. He said that Soviet Russia was like a jellied mass dropped on a table top: it would spread out until it reached its natural limits of expansion, after which a lasting peace could be negotiated. When he was reminded that Nazi and Japanese aggression had had no natural limits, he angrily replied: "What do you want, war?" The clear implication was that this State Department representative refused to face not only the possibility, but also the fact that there is no limit to Soviet expansion.

Late in 1947 General Wedemeyer was sent to Korea and China to study the situation and bring back a recommendation for future action. Wedemeyer wrote General Marshall from the Orient that it increasingly seemed to him that we must aid all anti-Communist governments in the Far East as the only alternative to Soviet conquest of the whole area. Marshall replied that this might be embarrassing since we had so vociferously denounced Chiang Kai Shek and other leading Asiatic anti-Communists. By the time Wedemeyer returned with his on the spot findings, an American decision—forced on the President by Dean Acheson—had already been made to abandon both China and Korea. The Wedemeyer report was given the cold storage treatment. In criticizing the Department of State and others for ineptitude in Korea, however, we must remember that the average American citizen has contributed much to the weakness of America, too. Remember the "Bring the boys back home" cry of 1945?—the vociferous demands for lower taxes, fewer controls, and more consumer goods? In large part, the mistakes in American foreign policy are traceable directly to the fact that the whole of our people have had to learn slowly that what affects the rest of the world also affects us.

Prior to dealing with Korean developments since June 25, 1950, let us look more closely at certain events before that time. In south Korea, the American Military Administration of General Hodge repeatedly rebuffed nationalist elements which wanted a free election, and often favored pro-Soviet elements who had no popular backing, because they also opposed elections and favored a trusteeship agreement for Korea rather than independence—a trusteeship agreement which would permit Russia a voice in the affairs of all of Korea, both north and south. Hodge and his advisors appointed both nationalists (led by Syngman Rhee) and so-called leftists (led by Kimm Kuisic), as though democracy could be achieved by enforcing an equality over two opposed political groups, even when one of them, the so-called "leftists," had almost no popular backing, and were not really leftists, but rather Soviets. Travelling left politically just does not happen to be the same thing as travelling east geographically. But General Hodge insisted on calling the local Soviets "leftists" by which term they presumably became respectable. In March, 1947, the Military Government conducted a poll which showed that 92% favored the nationalist-supported independence plan, and only 2% favored the leftist-supported trusteeship plan. And yet the American Occupation went on treating both factions as being equal in strength. (See Robert T. Oliver, *Why War Came to Korea*, Fordham University Press, 1950).

If the American Military Government was bumbling in its lack of planning and *naivete*, the Soviet occupation was ruthless in its totalitarian "efficiency." To front for the Russians, a 35-year old expatriate was picked up and given the name of Kim Il-sung (a defunct patriot who had gained fame fighting the Japanese). Wearing this proud name, together with a chestful of Soviet medals, Kim Il Sung was pictured all over north Korea on big posters, along side that of that other great Liberator—Joseph Stalin. On November 3, 1946, an "election" was held—without benefit of foreign observers. This election consisted in the presentation of a slate of 41 candidates to fill 41 positions on the "Interim People's Committee of north Korea." The voters could walk up to a public booth surrounded by Soviet guards and approve the slate, or disapprove it—through open voting. The result was that the slate won 92.2% of the popular vote—the remainder being declared either void, or consisting of people who had had enough of life. Kim Il Sung declared as follows upon hearing the results: "Although I won the election, I will never forget the Red Army." From this time forth, north Koreans were told all about their new democracy, and also about the bloodthirsty imperialism of south Korea, imposed by the American occupation. Some north Koreans, who had no way of getting any other point of view, absorbed at least a portion of this hate

America propaganda. Many of the soldiers in the army that attacked south Korea were mere children when the Communist barrage of propaganda was loosed upon them, and never had an opportunity to view world conditions except as Moscow chose to present them.

Militarily, north Korea was subjected at once to conscription of its young men into an army that soon reached a force of 200,000 men (this at the same time that south Korea was denied any army at all on the American explanation that to do so would violate agreements made with the Russians, and might antagonize north Korea's Soviet regime into attacking). This north Soviet army was armed at first with Japanese weapons, then with Soviet weapons—tanks, planes, and heavy artillery. It was given battle experience not only with the Chinese Communists in China, but also by frequent raids into south Korea. Meantime, the Americans refused to allow the Republic of Korea to build up an army equal to it, prevented the Republic army from having tanks or heavy artillery, and instructed south Korean units not to pursue north Korean raiders when they got back near the 38th parallel. As the price for providing light arms to the troops of the Republic, the United States exacted a solemn promise that under no provocation whatsoever would Republic troops ever set foot on the northern side of the 38th parallel. To minimize any possibility of clashes, they were told to hold defensive positions from one to three miles south of the line, and they were absolutely forbidden from attacking the bases from which the Communist advances were made. In May, 1949, Republic of Korea troops were reprimanded by the United States for chasing north Korean invaders back into north Korea, and simultaneously occupying a hill which, although just inside south Korean territory, permitted the Republic troops to view north Korean Communist troop dispositions. Accordingly, the Communist forces could choose the time and place of attack, and carry out hundreds of such attacks in the certain knowledge that there would be no retaliation for such moves.

Another factor weakening the Republic of Korea was the fact that the American Occupation prevented the Korean Government from screening men who volunteered for service in the small Korean Army. The result was that for some months Communists and their sympathizers slipped in and wreaked havoc with the development of an efficient and loyal Republican Army. At the same time an American General had the audacity to proclaim the south Korean Army "the best fighting force of its size in all Asia."

The military disparity between north and south Korea was but one of the many differences between the two areas. The Communist north hastened to put into effect a widely advertised "land-reform" program:

for which many half-informed Americans had nothing but praise. Since this Communist-type "land-reform" is presumed to be the greatest single appeal of Communist rule in Asia, a brief description of its operation is in order. When the Soviets entered north Korea, they seized the land, drove out or killed the landlords, and established Communist-manned "land-reform" committees in each district. These committees distributed land to farmers who proved to be "cooperative." In no instance, however, was the land given or sold to the farmers, and no farmer received title to such lands as were distributed. Farmers merely received the land in trusteeship from the committees, and paid taxes to the Communist state in the form of the produce of the land. Farmers who "cooperated" with the Communists had lower assessments than farmers who failed to "cooperate." Land-reform thus became a major weapon for holding the peasant masses under subjugation. The north Korean Communist regime also made an agreement with the Soviet Union to supply an annual labor force of 50,000 young men, which not only proved to be a drain on the resources of the north, but also a most effective way of subjecting the populace. The Communist rulers could always use the threat of conscription of the sons of a family to gain and retain political obedience.

Near the end of 1949, the Soviet Government began intensive training of Korean and Chinese Communist troops for the attack on the Republic of Korea. Soviet Marshal Malinovsky was put in charge of the operation. Russian T-34 tanks, burp guns, bazookas, artillery, and MIG-15 planes were channeled to Soviet Siberia and Manchuria by way of the Trans-Siberian railroad and connecting lines between Irkutsk and Mukden. On January 12, 1950, American Secretary of State Acheson declared Formosa and Korea to be outside the American Pacific security line. American troops were withdrawn from Korea, and President Truman announced the end of all aid to the Republic of China, located on Formosa.

Early in June, 1950, President Truman announced: "We are closer to peace now than we ever have been before." On the 25th of June Communist armies crossed the 38th parallel and poured into south Korea. Soviet policy for Asia had passed on to the military phase. The attack was planned in the Kremlin, and equipment and arms were Russian.

Upon General MacArthur's recommendation, President Truman ordered American air and sea forces to help defend south Korea. The same day the UN Security Council asked UN members to assist the UN-sponsored Republic of Korea against Communist aggression. United States ground forces were committed to the Korean war on June 30th.

Whereas only a few of our European UN allies responded to the UN call for collective security, sending small token forces, the Republic of China (a permanent member of the UN Security Council) offered 33,000 troops. This offer was unilaterally turned down by the United States, which suggested that Nationalist forces were needed for the defense of Formosa. At the same time the United States Seventh Fleet was sent to the straits of Formosa, thus breaking the Nationalist blockade of Communist ports, and rendering Mao Tse-tung's coastline immune from Nationalist hit and run raids. It was also suggested that to accept Chiang Kai-shek's manpower offer might antagonize Communist China into entering the war.

By the end of September, after MacArthur's dramatic landings at Inchon, the American, Korean, and token UN forces were ready to push north of the 38th parallel and liberate north Korea from the enemy. On October 7, 1950, the UN General Assembly voted that "the unification of Korea has not yet been achieved. . . . Recalling that the essential objective . . . was the establishment of a unified, independent and democratic Korea," the resolution recommended liberation of north Korea, and authorized the Allied Commander to proceed with this essential task. Great Britain, chief sponsor of the October 7th resolution, interpreted it as follows: "After adoption of the resolution, the authority of the UN forces to restore the situation in Korea as a whole was clear . . . and on October 9th the UN forces began their advance across the 38th parallel." From British State Paper dated October 31, 1950, entitled "Summary of Events Relating to Korea, 1950," as quoted by Robert T. Oliver in his *Verdict in Korea,* State College, Pa.: Bald Eagle Press, 1952, p. 47). Just how clear it was to the UN delegates that Korea must be reunited by force of arms in order to accomplish its goal of "a unified, independent, and democratic government in the sovereign state of Korea" was well stated by Percy Spender, Australian Minister for External Affairs in a talk over the UN radio October 5, 1950: "The UN would be courting disaster . . . if it were for one moment to contemplate stopping short at the 38th parallel. . . . Why on earth go through all the effort and bloodshed of the last three months if we were going to do no more than restore the status quo."

General MacArthur's forces liberated north Korea up to the Yalu river by October 26th. While few (including MacArthur) thought that the Chinese Communist troops would directly intervene in great numbers MacArthur did ask for permission to bomb Manchurian "privileged sanctuaries" in the event Mao's armies did cross over into north Korea. This permission was not given by the UN. A month later the bulk of the Chinese Communist armies attacked the Allies, and rolled them back into south Korea. MacArthur and his air commanders asked permission to bomb the Manchurian sanctuaries, but were again denied permission. Mao Tse-tung was immune from attack, either from the land or the sea.

The reaction of the UN was different in November than what it had been in June. Instead of labeling the Chinese Communists the aggressors, the UN asked Communist China, which had the blood of American, Korean, and UN soldiers on its hands, to come to Lake Success (sic) to discuss the matter. Debates in New York saw the UN offer many concessions to the Communists, but apparently not enough. In January, 1951, the Chinese Communist delegation left New York, and shortly thereafter the UN got around to labeling Communist China the aggressor. However no sanctions were applied, largely because Britain, India, and other UN members were fearful that such action might "spread the war." On the other hand, leaders in the United States and the Republic of Korea, whose troops constituted 95% of the total, were anxious to adopt some effective military steps to take the pressure off their hard-pressed forces.

On January 12, 1951, General MacArthur and the Joint Chiefs of Staff agreed on a four point program to win the war. These points were: 1) Economic sanctions against Communist China, 2) Naval blockade of Communist China, 3) Use of Republic of China forces against the common enemy, and 4) Air reconnaissance over Manchuria and Chinese coastal areas. These recommendations were shelved by the National Security Council of the United States Government. Proposals for "hot pursuit" of enemy aircraft north of the Yalu were also abandoned, even though a UN majority favored such a proposal. Irked by the crippling restrictions on offensive military operations, MacArthur made no secret of the fact that he disagreed with the policy of the politicians and diplomats in Washington and New York. He accordingly told the enemy that either they must agree to peace on terms set forth by the Allies, or face the military consequences. He was immediately denounced as a "warmonger" not only by the Communists, but also by the British, the Indians, and many Americans. On April 11th President Truman dismissed General MacArthur from all his commands.

By the end of June, 1951, Allied forces had again pushed the Communists back into north Korea, and were in the process of liberating this territory again, when the Soviet Union's Jacob Malik called for a cease fire. Instead of pursuing their military advantage the Allies called a halt to their victorious march, and began to debate with the enemy instead of defeating him. It was recalled that the Communist armies in China had followed much the same tactics in their battles with the Nationalist Government. Whenever they were losing a battle, they would call for a cease fire, and build up their strength during the ensuing debate, to resume the fighting at a time of their choosing.

The Allied Commander General Ridgeway suggested cease fire talks aboard the hospital ship *Jutlandia,* in Wonsan harbor. The Communists insisted on Kaesong, alleged to be an "open city." The Allies accepted Kaesong, but upon arriving there found it to be in Communist hands. UN negotiators were forced to approach the city bearing white flags, escorted by armed Communists. While Communist photographers had a field day taking pictures of the "surrending Americans," Peiping radio gleefully claimed victory. Later the talks were transferred to Panmunjom, at Communist insistence. Allied negotiators made every importance concession. Ridgeway, after insisting that Kaesong was necessary to the defense of Seoul, agreed to leave it in Communist hands. Allied negotiators capitulated to the enemy, allowing them to build airfields in north Korea during a cease-fire, recognizing Communist Poland and Czechoslovakia as "neutral" truce observers, and conceding to their demand that only four points of entry, and not twelve, be watched in north Korea during a cease-fire.

In April, 1952, the Allied Command tried to discover how its prisoners of war felt about being repatriated to their Communist homelands. However, these prisoners were not simply asked "Do you want to go back to Communism," but rather "What would you do, if in spite of your refusal, you were repatriated?" 100,000 prisoners out of 170,000 indicated that they would forcibly resist repatriation. The number would no doubt have been larger had the Allied Command broken up Communist control of several camp compounds, and had the question simply been phrased to elucidate a preference. Upon learning about the prisoner poll, the Communists demanded that their 11,000 prisoners be traded for our 170,000. Since this would have meant forcible repatriation for at least 100,000 war prisoners, Allied negotiators turned down the enemy demand. The enemy failed to tell the Allies what happened to 9,000 American war prisoners and 164,000 Korean prisoners previously believed to be in Communist hands.

Throughout the long and interminable debates at Kaesong and Panmunjom, the fighting was sporadic. In the fall of 1951 and 1952 it broke out into very bloody combat, with Allied losses reaching as high as 5,000 a week several times. By the end of 1952 the American casualty list had reached 130,000 dead, wounded, and missing. The Republic of Korea list was at least twice that size. Thousands of men were killed losing and retaking Heartbreak Ridge, Sniper Ridge, and other promontories. The Allied Command was still denied permission to use Nationalist troops, bomb enemy privileged sanctuaries in Manchuria, or blockade the coast of the enemy in China.

In the fall of 1952, the United States conceded to UN pressures to transfer the talks to UN headquarters in New York. There British, Indian, and other pressures forced the United States and the Republic of Korea into further concessions to the enemy. On December 3, 1952, a so-called "compromise" Indian "peace" proposal was adopted by the UN General Assembly. This proposal would have sent Allied prisoners to an island governed by Sweden, Switzerland, Poland, and Czechoslovakia. Those wishing to go back to Communism could go back, and transportation would be provided them. However those wishing to go to Formosa, south Korea, or elsewhere would be forcibly detained for three months, then for an additional month by a larger far eastern political problems commission, and finally they would be turned over to the UN. The United States, which originally insisted on the principle of no forcible repatriation, and which had encouraged enemy soldiers to surrender so that they could go where they desired, capitulated to British and Indian pressures, and voted for the Indian proposal. The Soviet bloc, observing the weakening position of the United States delegation, decided to oppose the Indian resolution as not going far enough to meet Communist demands. Apparently the Soviets reasoned that if the United States was willing to abandon principle to the extent of agreeing to the Indian proposal, it might easily compromise even further.

February, 1953 saw a Soviet increase in jet bomber strength in Manchuria offset in part by the strategy of newly inaugurated American President Eisenhower. The President announced that the U.S. Seventh Fleet would no longer "be employed to shield Communist China." This move permitted Nationalist China to make hit-and-run raids on the mainland, thus relieving the pressure in Korea. Shortly thereafter, however, General Van Fleet was allowed to resign his command under circumstances which made it appear to be a re-enactment of the MacArthur dismissed. Van Fleet testified that he was prevented from achieving military victory in June, 1951, when he had the enemy on the run. He also testified to serious ammunition shortages in Korea.

8

Communism in India and Pakistan

The Soviet Embassy in New Delhi, India, is in the habit of sending out its members to outlying cities at times that coincide with crises among Communist organizations throughout the country; for the Indian Communists, together with all other orthodox Soviets, are completely under the thumb of Moscow. Soviet Ambassador Konstantin Novikov, and his First Secretary, P. D. Erzin, are not only at work keeping the local Communists in line, but also spend considerable time encouraging Indian neutralist, pro-Soviet, pro-Chinese Communist and anti-American thinking. Madame Alexandra Erzin, during 1950, initiated a series of social functions at the Soviet Embassy designed to widen the contacts of local Communists and fellow travelers with well-known persons inclined in a pro-Soviet direction.

On March 10, 1951, Indian Home Minister Chakravarty Rajagopal-achari declared that in "each single member" of the Communist apparatus the "sense of scruple or moral hesitation is totally wiped out." (Robert Trumbull, *New York Times*, March 11, 1951).

Three leading Indian Communists issued a statement to their comrades on September 23, 1950, stating that the party should "put the peasant movement progressively on the rails of the armed struggle, and that in agrarian relations they should, by mass mobilization and direct action, as in Telengana (Hyderabad) create armed forces in rural areas and strong bases for their operation. . . . it is a question of raising the movement in the rest of the country to the level of Telengana." (*Loc. cit.*)

The Indian Communist Politburo issued a policy statement on November 15, 1950, declaring: 'Finally it is necessary to clearly grasp the truth that the armed struggle has become the principal form of struggle in the present agrarian revolutionary stage that our national liberation movement has grown to." This statement went on to urge Communist organization to "adopt and coordinate all other conceivable forms of struggle such as economic and political strikes, demonstrations, agricultural, labor, and tenant struggles, signature collections for peace pledges and election contests . . ." (*Loc. cit.*)

A Soviet agent told Indian Communists in December, 1950: "It is the task of the Communist party to skillfully utilize the stand of the Nehru Government on questions like Korea and the atom bomb. Re-

garding the armed struggle, we do not deny that ultimately the revolution in India will and must take the form of armed struggle. It is
hardly to be debated." (*Loc. cit.*).

Bombay is one of the most active areas of Communist concentration.
It is here that many of India's writers, film stars, and cultural leaders
are recruited to visit Communist China and the Soviet Union on carefully supervised tours. At the end of January, 1952 Bombay was host
to an "International Film Festival" in which Soviet productions pre-
dominated. Russian film personages had previously made an impression
on the large Indian film colony of Bombay, capital of India's motion
picture industry, second largest in the world. Continuing its cultural
and economic propaganda assault, the Soviet Union opened an art ex-
hibition in New Delhi on March 5, 1952, and leading Indians attended
the Moscow Economic Conference in April. At the same time Bombay
was flooded by Soviet cultural representatives winning friends and influencing people at the Soviet-dominated Bombay Industrial Exposition
and India's Film Festival.

In August of 1951 the Indian Communist party was recognizd by the
Election Commission as one of the nine parties qualified to contest
India's first national elections. The results were anything but comfort-
ing for Nehru. The Communists made strong showings in the economic-
ally impoverished states of southern India: Madras, Travancore-
Cochin, Hyderabad, West Bengal and Tripura. Twenty-seven Com-
munists were elected to the lower house of the Parliament (House of
the People), and nine were elected to the upper house (Council of
States). Communist tactics followed the line of out-promising the
Congress Party and embarrassing the Congress Party. In order to
maintain effective rationing of food grains, the Government (Congress
Party) had what was known as a "procurement of food grains policy."
Under this policy the rural producer was compelled to sell his produce
to the Government at a price fixed by the Government, after keeping
a certain quantity for his own purposes. The Communists incited the
farmers not to deliver their grain to the Government, but rather to
hide or burn it. The farmers who refused paid heavily with life and
property. At the same time, the Communist in the cities, where rationing was dependent on the rural procurement, went around shouting
about the inefficiency of the Government procurement machinery.

The Communists formed electoral alliances with any and all anti-
Congress political factions, be they radical or conservative. They exploited the failure of the Congress Party to solve the food problem, and
manipulated to their advantage such other factors as provincialism,
communalism, and linguism. Thus, to the sections of people in Thami-

land who opposed the so-called "domination of South India by the North," the Communists offered a platform of united front with the Dravida Khazhagam and a manifesto which supported the formation of a separate Dravidian state. Communists went to considerable lengths to cooperate with the Dravidian Federation, an ultra-conservative landlord's organization. (See Atreya, "Why the Communists Gained in India," *New Leader*, March 24, 1952). Nehru went out of his way to campaign against A. K. Gopalan, a Communist leader in Madras. When the balloting was over, Gopalan was found to have achieved an 87,000 vote margin over his Congress Party opponent.

In April, 1952, the Communists succeeded in ousting the Congress Party from control of the "Pepsu" (Patiala and the East Punjab States Union.). This gave the Communists an important bridgehead in northern India. This development was symptomatic of Communist tactics in exploiting differences between the Congress Party and opposition groups. In this instance the Communists, with only three seats, joined the Akali party, with twenty-seven members, and three dissident Congress representatives, to form a bloc which upset the Congress-dominated government. Much the same was accomplished in the state of Madras. The Madras Communists, with sixty-two members in a legislature of 375, worked with T. Prakasam, leader of the leftist Peasants, Workers, and Peoples Party to effect a coalition of 169 members against the 152 Congress representatives. On July 16, 1952, the Communists induced the Peasants, Workers, and Peoples Party and left-wing Socialists to join them in a united front against the Congress Party in Bombay.

India's Communist leaders found themselves immensely strengthened following the national elections, and practically guaranteed of five year's financial prosperity at the expense of the Indian Government. It irritates anti-Communist Government officials that the law compels support of the Communist opposition in a style to which neither they nor the average Indian has ever been accustomed. Twenty-seven Communists in the national House of the People, and nine in the Council of States are entitled to occupy Government-owned five room bungalows for less than $30 a month rent during their five year tenure of office. Communist members immediately stuffed these houses with the party faithful, and used them as bases for propaganda and even guerrilla activity. Additionally, they devoted some of their newly acquired luxurious space to a party headquarters with highly organized sections for research, statistics, press relations, and other political units. Most galling of all, to officials who previously were concerned with keeping Communists in jail, was the fact that the Indian Government

was compelled directly to subsidize Communists—who were dedicated
to the overthrow of the Government—to the extent of about 50,000
rupees ($10,000) monthly in pay and allowances to the Communists
and their allies in Parliament. (Trumbull, *New York Times,* April 16,
1952).

Communist successes at the polls were somewhat dampened, however, by the startling revelations made to the Indian Parliament on
June 3, 1952. Dr. S. N. Sinha, former Soviet Army Captain, revealed
that the Indian Communist Party was working under direct instructions
from the Cominform. Armed with documents, maps, and several secret
papers, Sinha told the Parliament that Communist insurrections in
Telengana had been planned in Prague, Peiping, and Moscow, and
directed from there, and that the insurrectionists maintained "direct
radio communication with their headquarters in central Europe." In
the face of angry protestations from Communist members, Sinha read
the following excerpt from the secret protocol of the Hitler-Stalin
pact: "The Soviet Union declares that the center of gravity of its
territorial aspirations lies in the south . . . in the direction of the Indian
Ocean." Sinha warned the Parliament to become more alive to the
dangers of Soviet expansion, particularly into the neighboring Himalayan states of Tibet, Nepal, and Bhutan. (*New York Times,* June 4,
1952). Sinha charged that Communist member Mrs. Renu Chakravarty,
to take a specific example, had carried out orders given her by Soviet
agent Lemin, said to be a Cominform member in charge of operating
Communist strategy in India.

During September, 1952, Soviet policy determined to send Indian
Communists and their allies to an "Asian and Pacific Peace Conference"
in Peiping, at the same time that top Chinese Communist and Soviet
officials met in Moscow. The Indian delegation was led by Dr. S. D.
Kitchlev, President of the Soviet-controlled All-India Peace Council.

Indian Communists operate not only on the legal level, but also on
the guerrilla level, as indicated by the above-mentioned party directives. During the first two months of 1951 Communist groups ruled in
defiance of the Government in parts of India's northeastern state of
Assam, on the borders of Tibet, China, and Burma. Well organized
and heavily armed Communist bands, with college-trained leaders
(many from the Communist dominated All-India Student's Federation),
and trained in military tactics by former Indian Army leaders, repeated
the tactics so successfully carried out in the rural revolt of Telengana.
A correspondent of the *Times of India* described conditions in Assam
as being "almost a replica of the Communist-infested areas of Malaya."
One important Communist leader of the area, later killed, organized

a Soviet state in upper Assam. This man, Anil Roy, recruited also an army "for the liberation of masses from the tyranny of the present swindlers at the helm of the administration." Considerable tribal territory, including a part of Assam's Sibsagar, lies in an area above the Brahmaputra river, and claimed by Communist China in new maps drawn up by Mao's cartographers. (Trumbull, *New York Times,* March 2, 1952).

Daniel Poling, after a visit to India in 1950 (after the beginning of the Korean war) quoted an American correspondent as saying that Nehru "is a more effective spokesman for Moscow at Lake Success than Vishinsky, because he is not a Communist but supports Communist policy. His motive is different but the effect is the same." (See letter to *New York Times* dated January 23, 1952). On March 13, 1951 Nehru declared: "My policy is not governed by continuous talk about Communism, either in India or abroad. It is a bogie which confuses thinking . . ." Typical of the Nehru Government's appeasement of external Communism was the public reception given on October 10, 1951 in New Delhi for the Chinese Communist cultural mission. The Communist visitors stayed at the home of Indian President Prasad, and were met by Foreign Secretary Menon. India's Ambassador to Peiping, Sardar Panikkar (who previously had been lavish in his praise of the new Chinese regime) delivered a eulogistic speech in behalf of his Communist Chinese friends. An audience of 1,000, including leading Indian Communists and Government officials, welcomed the Chinese on behalf of the Government, the people of India, and the Indian Council of World Affairs.

At the same time that the Indian Government welcomed representatives of a regime condemned by the United Nations as aggressors in Korea, it refused to allow the anti-Communist Congress for Cultural Freedom to meet in New Delhi, and forced it to move its meeting to Bombay. There it forbade Indian civil servants from attending.

It seemed increasingly apparent that Nehru's refusal to line up with the collective security forces against Soviet expansion played right into the hands of Soviet policy-makers for India. In a dispatch from Darjeeling, dated August 25, 1952, *New York Times* correspondent Robert Trumbull stated that "The Chinese Communists now occupying Tibet plan to move 200,000 troops into the realm of the 'living Buddha' to dominate India's Himalayan borders. In the long-range plan of the Reds, Communist infiltration into Afghanistan, Nepal, and the states of Bhutan and Sikkim is to be followed by penetration of India itself." Reports of Soviet air-bases being built in Tibet and Sinkiang continued to flow into intelligence offices of the western powers during 1952.

Although temporarily alarmed at the Communist conquest of Tibet, the Indian Government recognized the new status quo, in its "peace-at-any-price" policy. The UN did nothing.

NEPAL

On January 23, 1952, Communist military forces under the leadership of K. I. Singh attacked the Nepalese capital of Katmandu, and seized it. It was a spectacular success, but short-lived. Twenty-four hours later they were driven out by the army of Nepal after a bitter battle in which the rebels lost over 500 men. Singh and his forces retreated into Communist-controlled Tibet, and have operated hit-and-run raids against Nepal ever since. Nepal, being a sort of buffer state between India and Tibet, is of prime importance to India. As a result, the Indian Government of Nehru intervened directly in Nepalese affairs to the extent of sending troops there in February, 1951, to see to it that local unrest did not accrue to the benefit of the Communists. Following the Communist uprising of January, 1952, the Nepalese Government outlawed the Communist apparatus of that strategic Himalayan kingdom. On August 2nd, the Government arrested fourteen exiled Communist leaders who had been trying to return from Tibet; documents found by Government officials revealed that another armed Communist move was in the making, with aid from Tibetan Chinese Communist authorities. Unfortunately for the anti-Communist cause a feud between Prime Minister M. P. Koirala and his brother, B. P. Koirala, president of the Nepalese Congress Party, threatened the stability of the regime.

KASHMIR

Insofar as anyone understands Kashmir's problems, the comprehension in the minds of most people is in terms of issues like India vs. Pakistan, Moslem fanaticism or communisation, Indian secularism and UN mediation. The fact is that indications in Kashmir point to a planned Soviet strategy aimed at using Kashmir in relation to India in the same way it used Yenan in north China in relation to the Chinese National Government.

Not long after the Korean war started, Radio Moscow began paying compliments to the Kashmir National Conference—the largest political faction of Kashmir—as representing the people's will to self-determination and national liberation. The National Conference is riddled from top to bottom with Communists, who command considerable influence on the Kashmir government. Led by Sheik Abdullah, probably not himself a Communist, the chief lieutenants of the Conference have increased their pressure on him to toe the party line.

Two important Government leaders, G. M. Sadiq and Mirza Afzal Beg, have often followed the Communist line. Sadiq, president of the Kashmir Constituent Assembly in 1952, was actively associated with Soviet "peace" movements and other front organizations. On April 14th, 1952 Sadiq stated: "The new constitution of Kashmir . . . will be after the pattern of New Kashmir. . . . It will be a democratic constitution where more emphasis will be laid on the economic aspects of our democracy. Kashmir is not according to the Government of India, but to the people of India. . . . In India we find a gigantic movement not only of the Congress, but of other progressive forces, and in that atmosphere the new Kashmir movement can not only be sustained but also strengthened . . ." (Quoted by Atreya, "Kashmir, India's Yenan?", *New Leader*, August 18, 1952). On January 17, 1952, Soviet UN delegate Malik had urged that Sadiq's Constituent Assembly be allowed to determine its own political future.

Another straw in the wind was the demand of the Kaushak Bakula, head Lama of Ladakh to break away from the state of Kashmir and join Tibet. The Ladakh Lama is known as a protege of Sheik Abdullah and the National Conference.

In the spring of 1952, the pro-Communist journal *Blitz* of Bombay demanded: 'Why should Kashmir have choices of accession between India and Pakistan; why not independence or accession to the U.S.S.R. or New China?" The same publication declared, in an article dated May 3, 1952: "It was generally believed that the lion of Kashmir (Abdullah) was a good circus lion owned by Nehru. Now they know that it is not a circus lion whom they have to deal with. . . . In this connection, the references made by Mohammed Sadiq, President of the Kashmir Constituent Assembly that the people of Kashmir looked to the entire democratic movement in India and not only to the Congress has given new meaning to Sheik Abdullah's stand. . . . There is little doubt that this stand will win more friends for India and firmer support from the democratic camp . . . The Russians will veto anything against the democratic movement in Kashmir as it is now clear that Sheik Abdullah's democracy is different from the Mountbatten-Nehru brand of freedom and democracy . . ." (*Loc. cit.*).

Kashmir, bordering on Soviet-controlled Sinkiang, and touching the U.S.S.R. at the Baroghil Pass, may easily become the Achilles heel of India, and the path of entry of Soviet power south to the Indian Ocean, as Stalin indicated in 1939.

PAKISTAN

Premier Liaquat Ali Khan told the Pakistan Parliament on March 21, 1950, that high army officers were arrested for plotting to establish a military dictatorship "on the Communist model." Twelve days earlier the Premier announced the arrest of General Akbar Khan, Chief of Staff, General M. A. Latif, commander of a strategic city near the Afghanistan frontier, and Faizahmed Faiz, editor of the *Pakistan Times*. The Premier said that Khan and Latif were leaders of a plot which "planned to resort to force, with the support of Communist revolutionary elements, and making use of such members of the armed forces as they could tamper with . . ." (*New York Herald Tribune*, March 22, 1952).

Communist operations in Pakistan broke out into violence in early March, 1952, when professional agitators took advantage of student riots at Dacca University, East Pakistan. The result was a reported twenty-nine lives taken in the violence, and a near Communist-coup in East Bengal (East Pakistan). Since 1950 Communist military groups have been active in the south-eastern section of East Pakistan, along the border of Burmese Arakan. The geographical separation of East and West Pakistan makes it all the more difficult to deal effectively with the Communist problem.

Soviet efforts to bolster local Communist operations with propaganda were very successful between 1947 and 1951. Soviet publications were made available in very cheap editions, and seemed to be having a considerable effect on fellow-traveler elements in Pakistan, when the Pakistan Government moved in at the end of the year 1951 to stop the flow of Soviet materials.

Soviet policy for Pakistan, by the end of 1952, seemed to have accepted the Pakistan Government as too strongly anti-Communist. Moscow is now concentrating its efforts upon India, Kashmir, and Iran.

9
Communism in Iran

During World War II, the Soviet Government was busily engaged in building in Iran a machine which it hoped would take advantage of that country's weakness, and ultimately transform it into a Soviet colony. The center of Soviet propaganda in Iran lies in the Embassy of the U.S.S.R. in Teheran.

This propaganda is directed by a foreign affairs officer named Danil Kommissarov, who was press-attache during World War II. Due to his initiative, numerous Iranian newspapers, especially in Teheran, have been won over to the Soviet cause. He was the brains behind the founding of the so-called "Peace-Front" of 1943, a group of about 40 newspapers which followed closely the Soviet line. Public propaganda and cultural infiltration, directed by Kommissarov, utilize the radio and travelling preachers or "Kalendars" quite effectively.

During World War II, the U.S.S.R. succeeded in winning for her purpose a considerable number of Iranian papers. These papers, which since 1943 were united with the party-owned Tudeh Press in the "Peace Front," received paper supplies and financial support from the U.S.S.R. The paper shipments ceased after the withdrawal of the Soviet army in 1946, but financial support continued. By maintaining close contact with journalists through press conferences, intimate personal connections, and wide distribution of the bulletins of the Russian news agency *Tass*, the Soviet Embassy in Teheran reached many persons.

During the war, news delivered by Tass was usually preferred to that provided by Reuter-Agency, probably due to the fact that the Russian Agency distributed its news free of charge and Reuters did not. From 1946 to 1950, *Tass* influence declined, but by the end of 1950 a new cordiality in Russo-Iranian relations found its expression in the Iranian Press. After the signing of a commerical treaty on November 4, 1950, the Iranian news bureau *Pars* again began using the material furnished by the Russian *Tass* Agency.

Strong Soviet influences manifested themselves even in those papers which remained ostensibly anti-Communist, or non-Communist. As everywhere else in the Middle East, the strongly nationalistic newspapers gradually came to adopt typical Soviet slogans such as "Fight Against Western Imperialism," "Persia not an American Colony," "Imperialistic Aggression," 'Fight Against Americanization," and so on.

After the banning of the *Tudeh* (Communist) party on February 6, 1949, the Communist press was made illegal, but numerous Tudeh papers continued to appear, more or less concealed; the most important of these, *Mardom,* achieved a circulation of approximately 10,000.

In the field of cultural propaganda, an important vehicle of Soviet influences is the so-called "Soviet-Iranian Society for Cultural Relations" in Teheran. This society is a branch of the Russian cultural organization "VOKS," which is dedicated to supporting the Soviet line through cultural media. This society has founded "Cultural Centers" in Iran with libraries, lectures, concerts, art exhibitions and theatrical perform-ances. These "Centers" have become a rendezvous for many young Persian "intellectuals." However, several of the "Centers" were closed down by the Iranian Government simultaneously with the banning of the Tudeh Party in 1949.

Due to the high number of illiterates in Persia, the radio has increas-ing importance as a propaganda medium. During World War II, the Iranian Government granted permission to Great Britain and the U.S.S.R. to use Radio Teheran for certain programs. The U.S.S.R. took advantage of this to broadcast programs which were not only anti-West, but also anti-Iranian Government. All such broadcasts were stopped with the end of the Occupation.

Since 1946, Soviet radio propaganda has been conducted by Russian broadcasting stations. In addition to Radio Moscow, two other stations, those of Baku and Tashkent, are involved in this type of broadcast. Radio Baku serves mainly as a vehicle of Soviet propaganda among the Kurds. This station conducts daily broadcasts in the Kurdish language. Besides the official broadcasting stations, a great number of secret Communist stations are in operation. They are mainly concerned with Soviet propaganda in Azerbaijan province, and operate near the Russo-Azerbaijan border. All propaganda broadcasts, official or clandestine, are directed from Moscow and carefully follow all fluctuations of Soviet foreign policy.

One of the sections of Iranian society to which the Soviets have paid particularly close attention has been the Kurds. During World War II, the Russians took great pains to win the support of the Kurdish sheiks. The chiefs of several tribes were invited to the U.S.S.R. and supposed-ly, given the full Communist treatment. They received backing from the Soviet Embassy, particularly though its propaganda boss, Danil Kommissarov.

At the time of the Communist rebellion in Azerbaijan, the Soviets sought also to detach the Kurd territory from Iran by proclaiming a so-called "Kurdish People's Republic." Announced on December 15,

1945, this puppet regime was supported by the U.S.S.R. until Russian occupation troops were finally prevailed on to leave Iran in December, 1946.

One of the leaders of this short-lived Soviet satellite, Mulla Mustapha Barzani, escaped to Russia, and today spearheads the Communist rebel movement in Kurdish territory. In radio programs broadcast regularly over Radio Baku, he encourages the Kurds not only of Iran, but also of Iraq to rise up and overthrow their governments. In addition to the broadcasts, well-schooled propagandists are sent out to serve the Kurdish project. The theme enunciated by Radio Baku is as follows: "The Soviet Union has long become the true homeland of all Kurds. On Soviet soil the Kurdish worker, farmer and intellectual peacefully and cheerfully perform their daily work." The Soviet propaganda leads the Kurds to believe that they should become independent from Iran and Iraq, although not from Soviet Russia.

In Iran, as in all Middle East countries, the Soviets utilize the personal, or oral approach in their psychological warfare. This is all the more important in Iran since the banning of the Tudeh party and most of its press in 1949. Soviet propagandists mostly appear as travelling preachers, called "Kalendars." Their outer appearance and bearing differs very little, if at all, from the genuine "Kalendars" and they usually disguise their Communist propaganda skillfully behind religious camouflage. They are extremely difficult to recognize and apprehend, while their influence among industrial workers and the uneducated country population seems considerable. Whisper-propaganda originating from the activity of these false "Kalendars" is one of the most important current means of Communist propaganda in Iran.

Soviet propaganda in Iran utilizes only a few basic propositions, repeated over and over again. These include: (1) Praise of the U.S.S.R., her social achievements, her "peace policy," and so on. (2) Appeal to the conscience of the Communist and fellow traveler elements in Iran in behalf of the following considerations—(a) nationalism, including nationalization of natural resources and "Iran for the Iranians;" (b) local autonomy and favored treatment for national minorities; (c) an attack on disgraceful social conditions—utilizing some scapegoat upon which to attach all the blame—the British, the Americans, the landowners.

Eloquent praise of the U.S.S.R. is one of the most important and constantly repeated propaganda topics. For example, if propaganda is mainly directed toward the industrial workers, the modernization of the Russian industry or social justice are emphasized. On the other hand, if the propaganda is meant for the ears of the farmers, the line stresses agricultural collectivism, mechanization of agriculture, new reclamation and irrigation projects, and other "advances" in the U.S.S.R.

How, precisely, is the Iranian Communist movement organized? How strong is it? How is it controlled from aboard? On October 13, 1941, the Iranian Communist leaders revived their party, which had been banned during the Hitler-Stalin pact and even before, and gave it a new name—the Tudeh party. The term Tudeh means people. The organization of the Tudeh party followed the example of the Communist parties in other countries. It had a Central Committee consisting of ten members, a Control Commission of eight members and three party secretaries who conducted current party business.

In its official program, the party carefully avoided mentioning any revolutionary goals. The new party name did not mention the word "Communist." The program originally called for neither nationalization of private property nor agricultural collectivization, but rather stressed programs to which any liberal might be attracted. But the Tudeh tried to give the impression that it was willing to do more to achieve these goals than the other parties. Also, the Tudeh party would pitch its propaganda to the lowest common denominator, while most so-called "liberal" elements would talk in terms way above the heads of the average person.

From the beginning the industrial worker stood in the center of the party's attention. Communist-dominated unions were created in Teheran, Tabriz and Isphahan, especially among the textile workers, and among workers in the Anglo-Iranian Oil enterprises. Next to the workers, special attention was paid by the Communists to the intelligentsia of the country, especially the younger members. Interestingly enough, many of those thus appealed to had had American or British educations, which frequently seemed to act as a softening process for the local Communists. Strongly idealistic, these people fell for the Communist reform line without stopping to consider the black reaction of the Soviet system itself.

The Tudeh party also appeals to dissatisfied minorities in Iran, such as the Kurds and the people of Azerbaijan. The separatist movement in Azerbaijan proved very favorable for the reception of Tudeh party propaganda. It was in this part of the country that the first open contest between the Tudeh party and the central government in Teheran took place, namely, the Azerbaijan rebellion of 1945-1946.

In 1944, the Tudeh party polled 300,000 votes and sent eight members to the new parliament which contained a total of 136 representatives. Highly disciplined and well-trained parliamentarians, the Tudeh people often were able to act as a key voting bloc to swing legislation and propaganda their way. The Tudeh party reached a high point of influence when four of its members were included in the government of Premier Ghavam from August 2, 1946 to October 17, 1946.

Perhaps the most characteristic technique of the Tudeh has been the stimulation of mass demonstrations followed by staged riots. While other political parties of Iran anxiously avoided the use of any kind of force or violence, the ruthless leadership of the Tudeh party called on its members to break their heads and risk loss of life and limb on many an occasion. Newspaper articles and speeches of the party leaders usually were strongly demagogic and aggressive in character. Special slogans were coined for every meeting. Political enemies were subjected to the character assassination technique. Storm troopers broke up or disturbed meetings of the opposing parties and several times actually physically assaulted the persons of political enemies. Holidays, such as the anniversary of the Tudeh party or official holidays of the Soviet Union, were celebrated with a maximum of fuss and feathers.

The Tudeh party made it clear from the start that it was against any government or movement which opposed the Soviet Union. As one Tudeh spokesman declared: "Every government that acts against the Soviet Union is fascist." Although in 1944, the Tudeh party was able to take in many fellow travelers and members of the lunatic fringe—people peculiarly susceptible to Soviet causes—the behavior of the U.S.S.R. and its Iranian agent, the Tudeh party, soon led to a clear-cut isolation of the Iranian Communists and their hangers-on from the loyal Iranian population.

The Tudeh movement had become so blatantly pro-Soviet Union by 1949 that it was outlawed on February 6, 1949, as a political movement outside the pale of the loyal opposition. Since that time it has been hard to estimate the exact number of party militants, although it is known that the party paper *Mardom* has a circulation of 10,000. General Razmara declared in September, 1950, that there were only 200 real Communists in Iran. This appears to have been a slight underestimation, however, even assuming a large number of misguided fellow travelers.

By the fall of 1952 the Tudeh party stood openly as the possible successor to Premier Mossadegh. It showed its greatest strength in the rioting of mid-August, 1952, when it joined a united front with nationalist extremists led by the Moslem Mullah Ayatollah Kashani to overthrow the short-lived government of Ahmad Ghavam. The fact that Kashani then became President of the Chamber of Deputies indicated the measure of influence which the Communists had with a man near the summit of political power in Iran.

The only thing that is secret about the Tudeh Communists is their leadership. It is drawn from a panel of men who are hiding—some of them in Moscow, Prague and Baku, and others perhaps in Iran proper. Among these leaders are Mortaza Yazdi, former Minister of Public Health in the post-war Ghavam cabinet; Dr. Kia Nuri, one-time professor of Science at the University of Teheran (a hotbed of Communism); Ali Ghasemi, journalist, writer, and speaker; and Captain Khosrow Roozbeh, who wrote military textbooks and tried to establish a Communist core within the Iranian Army. There is also Dr. Feridon Kashavari, Minister of Education in the old Ghavam cabinet, and Ali Kambarsh, former deputy from Kazvin and former aviation officer.

The two principal Communist fronts include the Partisans of Peace, headed by Mahmud Hormoz, lawyer from Azerbaijan, and the Association to Combat Imperialism in Iran.

In their bid for power in Iran, the Soviets and their local Communist followers have attempted to channel Iranian nationalim in a pro-Soviet direction. Like all states of the Middle East, Iran has striven for several decades to attain an active national policy of its own, and to cease to be the object of Great Power politics. The reason for the particularly strong nationalistic tendencies in Iran lies in a natural reaction against a long history of foreign interference. In 1907, the country was divided up into two "spheres of interest," one dominated by Britain, and the other by Russia. For many years Iran was subjected to various pressures by these two powers. Both sent occupation troops to the country whenever their political interests seemed to require it. During the first world war Iran was occupied by English, Russian and Turkish troops. During World War II, Iran was occupied largely by British and Russian troops in the guise of allies. The economic consequences of this occupation were extremely severe. The general dislike of Great Britain was only over-shadowed in 1946 briefly, when Iranian public opinion became incensed at the refusal of the Soviet Government to withdraw its troops.

Since that time anti-British feeling has been whipped up by nationalist fanatics. The Iranians are no longer willing to accept the old conditions of the Anglo-Iranian Oil Company for the exploitation of the oil fields. The argument that the share of profits received by the Iranian Government was less than the taxes which the Anglo-Iranian Oil Company has to pay to the British Government has for a long time provided the fuel to heat Iranian nationalism to the boiling point. Timely concessions on the part of the oil company could have disarmed this argument to a certain extent. Meanwhile, however, public opinion had developed from the demand for better contract conditions to all-out nationalization of the oil fields.

During World War II, not only Britain and the Soviet Union, but also the United States promised to give economic aid to Iran in order to make up for the damages inflicted on the economy of the country by the allied occupation. Again and again the Iranian press, the government and the Shah himself pointed out that the economic crisis of the country was the direct result of the occupation and that Iran had the right to demand the promised economic assistance. The subsequent trip to the United States by the Shah mainly served to support this request for help and to make it more effective. The confidence of the Iranian people in American had been great and expectations were high.

These feelings of expectation, originally prevailing in Iran and encouraged by the joint statements of the Shah and President Truman, were deeply disappointed when, in spite of all promises, no assistance was given beyond a few shipments of war material. This default of American support had very important repercussions on the growth of Iranian nationalism. The existing dislike of Britain was extended to a general dislike of the great Western Powers, including the United States.

It is evident that, after this development, Iranian nationalism, with its anti-western attitude, was courted by the Soviets. Communism sought to enter into an alliance with nationalism, and, in that way, the Soviet Union hoped to secure advantages for itself. Russia had bound herself to those elements in Iran which desired a political and economic breach with the Western Powers. This meant that the U.S.S.R. could leave the fight against the position of the Western Powers entirely to the Iranians themselves. Thus Iranian nationalists increasingly began to play into Soviet hands, however unintentionally.

Next to the oil dilemma in Iran, the field of agriculture presents the most enticing picture for Soviet propaganda and Soviet action.

The bulk of Iran's agricultural possessions are in the hands of the dominant landowner class. These landowners lease their land to the peasant in accordance with the old five-point system. The share of the peasant in the five factors—land, water, draft animals, seeds and manpower—determines the percentage of the crop which has to be paid to the landowner. For instance, if a peasant has nothing but his own manpower to contribute, he must hand over four-fifths of his crop.

Thus the average income of the Iranian peasant amounts to approximately $110 per year. In years of crop failure, such as 1948 and 1949, the poverty of the farm population becomes unbearable. During these years, whole villages were deserted because the inhabitants, after eating their seed grain for the next year and their livestock left their villages and went to the cities to find another means of livelihood.

Plans to reform Iranian agriculture were designed by the Shah himself, who is the largest landowner in the country. In 1949, he outlined a plan for the agricultural reform—division of the largest estates for the benefit of the farmer, the formation of agricultural unions and the introduction of modern agricultural methods. The government of Razmara tried for many months, without success, to make parliament accept the land reform suggestions of the Shah. Finally the Shah began on his own initiative the division of his personal estates in order to set an example for other landlords.

The resistance of the Iranian landlords is concentrated in the parliament. The majority of the representatives either belong to that class themselves or depend on it. This fact makes land reform all the more difficult to achieve. Additionally, the fact that many peasants have now seen fit to go to the cities for work due to depression in farm areas, has led to a glut of the industrial labor market, and to consequent unemployment.

The Shah not only attempted to give the general signal for agricultural reforms, he also planned extensive economic reforms to improve Iran's industrial situation. The Iranian government conducted surveys and research envisaging a seven-year improvement program involving reforms. In October, 1949, the American engineering consortium Overseas Consultants Inc., drew up a report based on studies to carry out such a plan. This report recommended social and public health measures as prerequisite for a later industrialization. This long-term plan envisaged the construction of modern means of communication, irrigation, reforestation, and the building of cement and textile factories.

The total cost was to be $650 million, of which agriculture was to receive $200 million, and industry, mining and transportation each $70 million. Approximately one-third of the cost of this project was to be borne by the oil income, and the remainder by raising the taxes in the higher income brackets, especially those of the large Iranian landowners.

Since it was extremely unlikely that the parliament would approve a bill providing the financial means for the reforms, the country began to look abroad, and particularly to the United States for assistance. This was the natural consequence of the thought that the United States still owed Iran the fulfillment of the war-time promise of economic assistance. The disappointment resulting from the non-arrival of the

American loan was an important factor in the sudden change of political attitude which took place in the summer of 1950 in Teheran. This found its reaction in a commercial treaty with the U.S.S.R. in November, 1950, and in measures against the Western Powers. The fight of the Iranian privileged classes against the Shah's reforms reached its climax with the assassination of Premier Razmara. According to the available information, it is probable that behind Moslem religious fanaticism stood both reactionary landlords and the Tudeh party.

In spite of bad agricultural conditions and Soviet propaganda, the farm populations of Iran have shown a singular contempt and disregard for Soviet machinations. Habit, personal loyalty to the landowner and the influence of the Mohammedan faith can, at least partially, be held responsible for this attitude.

Conditions in the cities, are, however, different. Many industrial workers are entirely under the influence of the propaganda from the Tudeh party and the U.S.S.R. Many workers in the textile center of Isphahan are among the most susceptible to Communist propaganda. The result has been an increasing number of strikes, demonstrations and riots, which only Premier Mossadegh's oil nationalization policy was able to overshadow.

The real beginning of the Iranian crisis dates back to November 4, 1950, when the Iranian Government, despairing of American loans and British concessions, was approached by the Soviet Government. A trade agreement resulted. As usual, the Soviets sat back to await a Western mistake, and then, at the precise moment moved in with the offer of badly needed trade with Teheran. From that date to this, the Soviets have concentrated on detaching Iran's oil from the West, and perhaps ultimately getting some part of it to the Soviet Empire.

The natural oil resources of Iran presently under exploitation lie in the southwest part of the country in the region near the Persian Gulf, in the province of Khuzistan. The first oil concession signed by the Persian Government was granted to an Australian in 1901. In 1908, the first oil well was operating. The Anglo-Persian (later Anglo-Iranian) Company was founded with British capital and management to undertake the further exploitation of the resources. The British Government has been in possession of the majority of shares since 1941. In addition to Khuzistan province, geological research has disclosed the existence of other extensive oil resources in the northern part of the country in the provinces near the Caspian Coast. These resources have not as yet been claimed for exploitation in spite of repeated attempts by the British, Americans and Russians to secure concessions in this area.

The rights of the Anglo-Iranian Oil Company were based on a concession contract concluded on May 28, 1933, between the company and the Iranian Government. According to this contract, the activities of the company were restricted to an area of 100,000 square miles in southern Iran. The financial provisions of the contract were extremely favorable for the Anglo-Iranian Company. On July 17, 1949, they were somewhat altered in favor of the Iranian Government, mainly by raising the amount of oil turned over to Iran per ton of oil sold or exported. This agreement was to be retroactive throughout 1948. This concession was, however, far from sufficient to satisfy the Iranian Government.

For over ten years Iran had tried to improve the conditions of the contract. The public became more and more convinced that the obligations of the Anglo-Iranian Oil Company toward Iran were proportionately low compared to the profit of the company. During the years 1933-1947, for example, the company paid to the Iranian government 60 million pounds sterling, while the Anglo-Iranian Company paid 72 million pounds sterling to the British Government in taxes.

After 1945, the example of the economic policies of the British Labor Government had its effect in Iran. The call for the nationalization of oil became more and more urgent and energetic British concessions in 1949 were considered insufficient. Iranian nationalism was already in full blaze and the British concessions could not satisfy the people as they probably could have done a few years earlier.

In 1950, the parliament of Iran established an Oil Committee under the supervision of Dr. Mossadegh, leader of the National Front party. This committee was dedicated to the study of questions connected with the nationalization of the Iranian oil. Premier Razmara was opposed to the planned nationalization, wanting to use the increased payments of the Anglo-Iranian Oil Company for financing the seven year reform program. Razmara was aware of the almost insurmountable technical obstacles which would be connected with the nationalization of the oil fields, a situation not appreciated by members of parliament overheated by nationalism.

The assasination of Razmara in early 1951 removed the main resistance to nationalization, and Mossadegh became the new premier. On March 15, 1951, the Iranian parliament unanimously accepted the project for nationalization of the Iranian oil fields. The British Government considered nationalization a violation of the 1933 contract, which provides in article 22 that the agreement cannot be changed, without the agreement of both parties. The British-owned Abadan refinery produced 20 million tons annual capacity. Until very recently Iranian oil provided most of the fuel for the British fleet.

Although the Soviets would be unable to utilize the oil of south Iran after the expulsion of the British, due to lack of means of transporting the oil to Soviet Russia, the oil of northern Iran does present a real potential asset to Soviet strength. The exploitation of the northern Iranian oil near the Soviet frontier would considerably strengthen the U.S.S.R. economically, as well as militarily.

The problem of the oil transport to Russia from this area could be solved more easily and quickly than in the south by creating a railroad connection between the oil region and the extensive railway system which has its center in Baku. In 1925, the Soviet Union became part owner of the Kavir-Kurian Oil Company by securing 65 per cent of its shares through indirect purchase. Until this day, however, the oil fields and output of the northern oil company remain small.

Russia's maneuvers to hinder the granting of oil concessions to the Western Powers are more important than attempts to secure oil concessions for herself. In 1922 and 1937, the Soviet Union succeeded in influencing the Iranian Government against the granting of oil concessions to American oil companies. In September, 1944, the U.S.S.R. demanded oil concessions in the five Iranian provinces near the Caspian Sea. The Soviets probably knew that their demand would get them nowhere, but they also heard rumors that the United States was simultaneously negotiating with the Iranian Government for oil concessions. Indirect Soviet pressures resulted in the Iranian Government refusal of concessions to either side—which in fact amounted to a Soviet victory.

With the British expelled from Abadan, the West was cut off from Iranian oil, and to this extent the Soviets gained an advantage. There remained the question of what Iran would do with the oil fields, lacking the technical direction. A few thinking Iranians were aware of the fact that Iran was not yet able to fully exploit her oil fields without foreign aid, and realized the serious consequences for the Iranian economy following a complete breach with the Anglo-Iranian Oil Company.

Iran, with her need of one million tons of oil per year, depends on the efficient operation of the oil fields. Equally severe financial consequences are expected from nationalization. Such arguments have to face the opposition of the most fanatic Iranian nationalists who would rather set the refineries of Abadan afire than leave them any longer in British hands. It is the task of the Tudeh party to inflame this fanaticism.

With the British finally and completely expelled, the Soviets realize that the Iranian Government will be far more susceptible to Soviet pressures than previously. The Western Powers are also weakened further by the spread of anti-British feeling throughout the Middle East, notably in Egypt. Opportunities in the Middle East are no doubt tempting Soviet policy makers into playing an ever-increasingly forceful game. With Western leaders still almost entirely preoccupied with Western Europe and the Far East, the extension of Soviet power southwards to the Indian Ocean appears more likely than ever before.

10

Communism in the Middle East and Africa

Apart from Iran, Soviet influence in the Middle East appears to be rather weak. Communist groups in the other states of the area pale in significance in comparison to the militant and well organized *Tudeh* (Communist) party of Iran. Furthermore, Iran is the closest of these states to the Soviet frontier. Indeed the Soviet-Iranian frontier extends some 500 miles between the Caspian Sea and the Afghanistan border.

A major factor in reducing the Soviet penetration of the Middle East is Turkey—that great bulwark of long standing against Russian encroachments to the south. Should, however, the Iranian situation deteriorate and the Soviets gain Iran, the men of the Kremlin would find themselves on the Indian Ocean, and adjacent to Iraq. This position would enable the Soviets to outflank Turkey, and gain control of the entire and strategic Middle East area.

Soviet policy here exploits the incipient nationalism and frequently anti-western feeling of the population. The Soviets pose as the champion of the "colonial" or "semi-colonial" peoples of the Middle East against British, French, and American "imperialism." Communist agitators and Soviet radio programs appeal to the masses in simple terms designed to win sympathy for the Soviet Union and hatred of the western powers. Abd el-Krim el-Khatabi, famous Riffian warrior and president of the National Liberation Committee for North Africa, once told C. L. Sulzberger of the *New York Times* that in his anti-western struggle ". . . we would gladly accept arms or support from any quarter, even the Communists and Russia." (C. L. Sulzberger dispatch to *New York Times,* October 27, 1951).

Nationalism has been a favorite force with which Communism has sought to associate itself. In 1949 Communists gained 43% of the Greek vote in the British colony of Cyprus—because the Greek majority population wants the island to belong to Greece. Communists agents have penetrated every nationalist movement within the Middle East—from Cypriotes demanding union with Greece to Moslem movements in North Africa and the Middle East. One example of such penetration is Dr. Khalil Budayri, one of the leading Arab Palestine Communists, and nephew of Haj Amin al-Hussaini, exiled Grand Mufti of Jerusalem.

Communist parties have been outlawed in most lands of the Middle

East except in Lebanon, whose capital is believed to be the center of the Soviet activity in the area. Throughout the Middle East the Communists have fostered riots, held secret meetings, distributed pamphlets, and with considerable success have sought to capture the support of university students. Whenever crises have developed, as in Iran, Egypt, Morocco, and Tunisia, Communists have put their best foot forward to guide mass emotions along lines useful to Moscow. Increased Arab unrest since 1950 has led to a definite switch in Soviet policy in favor of gaining friends among the Arab states. Soviet broadcasts in Arabic have been speaking of a regional "peace conference" for the Middle East and Africa—without mentioning the date or locality —and declaiming meanwhile against the "colonizers." Even among the Christian minority Soviet policy wins allies. Alexandros, Patriarch of Antioch, visited Moscow in the summer of 1951 where he was promised monetary compensation for confiscated church property (in Syria). Alexandros speaks for some 250,000 Orthodox Christians in Syria, Iraq, and Lebanon.

IRAQ

Iran's oil nationalization frenzy did not spread to Iraq. This did much to assist that country's anti-Communists. Members of a Communist organization formed in the summer of 1951 were rounded up as soon as they began their activity.

As far back as 1938 the Iraqi Government found it necessary to outlaw Communism, and, in an amendment of the Penal Code by act of Parliament, made Communist activity a criminal offense, involving the death penalty in certain cases. There was little Communist activity until World War II, when Soviet influence increased—notably after 1942. Iraq did receive quite a scare when Mullah Mustapha Barzani led a Communist revolt among the Iraqi Kurds, concurrently with the Soviet move in Iranian Azerbaijan. Then at the beginning of 1948 Communist organized riots shook Baghdad, culminating in the overthrow of strong man Salih Jabr's government.

Communism first appeared in 1923 as an idea which appealed to a handful of middle class intellectuals—by way of France and Britain. At that time a Communist group was organized with an unlicensed, privately circulated organ called the *People's Struggle*. Next, the Iraqi Communists tried to expand through infiltration into an authorized political organization. The National Reform Society, formed at the end of 1936 by Baghdad "progressives," was the Communist objective. However this effort was defeated, and the Communist leader Abdel

Kader Ismail was banished to Damascus, to work with the Syro-Lebanese Communist party.

Upon the outbreak of World War II, Communist activity resumed, under the leadership of Moscow-trained Salman Yousif, popularly known by the alias "Fahad" ("the Leopard"), who became the brain behind the movement. Following the Moscow line, a new party organ, *Al Sharara*, denounced western resistance to German aggression as "British Imperialism," and Fahad and his party, taking their cue from Moscow broadcasts, supported Rashid Ali's Nazi-sponsored revolt of 1941. When the revolt collapsed, its Communist supporters were jailed together with their Nazi comrades, but were released after the German attack on Russia. The Communists took advantage of this situation to further their own aims, making full use of all available facilities to spread their propaganda. The Russian occupation of Iran, jointly with the British, opened a direct route for Soviet propaganda into Iraq, and in 1943 the first Russian legation was opened in Baghdad. Moscow newspapers and periodicals, in Arabic and in English began arriving in large numbers. The pamphlet *Constitution of the Soviet Union*, issued in Arabic, quickly sold 40,000 copies at a reduced rate, as did the English edition of the *History of the Communist Party*. With the Iraq Government winking its eye and the wartime atmosphere highly favorable, the Communist movement gained momentum. Emulating the western press, local Iraqi papers went overboard in lavish praise of the Soviet Union. Two local Communist publications—*High Ideals* and the *Journal*—appeared in Baghdad under government license. Fahad himself wrote extensively under the pen name Yasin Khalaf.

During this period Communist party membership increased tremendously, and practically anyone was admitted into the party. Canvassing went on through public meetings, and party leaders travelled the length and breadth of the country spreading the Communist doctrine among students and teachers, workers and peasants, government officials and businessmen, in cities, villages, and throughout the countryside. Iraqi Communists established contact with British and Indian Communist military personnel, and the contamination spread deep into British troops stationed in Iraq. Considerable gains were made in Najaf, religious and intellectual center of the Orthodox Shiah Moslem sect in Kerbala province, as well as in Iraqi Kurdistan, where Mullah Mutapha spearheaded the Soviet drive.

Political conditions after the war in 1945 continued favorable for the Communists. Particular gains were made through the Society for Combatting Zionism, which denounced Zionism as a front for "western imperialists." However, a split in Communist ranks soon developed, and a dissenting group formed the underground Iraqi Communist League. This family dispute soon reached outside ears, and early in 1947 Iraq, together with other Arab states, cracked down on the local Soviets, and arrested Fahad and other leading Communists in Iraq. The death sentence passed during the premiership of Salih Jabr on Fahad and several other top Communists was commuted as a result of foreign pressures. Fahad continued to lead the movement from his prison cell.

In January, 1948 the pro-western premier Salih Jabr signed the Portsmouth Treaty in England, and this was immediately the signal for a Communist-nationalist alliance based on the proposition that Iraq's sovereignty had been impaired by the treaty. The Salih Jabr government was toppled, but the Communist objective fell short of its mark. Although the Portsmouth Treaty was abrogated a demand to release the Communists from jail was turned down by the new government.

As of May, 1948, Iraq was placed under martial law, as a result of the war in Palestine. This enabled the government to operate more successfully against local Communists. In October, 1948, the police tracked down the party hideout in Baghdad, and captured most members of the Central Committee, with their printing press, a complete register of party members, coded instructions which Fahad had issued from jail in invisible ink, and other documents of interest. Members of the party were rounded up from all over Iraq, and Fahad and the other Communist leaders (four others—two Moslem and two Jews) were hanged.

Practically all active Communist work in Iraq has been at a standstill since that time, thanks to the efforts of the strongly anti-Communist premier Nouri Pasha el-Said. Soviet efforts since the Korean war have centered in playing up to nationalist elements and creating a situation in Iraq comparable to that in Iran.

On November 24, 1952, a new Iraq Government came into power in the aftermath of a reign of rioting and bloodshed in Baghdad. Rioters smashed the United States Information Office and stoned the British Embassy, shouting "Down with foreign imperialism." Prince Regent Abdul Ilah called on General Mahmoud Nur Al Din to assume the premiership and restore order. All political parties were dissolved and several political leaders were jailed. These incuded: Kamel Chaderchi and Husain Jamil of the National Democratic Party; Kamil Samarrai, Saddiq Shanshal and Ismail Ghanim, of the Independence Party, and Razzaq Dhahir, of the United Popular Party.

SYRIA AND LEBANON

The Communist organization for Syria and Lebanon had one common headquarters and politburo until 1944, when two groups were created. Khalid Bakdash became leader of the Syrian Communists, and Farej Allah al-Hilu became Lebanon's Number One Stalinite. Communism in the Levant states first showed signs of life in 1922. It displayed some strength during the Popular Front period in France, 1936-1939, which carried over into the French-administered territories of Syria and Lebanon. In 1944, the local Communist groups received further encouragement when the Soviet Union became the first country to recognize the newly created independent states of Syria and Lebanon.

The Lebanese Communist movement was strengthened by its successes in seizing control of the Lebanese Syndicate of Labor Unions. The chairman of this syndicate was Mustafa el-Aris, a member of the executive committee of the Soviet-controlled World Federation of Trade Unions, and himself an acknowledged Communist. Another Communist group in Lebanon was the Friends of the Soviet Union, which appealed to "intellectuals" fond of dabbling in pro-Soviet activities.

In December, 1947, the Syrian Government outlawed the Communist Party, and the Lebanese Government followed suit a month later. This however did not mean the end of Communist activity in the Levant states. In August, 1951, the Orthodox Patriarch of Antioch, Alexander III, who represents nearly 500,000 communicants mostly in Syria and Lebanon, came out openly in support of Soviet policies, and against the United States and the non-Communist realm. *Pravda* and *Izvestia* published front page stories quoting the Patriarch's praise of the "Soviet peace policy" and his attack on the "attempts of the United States to attain world domination." These sentiments were expressed following a visit by Alexander to the Soviet Union as guest of Russian Patriarch Alexius I. Alexander coupled the names of President Truman and Pope Pius XII whom he described as friends and collaborators in a policy aimed at initiating a new war.

Meanwhile Syria underwent a brief period under the leadership of pro-Soviet premier Marouf Dawalibi. He succeeded the pro-western premier Hassan el-Hakeem on November 10, 1951, but retained power only twenty days. Dawalibi, leader of the Populist Party, was overthrown by a swift, bloodless coup d'etat led by Colonel Shishekly, a power behind the scenes in Syria since 1949. The new premier was Hamad el-Khoudja, favorable to a Near Eastern Defense Pact against Soviet aggression.

Soviet policy resorted to an old trick in April 1952, by playing upon anti-western feelings of the Arab peoples. A World War II nationalist-liberation group called the *Muktamar Al Watani*, was reactivated as a Communist front organization. This group originally had considerable prestige as an anti-French movement ostensibly devoted to achieving Lebanese independence. When it re-appeared in 1952 it was headed by a well-meaning non-Communist nationalist named Dr. Salim Idriss, and included two non-Communist groups—the Moslem *Haia Al Watania* (National Society) and the Maronite Christian Falange. There was no doubt, however, that the organization was Communist-controlled. It began to attack the United States Point Four program in the Levant states as a front for "imperialist spies" and "imperialism." The group represents the Soviet Middle East tactic of using anti-western nationalism as the spearhead of the Communist movement.

EGYPT

Prior to the coup d'etat which expelled King Farouk from Egypt in July, 1952, the principal Communist tactic involved the prevention of any Egyptian cooperation with the West, and pressure to achieve an Egyptian-Soviet pact. Pro-Soviet groups and publications were naturally in the forefront, but the movement had the backing of Hafez Rama-dan Pasha, president of the Nationalist party. The most important stim-ulus to the campaign came from *Al Misri*, principal organ of the Wafd party. On October 22, 1951, the pro-Soviet newspaper *Gomhur Al Misri* published the text of a telegram from Mohammed Darwich, president of the "Movement for National Struggle," to the Soviet Am-bassador in Egypt. It asked for Soviet aid to overcome "British imperialism and barbarism."

The Egyptian Communists had previously infiltrated the Moslem Brotherhood, a terrorist organization which led to bombings and assassinations in Egypt in 1948. The leader of the Brotherhood, Hassan Al Hadabi Bey, refused, however, to join the Communists in the cam-paign for a pact with Soviet Russia.

Pravda's advice to Egypt, as expressed on January 25, 1952, outlined the Soviet propaganda line. It sympathized with Egypt's struggle for "freedom and independence" and mourned that its people had "fallen into misfortune under foreign occupation." *Pravda* urged all Egyptians to turn their thoughts "to the Soviet Union, to Moscow, and to Stalin." The author of the article, Mr. Rassadin of the paper's Cairo staff, at-tacked "the aggression of English imperialism against the Egyptian people," and encouraged nationalist groups to seek common cause with the Soviet Union as the ideal solution to their ills. (*Pravda,* January 25, 1952). The day after this article appeared in *Pravda,* Cairo was shaken by one of the worst outbreaks of violence in Egypt's history. Thirty people were killed, and 700 buildings were destroyed as mobs of fanatics burned and looted, and attacked all foreigners that came in sight—notably Americans and Britishers. Ahmed Hussein, chief of the Egyptian Socialist party, whose features are at the same time Communist, Fascist, and nationalist, was charged as being chief instigator and organizer of the violence, along with five of his associates. A Fascist at the time of Rommel's advance on Cairo during World War II, Hussein took on an increasingly Communist line after returning from a visit to New York in 1947.

King Farouk was ousted from power on July 22, 1952, by the military coup of General Naguib Bey. Neither Communism nor Communists appeared to have played any role in the change of power, although Naguib went out of his way to state at the time: 'I would like to assure the world that the evil-intended propaganda that Communism is widespread in the Egyptian army is utterly false and untrue." (*New York Times,* July 24, 1952).

Although there have been some charges that pro-Communist intellectuals have achieved a position in Naguib's entourage (*The Freeman,* September 22, 1952, p. 876) there seems to be little to support the charge. Indeed there exists considerable evidence that since Naguib came to power, the strength of the Communists has waned. It is true that Naguib did release many Communists from the Huckstep detention camp where they had been interned by Farouk. On July 29th, Youssuf Hilmi, a member of the Egyptian Communist party's Central Committee, as well as secretary general of the "peace" movement, was released from a detention camp along with Fathi Ridvan, an Egyptian pro-Soviet sympathizer and deputy president of the "peace" movement. Both men came out in support of Naguib. Their action was followed a few days later by the president of the "peace" movement, Kamel el Bindari, a rich landowner known as the "Red Pasha" since he was ambassador to Soviet Russia in the 'forties. In September, Fathi Ridvan joined the Naguib cabinet as minister without portfolio in charge of propaganda.

The Communist party itself, alarmed at defections of pro-Soviet elements to the Naguib movement, joined a number of leading anti-Naguib landowners and industrialists in efforts to provoke industrial unrest. One of these efforts resulted in considerable bloodshed at Kafr Dawa, when six workers and soldiers were killed, and many others wounded The Communists called Naguib a "Fascist" for awhile, but subsequently have sought to employ the united front tactic, through a group led by Fathi er Ramle. This group, called the "popular socialist party" has an organ named *Al Moarada*. When the showdown occurred between Naguib and the Wafd party in October, 1952, however, the Communists lined up with the Wafdists, whose youth groups they had infiltrated. The resultant Wafd defeat reflected little glory on the Communists, who decided to concentrate on influencing Naguib through the intermediary of pro-Soviet intellectuals like Fathi Ridvan. (See Mark Alexander, "Naguib Spikes the Communists, *New Leader,* November 3, 1952).

The Naguib Government discovered an important Communist cell in the northern Egyptian province of Dakahlieh in late August, 1952. The home of Fathy Soliman in the town of Faraskour was raided by police. Roger Vailland, noted French playwright and journalist, was among the twenty-four persons present. Two months later, the Government uncovered an espionage network which was charged with being a threat to the state. Twenty persons were held, including the Egyptian journalist Maurice Fahmy.

Communist tactics for 1953 took advantage of Soviet anti-semitism by fanning anti-Israeli sentiments in Egypt.

FRENCH MOROCCO AND TUNISIA

The difficulties between the French and nationalist forces in Morocco and Tunisia have been fully exploited by Soviet propaganda, which seeks to link nationalism with anti-western feeling, and present the Soviet Union as the champion of the "colonial and semi-colonial peoples." The Soviet organ *Izvestia*, on January 26, 1952, declared that uprisings in Tunisia were the direct result of France's denying independence to Tunisians. *Izvestia* charged that the French acted in the interest of the United States in allowing the territory to be transformed into a "base of imperialist aggression." *Pravda*, the same day, claimed that France was "renting" Tunisia as a site for United States air bases and as a "military *place d'armes* of the aggressive Atlantic bloc." It held that events in the French protectorate were "closely connected with the general rise of a national libration movement of hundreds of millions of people of Asia and Africa, and with a marked sharpening of the crisis of the whole colonial system of imperialism."

At the end of March, 1952, the French deposed Tunisian premier Mohammed Chenik, and arrested the nationalist Neo-Destour leader Habib Bourguiba. The French claimed that the nationalists had gone too far in extremist demands and actions for premature independence. Although friends of the nationalist Neo-Destour claimed Communism was not an issue and that they (the nationalists) were anti- Communist, it was noted that some Communist leaders were arrested together with the nationalists. It appeared that the Communists sought to make common cause with the nationalists, and to use the violence to further Soviet interests. Communist strength, however, seemed to be slight, and most nationalists apparently showed little interest in working with the Communists.

Communism in French Morocco is largely concentrated in the Moroccan section of the Communist-dominated General Confederation of Labor (C.G.T.). Moslem nationalists claim, however, that there are few Moslem Communists in Morocco, and that it was the French Communists who brought what Communist strength there is to Morocco. In November, 1951, French authorities intercepted a detailed plan for Communist infiltration in Morocco, where six new French-American military air bases were nearing completion. The plan included instructions from Etienne Fajon, permanent French Communist party representative to the Cominform, to Communist party leaders in the French protectorate, lying at the strategically vital western entrance to the Mediterranean. In the directive, Communist leaders in Morocco were urged to make ever effort to win for the "working classes" the support of the rural masses of Morocco, which, according to the directive, threaten to become the "allies of reaction." The plan called for the establishment under Communist direction of small friendly groups of the type known in France as "amicales." The population of Morocco is overwhelmingly Moslem and the Communist organizers of the *amicales* were cautioned to tailor their propaganda efforts to fit traditional Moslem antipathy for Communism as a doctrine. Fajon urged that great attention be paid to organizing the *amicales* in the "douars" or rural sections of the country—where Communism is not known. Fajon said that there should be two categories of Communists: the party stalwarts, and the more naive, presumably the French-hating Moslem fanatics, in the *amicales*. The leaders of the *amicales* were directed to be on the look-out for reliable material to recommend for regular party membership. It was urged that rallies of the *amicales* take place whenever there was any legitimate protest of neighborhood nationalists.

Antoine Pinay, French Minister of Public Works in the cabinet of Edgar Faure, claimed in New York in November, 1951 that Communist agitation was behind the unrest in Morocco. On the other hand, the *Istaqlal* (Independence) party, and its leaders Si Allal el Fassi and Ali Bargash have declared that they are anti-Communist, and that Communism and Communists are a French importation.

Communist influence along the Gold Coast (a British Dependency)
is known, but difficult to pin down, although Prime Minister Kwame
Nkrumah has Marxist roots. Soviet policy-makers are, of course, taking
advantage of the racial tensions in the Union of South Africa, but the
actual strength and identity of individual Communists is not clear.
More clear, is the extent of Communist strength in the British colony
of Kenya, on the east coast of Africa.

The Kenya tribe of the Kikuyu has become known to the rest of the
world through the ruthless activities of its secret organization, called
the "Mau Mau." The Mau Mau started, in the fall of 1952 a campaign
to drive the white man out of Kenya. This campaign included the
murder of white settlers and their families, as well as of native chiefs
who cooperate with the Kenya government. Mau Mau is a tribal
secret society which resorts to "practices that are a curious blending of
the twentieth century politics of revolt with the most barbarous of
jungle customs." (Douglas Hyde, "Red Thread in the Mau Mau Terror," *America*, November 22, 1952). Linked with the Mau Mau is the
Kenya Africa Union, which has important representation in several of
Kenya's most respectable organizations. Ostensibly devoted to improving the status of the Kenya natives, the KAU appears to be more of
a front for the Mau Mau and even more sinister groups. Leader of the
Mau Mau and the KAU is the handsome, bearded Jomo Kenyatta. A
man of intelligence and leadership qualities, he was a student in London before World War II. Drawn into left-wing circles, he gradually
became favorable to Communism, and went to Moscow. He returned
to Kenya to carry out "the African application of the Malayan Communist's jungle tactics" (*loc. cit.*). This has involved murdering white
settlers, terrorizing natives who collaborate with the whites, and killing
the white man's cattle, upon which he is dependent for a living. A
former British Communist leader, Douglas Hyde, has testified that in
1947 a conference was held in London at which representatives of
every Communist party in the Commonwealth met to work out their
tactics. In 1951 an Africa department was created in the London Communist headquarters. This department encouraged Kenyatta to infiltrate the respectable Kikuyu Independent Schools Association. The aim
of the KISA has become one of combatting government and mission
schools as purveyors of "imperialism." The KISA set up its own schools
to influence Kenya children against the "imperialists."

Through the Mau Mau and related organizations, Kenyatta is in a
position to continue to influence the natives of Kenya colony along

pro-Soviet lines. Another Malayan situation in Africa would seriously weaken the already embattled British.

ISRAEL AND OTHER MIDDLE EAST AREAS

The Israeli Parliament, called the Knesset, contained in 1952 four Communist members and nineteen members of the strongly pro-Soviet Mapam party. Between them, they exert a not inconsiderable influence on Israeli politics. Whether through their influence or not, Israel voted with the Soviet bloc or abstained in the United Nations on many issues dealing with Korea and the Far East. It should be made plain, however, that these Stalinites and their allies have been in the opposition to the governmental coalition of Prime Minister Ben Gurion.

One factor which has alerted citizens of Israel and their supporters throughout the world to the danger of Stalinism, has been the increasingly anti-semitic policy of International Communism. This anti-semitic policy came to a head in November, 1952, when the Czechoslovak Communist Government staged a shot-gun trial for former Jewish Communists and executed them a short time later. Among those purged were Rudolf Slansky and Vladimir Clementis, both of them former leaders in the Czech Communist regime. One of the witnesses against them was Mordecai Oren, leader of the pro-Soviet Israeli Mapam party, who failed to return to Israel in 1951 after a visit to a Communist trade union meeting in Berlin. Oren was well known in Israel for saying that Israeli workers would never fight against the Soviet Union.

The trials in Prague sought to prove that Jewish members of an alleged anti-Moscow conspiracy cheated Czechoslovakia and the Soviet Union for the benefit of Israel. At the same time the Czech Communist organ *Rude Pravo* launched a bitter attack on Zionism as the "tool of American imperialism." An editorial in the newspaper charged that the United States had turned Israel into a camp of aggression against the "peace camp and the enslaved Arab nations."

Israeli Foreign Minister Moshe Sharett told the Knesset on November 24, 1952, that the Prague proceedings were "a farce in the form of a legal trial. . . . history has already passed judgment upon those regimes which had recourse to the bogy of anti-semitism." He characterized the proceedings as "permeated with anti-semitism." On the same day Israel Goldstein, president of the American Jewish Congress, declared that the Prague trials proved that the Soviet-dominated countries were engaged in a campaign against Jews and the Jewish state. (*New York Times*, November 25, 1952).

Soviet policy for Israel seems bent on using the Communists and their Mapam allies to encourage anti-American sentiment in the UN and elsewhere, and on siding with Arab nationalism in at least a short term program of taking advantage of anti-western feeling in the Arab states.

Soviet policy for the Middle East has some support in other portions of the area. In Cyprus, the Communists to a large extent control the labor unions, and although representing less than ten percent of the islanders, have made a big noise against the building of western bases in Cyprus. In Afghanistan, the Soviets have attempted economic infiltration in the northern part of the country, while raising a large hue and cry over the American and UN technical missions in the Helmand Valley project. On September 19th, 1952, Afghanistan rejected a Soviet protest over the presence of these technical missions in the southern part of the country.

Communist influence in the Middle East increased noticeably during the second World War. Britain's wartime pro-Soviet attitude resulted in the lifting of the ban on Soviet diplomatic missions in Arab capitals, and from 1942-1943 Cairo, Baghdad, Beirut, and Damascus witnessed invasions of Soviet diplomats, commercial, and cultural attaches. Once established behind the cloak of diplomatic immunity, these Soviet agents became most active, noticeably in the trade union movement. The Soviet-controlled World Federation of Trade Unions took an active interest in the Arab and Iranian labor movement, sent visiting missions, and built up the prestige of such Communist labor leaders as Reza Rusta in Iran and Mustafa el-Aris in Lebanon. Pro-Soviet publications, friendship societies and numerous front groups began to appear throughout the Middle East. "Houses of culture," bookstores carrying Communist literature, exhibits of Soviet art, concerts, lectures, and motion pictures—all these were manifestations of Soviet infiltration. Arab intellectuals and artists were conducted on free tours in the Soviet Union, and lavishly entertained.

The Soviet paid special attention to minority groups. The Turkish-speaking population of Iranian Azerbaijan, the Turkomans of the Iranian and Afghan northern plains, and above all the Kurds, were consistently encouraged in their national aspirations. Soviet policy was most successful among the Armenians. Armenians are scattered throughout the Middle East, but are unpopular among Arabs, Iranians, and Turks alike. Exploiting this fact, Soviet policy influences Armenians through the Armenian Orthodox Church, with headquarters in Echmiadzin, Soviet Armenia. The Soviets encouraged thousands of Armenians to emigrate to Soviet Armenia, on the promise of a better life.

The U.S.S.R. has appealed to the Moslems of the Middle East, and has undoubtedly encouraged fanatical religious societies like the Moslem Brotherhood in Egypt and the Fadayan Islam in Iran in their anti-western tirades. British intelligence sources claim that the trouble-making Fakir of Ipi on the Afghanistan-Pakistan frontier was a recipient of Soviet subsidies. (See George Lenczowski, *The Middle East in World Affairs*, Cornell University Press, 1952, pp. 419-422).

11

Communism in Greece, Turkey, and Yugoslavia

Soviet policy for Greece saw an opportunity during World War II to wrest control from the exile Greek Government. In 1943 the Communist fifth column in Greece, known as the EAM, with a military arm called the ELAS, established a "provisional government" in the Pindus mountains, an act which flaunted the authority of the Greek exile Government. In August, 1944, a small group of Russian Army officers was dropped by parachute into ELAS headquarters. These agents had come from Moscow by way of Belgrade. EAM agents in Cairo sought to spearhead an army revolt against the exile Government in 1944. Failing this, the Greek premier was persuaded into including five members of the EAM in his cabinet. These five joined the cabinet on September 1, 1944, upon receiving instructions to do so from the Russian legation in Cairo. (William H. McNeill, *The Greek Dilemma*, Lippincott, 1947, p.144.).

When the Greek Government returned to Greece at the time of the liberation, and with the support of British troops, it found its authority challenged by the EAM, and its private army, the ELAS. Communist-incited violence in early December, 1944 led to a civil war, which the Greek Government, with the help of the British, put down after a month of fighting. According to the Varkiza Agreement of January 4, 1945, the ELAS agreed to surrender its arms and disband its forces.

In the elections of March, 1946, the Communist EAM urged its adherents to abstain. Only 9.3% of the Greek electorate did so. It was clear to the Communists that violent means must again be resorted to. About 4000 former ELAS soldiers had fled to Communist Yugoslavia in January, 1945, where they re-grouped, and received training and supplies. Aid also came to them from Soviet-controlled Albania and Bulgaria. Armed Communist raids began to take place on the northern and north-western Greek frontier at the end of 1946. The Greek Government asked the UN to investigate, and in May, 1947, the UN Commission reported that Greek Communist forces were receiving aid from the Soviet satellites of Yugoslavia, Albania, and Bulgaria. UN action against aggression, however, was paralyzed by the Soviet veto, and with the situation becoming more serious by the hour, Greece appealed to the United States for practical and immediate aid, which

130

was forthcoming in the form of the Truman Doctrine. General Van Fleet was sent to Greece to advise the Greek Army and help train it in its battle against the rebels in the north. By 1949 sustained military action against the Communist forces, together with Tito's defection from the Soviet Empire, caused Soviet policy makers to call off the effort, at least for the time being.

A United Nations Balkan "watchdog" commission, with headquarters in Salonika, has kept a watchful eye on Soviet pressures on Greece since the end of the civil war. In early August, 1952, Bulgarian Communist troops invaded and occupied for several days a small island on the Evros river, only to be driven off by Greek gunfire. A year earlier the Soviets had established a guerrilla-training network aimed at the overthrow of the Greek Government by force. (*New York Times*, September 16, 1951).

Considerable interest centers on the fate which befell the Greek Communist rebel leader General Markos Vafiades, who disappeared after the civil war. A leading Yugoslav specialist on Cominform matters charged that Vafiades was murdered by Nicholas Zachariades, Cominform agent in charge of the Greek rebellion after the rupture between Tito and Stalin in 1948. It was claimed that the Cominform's anti-Tito policy was best served by purging Vafiades, and preventing Greek Communist leadership from following Tito's path of secession from the Cominform. (See article by Ivan Karaivanov in *Borba*, Belgrade, December 4, 1951).

In March, 1952, a Greek military court sentenced eight persons to death and four others to life imprisonment on charges of espionage involving high treason. The ringleader of this group was Nicholas Beloyannis, who transmitted Greek security information to Cominform agents in Greece, Albania, and Bulgaria. Main points brought out by the prosecution were: 1) Intelligence communicated through secret radio transmitters in suburban Athens did not concern Greece alone, but her allies; 2) The Greek Communist party cannot be considered a Greek political party because it is an instrument of an organization outside Greece, namely the Cominform; 3) International Communism can exercise its power only by underground methods, and by hiding behind the facade of such groups as the Union of the Democratic Left. (*New York Times*, March 2, 1952).

The Greek Communist party was outlawed in 1948, and has resorted to operating behind front groups since that time. At the end of August, 1951, the United Democratic Front was organized to enter candidates in the September parliamentary elections. Its candidates included Colonel Stephanos Serafis, Andonis Abutielos, Nicholas Baloyannis, and Manolis Glezos. Serafis had been head of the ELAS Communist-controlled military group during the civil war; Abutielos, under death sentence for treason, was a prominent member of the Communist-dominated ENO(Greek Seamen's Union). Baloyannis had arrived from Prague in the summer of 1951 to reorganize the Greek underground. Glezos was imprisoned for treason.

The September 9, 1951, elections saw the Communist-controlled Union of Democratic Leftists win 10.5% of the popular vote and nine seats in the new parliament. During the next year this group won some friends in the coalition government of Plastiras and Venizelos. A year later, the Athens newspaper *Allaghi*, regarded as the organ of premier Plastiras's Progressive party, commended the old EAM and ELAS for their struggle against the then Greek Government. This paper, which also alleged that the United States was using germ warfare in Korea, is edited by Nicholas Papapolitis, brother of the Minister of Commerce in the Plastiras Government. Both Plastiras, and his deputy Venizelos, publicly dis-associated themselves from this editorial. (*Allaghi*, Athens, September 27, 1952).

The November, 1952, parliamentary elections saw the short-lived and unstable regime of Plastiras-Venizelos swept out of power by a landside victory for Marshal Alexander Papagos's Greek Rally party. One probable contribution to Papagos's victory was the fact that the Communist-controlled United Democratic Front sought to make common cause with the Progressive and Liberal parties of Plastiras and Venizelos. The Communist campaign was directed from abroad by the exiled general secretary of the Greek Communist party, Nicholas Zachariades. Candidates included Serafis, Glezos, and General Mihail Hadjimihalis(an ELAS leader in 1944, 1945). Whereas the Communists and their allies had polled 180,000 votes in 1951, they declined to 165,000 votes a year later (10.5%). Because the electoral system was changed from proportional representation to a majority electoral system, the Communist group failed to win a seat in the new parliament. The party of Papagos (military hero of Greece against both Fascism and Communism) won 49% of the vote, and an overwhelming majority in parliament. It is probable that Papagos' victory would have been even more impressive had not the Plastiras regime excluded soldiers and women from voting. The election seemed to be a mandate to deal more energetically with Communists and Communism.

TURKEY

Traditional Russian efforts to seize the Straits are but part and parcel of long standing Soviet-Turkish hostilities. During World War II however, Turkey took pains to assure Soviet Russia of her friendship. The Turkish Government outlawed the strongly anti-Soviet Pan Turanian Society. On January 12, 1945, Turkey agreed to open the Straits for the flow of supplies to Russia, but this and other steps did not seem to assuage Russian hostility. On March 21, 1945, the Soviet Government denounced the Soviet-Turkish pact of friendship and non-aggression, and made it clear that Turkey must grant the following concessions to remain in the good graces of the U.S.S.R.: (1) the return of Kars and Ardahan to Russia; (2) the granting of military bases in the Bosphorus and the Dardanelles; (3) a revision of the Montreux Straits Convention, and (4) a revision of the Thracian boundary in favor of Communist Bulgaria. During 1946 the Soviets demanded that the defense of the Straits should be jointly organized by Turks and Russians, and that the Straits should be controlled not only by Turkey but also by every Soviet satellite bordering on the Black Sea, and including, of course, the U.S.S.R. These demands were steadily rejected by the Ankara Government.

A mounting barrage of anti-Turkish propaganda, together with Soviet military demonstrations on the border, prompted the Turks to take countermeasures. In December, 1946, the Government announced the arrest of over seventy members of the Turkish Socialist Workers' and Peasants' party, and the Turkish Socialist party, for Communist subversive activities. The two groups were outlawed and their six news organs were banned. By the spring of 1947 Turkish-Soviet relations had reached an all-time low, and Turkey seriously feared a Soviet military move. Turkey's stand was supported by the Truman Doctrine, which was designed to back the anti-Communist governments of both Greece and Turkey. (See Harry N. Howard, *Germany, the Soviet Union, and Turkey During World War II*, U. S. Department of State 1948, 63 pp.).

YUGOSLAVIA

When Hitler attacked Stalin in June, 1941, the Croatian Communist Tito-Broz heeded the call of Moscow, and formed a military committee later known as the Partisans. On November 26, 1942, Tito created the "Anti-Fascist Council of National Liberation" (AVNOJ) in an effort to attract non-Communist "liberals" to his group. A year later the AVNOJ transformed itself into a sort of provisional government, and Tito acquired the dual title of "Marshal" and "Premier." Tito's Partisans were determined to ultimately wrest power away from the Yugoslav

Government in exile, and spent just as much time fighting the Chetnik group of General Mihailovich as they did fighting the Germans.

At first Britain and the United States aided Mihailovich, representative of the recognized Yugoslav Government. Gradually, however, Soviet pressure, together with pro-Tito reports from British agents in Yugoslavia, prompted Churchill after the Teheran Conference in 1943 to throw his support to the Tito group. Churchill forced King Peter of Yugoslavia to appoint a new premier who would be willing to discuss with Tito the formation of a new "coalition" regime. This new premier was Ivan Subasic, and he bent over backward in an effort to reach a satisfactory agreement with Tito. A series of conferences took place on the island of Vis, where Subasic, at the insistence of the British, capitulated to all of Tito's demands, while simultaneously cutting the ground out from under the exile Government in London. Precisely the same pattern was to be followed in Poland and in China.

The Yalta (Crimea) Conference, which took place in February, 1945, declared that a true coalition Yugoslav government, representing both Partisans and members of the exile Government should be formed. It was a foregone conclusion, however, that ever since Tito had followed the Soviet Army into Belgrade, there was no likelihood that he would allow representatives of the exile Government to assume any power in Yugoslavia. Tito did go through the motions of revising his cabinet, in an effort to persuade western leaders that he was establishing a coalition regime, but this move hardly changed the *loci* of power in Yugoslavia. Tito's close ties with Moscow were reflected in the Soviet names which Tito gave to all Yugoslav organs of government.

In August and September, 1945, Tito purged the hapless Subasic, as well as another non-Communist, Milan Grol. He then had his puppet "parliament" pass some election laws which would guarantee a victory for the Communist People's Front. The result was a typical Soviet election. The Popular Front won 475 seats in the new parliament, and granted 76 seats to splinter collaborationist groups—none of which has ever opposed the Tito regime. Shortly thereafter another purge removed the Serbian Peasant leader Jovanovic from active political life. The new parliament, in a remarkable show of unanimity, proceeded to vote for abolition of the monarchy, consecration of Yugoslavia to brotherhood with the U.S.S.R., and for the identification of the Communist Popular Front as the new government of Yugoslavia. Tito headed a politburo which included also Kardelj, Rankovich, Pijade, and Djilas. A Soviet-type federal system of government was created, with real power, however, remaining in the central government in Belgrade. Politburo member Pijade expressed the new philosophy of government as follows: "The altar lamp of terror must never be extinguished; the people must have fear. It is the duty of the police and the army to see that the people have fear." (Hal Lehrman, *Russia's Europe*, Appleton Century, 1947, p. 107; Martin Ebon, *World Communism Today*, Whittlesey House, 1947, p. 131). Tito added to this: "Those who persist in hindering the creation of something better and new will have to disappear from the face of the earth." (Ebon, p. 139). Among those who "disappeared" were General Mihailovich and Archbishop Stepinac.

Prior to the Tito-Stalin dispute of 1948, Tito's Foreign Minister Kardelj had this to say about the United States: "Between us and America there is an unbridgeable chasm. We are two worlds. They cannot be united. When we are victorious over the American world, the world will be one." (Ebon, p. 118). The same Kardelj later told a mass meeting of Communist Youth: "We have made several concessions to the capitalist world, in order to gain time. But when the hour strikes we must be ready to pass on to the offensive. The proletarian revolution is on the march. It is linked to the Soviet Union through agreements of mutual political and economic assistance. It is creating, as Stalin has said, a union of all the many parts of the Revolution . . . into one system. That Revolutionary system will go into a frontal attack against the Imperialist system." (*loc. cit.*).

Tito's regime adopted all the trappings of a Soviet satellite: slave labor, continuing purges, monopoly of political power by the Communist party, state control of the economy, thought control, and employment of former Fascists where feasible (among them Franz Pierts, Marko Masic, and Salejman Filipovic). It has also declared war on organized religion, and most particularly against the Catholic Church. The United States and Britain had ridiculed King Peter when he warned them: "Tito's Committee will end in the exercise of power by a single party." (Lehrman, *op. cit.*, p. 166). The United States and Britain sent Tito $88,000,000 worth of lend lease aid, as well as 420 millions worth of UNRRA supplies.

On June 28, 1948, following several sharp interchanges between Moscow and Belgrade, Tito was denounced by the Cominform as a "deviationist" and an "opportunist." It appeared that Tito had protested tight Soviet control of the Yugoslav economy, and that he thought it was possible to develop his own brand of Communism independently of Stalin's directives. This break did not immediately mean, however, that Tito had joined the western powers and their collective security efforts. Indeed Tito's Foreign Minister Kardelj, addressing the Fifth Congress of the Yugoslav Communist party, announced that the Yugoslav Government would continue to support Soviet foreign policy against the "imperialist powers." He also urged "Development of cooperation in all fields with the Soviet Union and the people's democracies with the common economic and cultural growth in the Socialist countries." Kardelj attacked the United States on the grounds that its "imperialism in western Germany had based itself on the same capitalistic monopolies as Adolf Hitler when he sought to achieve world domination." (*New York Times*, July 27, 1948).

It was not until several months later, in September, that Moshe Pijade, Tito's leading theoretician, attacked Soviet Marxist doctrines. He accused Stalin of mouthing "a sterile dogmatism that finds refuge in the past and turns its back upon the living reality of present day experience." At the same time three leading military and political personalities who tried to escape to Rumania and Hungary were caught and executed.

The increasingly anti-Tito stand of the Cominform, coupled with threats of sanctions against Tito, gradually forced the Yugoslav Government to acquiesce more gracefully to American economic and ultimately military aid. The United States felt that Yugoslavia's strategic location was vital to Mediterranean and central European defense, and accordingly it became fixed policy, both for America and Great Britain to court Tito diplomatically, and give him aid without conditions. Tito encouraged the new doctrine that the western coalition was not against Communism, but rather against "Russian imperialism." Many Tito supporters in the west simultaneously opposed American aid to Spain, on the grounds that Spain was a dictatorship, and the Spanish people did not like Franco. These partisans ignored Tito's even more stringent dictatorship, and that fact that Yugoslavs were escaping to Austria and Italy almost at the same rate as were people from Iron Curtain countries escaping into Vienna and Berlin. (See, for example, *New York Times*, July 22, 1952). Leigh White warned: "We must not make a false distinction . . . between Titoism and Stalinism. If we depended on Titoism to stem the advance of Stalinism, as we depended on Stalinism to stem the advance of Hitlerism, we shall end up by coming to terms with Titoism as we came to terms with Stalinism, to our undoing . . ." (Mr. White's *Balkan Caesar*, Scribner's, 1952, is one of the best descriptions of modern Yugoslavia. Other valuable reference works are David Martin's *Ally Betrayed*, Prentice-Hall, 1946, and R. H. Markham's *Tito's Imperial Communism*, University of North Carolina Press, 1947).

12

Communism in East Europe

POLAND

The Soviet conquest of Poland dates back to the Nazi-Soviet Pact of August 23, 1939. This pact, originally suggested by the Soviet Government in April, declared as follows in its secret protocol: "In the event of a territorial and political re-arrangement of the areas belonging to the Polish state, the sphere of interest belonging to Germany and the U.S.S.R. shall be bounded approximately by the line of the rivers Narew, Vistula, and San . . ." (U.S. Department of State, *Nazi-Soviet Relations, 1939-1941*, pp. 1, 2).

In the middle of September, 1939, Soviet troops invaded eastern Poland while German troops invaded western Poland. By the end of the month, the Nazi-Soviet Friendship Pact had been signed, and the Molotov-Ribbentrop line divided the German and Russian spheres of interest as planned by the agreement in August. The joint occupation of Poland ended in the summer of 1941 with the German attack on Russia. On July 30th, 1941, the Soviet Government re-established diplomatic relations with the exile Polish Government in London, and declared that "the Soviet-German treaties of 1939 as to territorial changes in Poland have lost their validity." (Quoted by William H. Chamberlin, *European Cockpit*, Macmillan, 1947, p. 248). The Soviet Government further adhered to the principles of the Atlantic Charter, outlawing territorial aggrandizement and recognizing the principle of national self-determination, when it signed the Declaration of the United Nations on January 1, 1941.

It soon became evident, however, that the Soviet policy for Poland was based on long range hostility to the exile Government and with a determination to create a Soviet puppet state in its place. During the year and one half of Soviet occupation, one and one half million Poles were deported by the Soviets to Russia and Siberia. The Polish Army Corps of General Anders, which put itself at the disposal of the Soviet Government after Germany attacked Russia in 1941, was cruelly mistreated. That the Soviets had no intention of working with the Polish Government was made clear when they created a Polish Communist front group originally known as the Union of Polish Patriots, and later, as the Lublin Committee. This Committee the Soviets were to foist upon Great Britain and the United States as the Government of Poland.

On April 17, 1943, the mass grave of 10,000 Polish officers was found in Katyn forest, near Smolensk. These officers had been captured by the Soviet Army in 1939, and the Soviet Army newspaper *Red Star* had admitted, on September 17, 1940, that they were being held in a Russian concentration camp. The Polish Government in exile repeatedly asked the Soviet Government for information relative to these Polish officers, but all to no avail. However, two days after the mass grave had been found by the advancing German Army, Moscow Radio declared: "There were, in fact, some former Polish prisoners in 1941, in the area around Smolensk. After the withdrawal of Soviet troops, they fell into the hands of the German Fascist executioners." (*Foreign Broadcast Intelligence Service*, April 19, 1943). This announcement was rather surprising inasmuch as the Soviets had said nothing about this for several years, and had not even bothered to answer Polish queries about the officers. When an International Red Cross inquiry was asked for, the Soviet Government broke off diplomatic relations with the Polish exile Government. Subsequent evidence points unmistakably to the Soviet Government as perpetrator of this crime of genocide (see the Van Vliet Report, findings of the Madden Committee, and testimony of former ambassador Lane).

By the end of July, 1944, the Soviet Army had pushed to the gates of Warsaw, and the Polish underground army (200,000 strong) could hear Russian artillery and see Russian planes over the city. The leader of the underground army, General Bor-Komorowski, representing the Polish exile Government, received word via Moscow Radio on July 29th to rise up in arms against the German garrison, at which time the Poles could expect aid from the Russian Army. A similar broadcast was monitored in London the next day. Molotov told Polish premier Mikolajczyk on July 30th that Russian troops were within ten kilometers of Warsaw's central district, and Stalin assured him that Soviet forces would aid the Poles against the Germans. On the basis of all this information, the Polish underground attacked the Germans on August 1st. Suddenly, however, the Russian artillery ceased firing, and Russian planes were no longer seen over Warsaw. The Soviet military forces sat by and watched the slow but certain liquidation of the valiant Polish soldiers. Molotov promised American ambassador Harriman on the 11th that aid would be forthcoming, but the promise was not carried out; three days later Harriman asked the Soviet Government for permission to use Russian airfields near Warsaw in order that American and British Commonwealth bomber crews flying aid to the embattled Poles might have fighter escort which could refuel. The

Soviet Government refused, even after a personal appeal by President
Roosevelt on August 17th. Molotov's answer to Roosevelt described the
Warsaw insurrection as "a purely adventuristic light-minded affair,
which was causing many sacrifices, and that Soviet support of it would
only lead to increasing sacrifices." (Arthur Bliss Lane, *I Saw Poland
Betrayed*, Bobbs Merrill, 1947, p. 46).

The unequal struggle lasted sixty-four days, and on October 3rd,
1944, the Germans wiped out the last pocket of Polish resistance. This
having been achieved, the Soviet Army could now proceed into Warsaw, for the last remnant of Polish governmental authority in the
capital had been wiped out, and the Soviet Government could install
the puppet Lublin Committee as the new *de facto* regime.

Churchill and Roosevelt, aware of the power discrepancy between
the Polish exile Government and the Soviet Government, and forgetful
of the principles of the Atlantic Charter, did what they could to end the
Russo-Polish problem. However, inasmuch as the Soviet Government
refused any compromise, the western leaders put pressure on the
Polish Government to give in to Soviet demands. Essentially these
demands were two: (1) recognition of the Lublin Committee as *de
facto* government, and (2) ceding to Soviet Russia the eastern Polish
territories Russia had occupied during 1939-1941. Although President
Roosevelt denied that any concessions had been made to Soviet Russia
in regard to Poland at the Teheran Conference in 1943, it is a fact
that a promise was made to Stalin to give him (Stalin) undetermined
Polish territory east of the "Curzon" line. (See Lane, p. 68, and Jan
Ciechenowski, *Defeat in Victory*, Doubleday, 1947, pp. 291-309). The
term "Curzon" line referred to a temporary armistice boundary between
Russian and Polish troops during the war in 1920. This line had never
been agreed to by either party as a final political boundary, and indeed,
it had been abandoned in 1921 for the Riga line (farther to the east).
Furthermore, the "Curzon" line had never run all the way down to
the Czech frontier—it had never included the Polish province of Galicia
as Russian territory.

Continued Soviet pressure on the Polish Government caused Roosevelt to beg Stalin on December 16, 1944 not to recognize the Lublin
committee as the legal Polish Government. Roosevelt pointed out that
the Polish exile Government of Mikolajczyk was the only legal government, as well as being one of the first United Nations. He further
reminded Stalin that Russian recognition of the Lublin group would
cause a split among the United Nations, and that it would give the
Germans considerable propaganda ammunition. Stalin rejected Roosevelt's warning and recognized the Lublin group on January 5, 1945.

The final betrayal of the Polish people came at the Yalta Conference. Here Churchill and Roosevelt capitulated to the two essential Soviet demands in Poland. A declaration was issued stating: "A new situation has been created in Poland as a result of her complete liberation (sic) by the Red Army. The Provisional (Lublin) Government should be reorganized on a broader democratic basis with the inclusion of democratic leaders from Poland itself and Poles abroad. This new government shall be pledged to hold free and unfettered elections as soon as possible on the basis of universal suffrage and secret ballot." (Lane, pp. 81, 82). By this declaration, the western powers abandoned the Polish exile Government, and paved the way for ultimate recognition for the Lublin Committee. In addition, the western powers recognized the Russian seizure of eastern Poland by agreeing to the "Curzon" line as the new boundary between Russia and Poland. This meant in effect, western recognition of the old Molotov-Ribbentrop line. Thus twelve million Polish citizens were turned over to Soviet tyranny without their advice or consent. Included were 70,000 square miles of former Polish territory, the all-Polish towns of Lwow and Wilno, and the Polish province of Galicia, which had at no time been Russian, and to which the Russians had not the slightest claim. There were no provisions for carrying out the promises for free elections, nor were there any guarantees for the safe return to Poland of the valiant fighting men of General Ander's Polish Army Corps.

President Roosevelt, weary, and near death, told Congress on March 1, 1945: "Our objective was to help create a strong, independent and prosperous nation. That's why we must always remember those words agreed to by Russia, Britain, and by me, the objective of making Poland a strong, independent and prosperous nation with a government ultimately to be selected by the Polish people themselves . . . the decision regarding the boundaries of Poland was quite a compromise. I didn't agree with all of it by any means." (*New York Times,* March 2, 1945).

Needless to say, the Russians never agreed to any real "broadening" of the Lublin regime. On April 1, 1945, but a few days before his death, President Roosevelt cabled Stalin: "Any solution which would result in a thinly disguised continuation of the present (Lublin) government would be entirely unacceptable, and would cause our people to regard the Yalta agreement as a failure." (James F. Byrnes, *Speaking Frankly,* Harper's, 1947, pp. 54, 55). During the UN Conference in San Francisco, Molotov announced blandly that sixteen non-Communist Polish leaders who had been abducted a month earlier, were being held in Moscow's Lubianka prison for "diversionist activities behind the Red Army." (Byrnes, p. 161).

The Soviet Government finally permitted Mikolajczyk to return to Poland, but granted him no real political power, and finally so harassed him and his Peasant party followers that he had to flee the country to save his life. The promised elections were delayed until such time as the Communist Security Police could guarantee that the results would be satisfactory. When the Peasant party refused to join the Communist-dominated Government Bloc in presenting a single slate to the voters, Mikolajczyk's two aides were murdered. Meetings of the Peasant party were attacked, and its supporters were intimidated and coerced. Thousands were sent to concentration camps in central Poland formerly maintained by the Nazis.

Not only were the Polish anti-Communists slowly decimated, but official Communist policy openly defied the United States by spying on the U.S. Embassy, threatening Embassy personnel, and during 1946 alone arresting eighty-four American citizens and executing several of them without their being allowed recourse to American consular and embassy authorities. In addition, American mail from Warsaw had to be routed through Moscow for censorship before reaching the United States. (Lane, *op. cit.*, p. 173, and pp. 198, 208).

The "elections" of January, 1947, were a sham and a fraud. Only the Communist Government bloc was able to campaign freely and with the aid of all the mass media. When Mikolajczyk protested the only satisfaction he got were empty notes of protest from the western powers to the Soviet Government. The Government bloc won 416 out of 444 seats in Parliament. A few months later Mikolajczyk had to flee for his life, and the Peasant party was destroyed. Poland was firm in the grip of the Soviet Empire.

CZECHOSLOVAKIA

Although the Soviet Union was one of the first states to recognize Hitler's puppet state of Slovakia, and concluded a trade agreement with it, Czech leaders were apparently more put out with the western powers because of the Munich Conference. Consequently Czech exile leaders in London, fully aware of the fate of Polish and Yugoslav exile regimes, bent over backward to accomodate the Soviet Government after June 22, 1941. The Czech Communist leader Klement Gottwald spent the war years in Moscow. The Czech leaders in London sent Eduard Benes to Moscow in December, 1943, as their representative, and he signed a treaty of friendship, mutual assistance, and post-war

cooperation with the Soviet Union. At that time the Communist Gottwald made demands on Benes which he turned down, but only
temporarily. It soon became evident that Benes was not a free agent,
and that he had best play the game as the Soviets desired. When
Polish premier Sikorski suggested a post-war Polish-Czech Danubian
federation, Benes originally agreed, only to reject the proposal when
told to do so by Stalin. (Martin Ebon, *World Communism*, Whittlesey
House, 1947, pp. 62, 63). Jan Masaryk expressed the new approved
"line" on December 31, 1944 when he said: "We want a strong and
democratic Poland, but only a Poland which will collaborate with the
Soviet Union. We have neither time nor inclination for a different
solution. . . . We want a decent and democratic Hungary which will
let us live in peace . . . a Hungary which will collaborate with the Soviet Union. The same is true for Yugoslavia, Austria, and Rumania."
(John F. Montgomery, *Hungary, The Unwilling Satellite*, Devin-Adair,
1947, p. 217).

Meantime the Soviets formed a front group called the Slovak
National Liberation Movement, and told Benes that he must capitulate
to all Soviet demands for Czechoslovakia or they would recognize this
group as they were to recognize the Lublin Committee in Poland. Benes
then gave in to the earlier Gottwald demands. Eastern Czechoslovakia
(Ruthenia, or the Carpatho-Ukraine) was ceded to the Soviet Union.
In addition, the so-called Kosice Agreement saw the Benes group
merged into the National Front Government; the largest pre-war
Czech party, the Agrarians, was banned, and restrictions were put on
free political activity. Non-Slavic minorities were to be expelled from
the country by force, if necessary, to make of the country a pure Slavic
race state. Industry was nationalized with the Communists holding
key positions.

Under these rules, and with the presence of the Red Army a constant
reminder to anti-Communists as to what might happen, the Communists gained a plurality of the votes in the May, 1946 elections.
However the four other parties had enough strength in the Parliament
to outvote the Communists. Premier Gottwald saw to it that Communists received important posts in government departments, and notably control of the ministries of Interior, Justice, and Education. Benes
and Masaryk hoped that Czechoslovakia could be a "bridge" between
the East and the West. Some observers even called the Czech Communists "agrarian reformers," just as they did in China. It soon became
clear even to the wishful thinkers, however, that Gottwald's Communists were no different than any others. When Benes and Masaryk
wished to join the Marshall Plan, Stalin told them not to do it.

Communist cabinet heads made themselves responsible not to the cabinet as a whole and the Parliament, but rather to the Czech Politburo. Communist para-military organizations were formed, with the aid of the nearby Soviet Army. The suicidal policy of trying to accommodate the Communists and please the Soviet Union came to an inglorious end in February, 1948. The Soviet Government, working through Soviet Ambassador Zorin, ordered Gottwald to move. The pretext was a parliamentary censure of the Communist Interior Minister for having hired nobody but Communists in the police and security departments. Faced with a Communist refusal to play the parliamentary game, the twelve non-Communist ministers resigned (except for two Socialists). On February 21st, Benes declared: "I will not now or in the future accept anything which will mean exclusion of one group or another from participating in the government." However Gottwald, and his lieutenants Nosek and Slansky had plans to enforce a one-party system. Armed Communists occupied all key areas of Prague, and then marched to the presidential palace of Benes. Meantime the anti-Communist front was weakened when the Socialists decided to play along with the Communists. Gottwald presented an all-Marxist cabinet to Benes and told him to approve it or the armed groups outside the palace would act. Benes gave in, after telling Gottwald: "You're talking to me like Hitler." (*Time*, March 8, 1948, p. 28). The week beginning March 7th was proclaimed Gottwald week, devoted to general rejoicing "to give the people a chance to express their gratitude." Gottwald declared: "If anybody thinks that an exchange of leaders is enough, and otherwise everything may remain as before, he is mistaken."

Benes had confidently said to Stalin in December, 1943: "Mr. Stalin, I have complete confidence that we have signed an agreement for non-intervention in domestic affairs, and I know you will keep it." He had apparently forgotten Gottwald's remark to Parliament in 1929: "You gentlemen ask me what we are here for. My answer is simple. We are here to break your necks." (*New York Times*, February 26 and 27, 1948). The Communist National Front thereupon passed a law which denied the franchise to "sinners against the republic or people's democracy." Czechoslovakia, a "people's democracy," was now behind the Iron Curtain.

HUNGARY

In the winter of 1944-1945, the Soviet Army entered Hungary, and in their wake followed Hungarian Communists who had spent the war years in Moscow, training for the "liberation." In the fall of 1944 Soviet parachutists had begun to lay the ground for Communist seizure of Hungary. Communist organizers were supplied by the Soviet Army with every conceivable aid: money, cars, radio sound trucks, gasoline, newsprint, literature and films in Hungarian language. In December, 1944, a provisional government was established at Debrecen, 116 miles east of Budapest, under Soviet aegis. The first act of the predominately Communist "parliament" was to approve a cabinet list prepared, appropriately enough, by Soviet Minister Pushkin. In January, 1945, an armistice was signed in Moscow forcing Hungary to pay Russia 200 million dollars worth of commodities, and 100 millions to Yugoslavia and Czechoslovakia.

When Budapest finally fell in February, the Communist members of the Debrecen cabinet followed to take possession. The new Communist mayor, Zoltan Vas, saw to it that the "right" people got food ration cards; that the "wrong" people were turned over to the Soviet Army as "collaborators." Anti-semitism was official Soviet policy, and former Fascists who were willing to help the Communists were readily accepted. Hungarian Communist leader Matyas Rakosi, speaking of the Fascist-like Arrow Cross leaders who had waged bloody anti-semitic campaigns a few months earlier, declared: "These little fascists aren't bad fellows, really. They were forced into fascism. . . . All they have to do is sign a pledge and we take them in." (Hal Lehrman, *Russia's Europe*, Appleton-Century, 1947, pp. 171, 187).

When the non-Communists from the Debrecen regime were finally allowed into Budapest, they found the political police already running the administration as a sort of super-government. The Communists again found that the key to control of east European governments were the ministries of Interior and Justice. Interior Minister Ferenc Erdei made plain what the new policy was when he said: ". . . it is better to make mistakes occasionally than to let one enemy of the regime escape." (*Ibid.*, p. 190). Hungarian anti-Communists were led by the courageous Smallholder party. The Socialists, for the most part, collaborated with the Communists, offering little resistance. The Smallholders looked to the American and British missions in Budapest to stand up to the Russians. At Yalta the Soviets had agreed to "assist the liberated peoples and to solve by democratic means their pressing political and economic problems." The Allies were pledged to jointly "assist such peoples to establish conditions of internal peace, to form interim governmental bodies broadly representative of all democratic elements." They were also pledged to "the establishment, through free elections, of governments responsive to the will of the people." The

Soviet Government, however, delights in such vague language, and carried out its plans without regard to American and British feelings. The so-called Allied Control Commission was run by Vishinsky. When American General Key protested Vishinsky's high-handed methods, and asked the U.S. Department of State for support, he was told by Washington to drop the matter in the name of "allied unity." (*Ibid.*, p. 194). Voroshilov seized American-owned oil fields at Lispe, and an American equipment plant near Budapest. He censored American correspondence, in violation of the Potsdam formula which provided for freedom of Allied newsmen to travel and report.

The only time any American official in eastern Europe stood up to the Soviets effectively was in the fall of 1945, when American political representative Arthur Schoenfeld told the provisional government that the United States would recognize it if free elections were held. The Soviet Government countered by immediately recognizing the regime, and then planning a semi-free election which, if won by the Communists, would have its position enhanced by the promise of American recognition. However, the Communist Government bloc had the full support of the Soviet Occupation forces, whereas the Smallholders and the few other anti-Communists lived a most precarious existence. Voroshilov tried to force the Smallholders into agreeing to a single slate arrangement, but for once the American and British missions protested effectively, and Voroshilov backed down. Voroshilov did succeed in terrorizing the Smallholders into agreeing to give the Communists fifty percent of the cabinet posts, regardless of the election results. The result was that although the Smallholders won 57% of the popular vote, and a majority in the parliament, the Communists received half the cabinet posts with sufficient strength to extend their power and ultimately coerce the Smallholders out of government entirely. They gained control of the key Interior post, and used this as a lever to terrorize the anti-Communists in and outside government. This maneuver had the full support of the Soviet Army and Occupation authorities. When Schoenfeld sought to protest, he was told by Washington that sufficient concessions had already been made by Moscow. The Communist-controlled Socialist vice premier Szakasits declared: "If the Smallholder party really wants democracy it must renounce the hope of governing with a Smallholder majority." He concluded that "electoral arithmetic cannot form the basis of our political life." (*Ibid.*, p. 209).

The Communist police and courts arranged numerous "plots" and "conspiracies" with which to discredit the Smallholder party. In December, 1945, three Smallholder cabinet ministers were forced to resign, and forty Smallholder members of parliament were arrested, as was the leader of the party, Bela Kovacs. A "confession" was extracted from the latter which implicated the Smallholder premier Ferenc Nagy. The Communists kidnapped Nagy's son, and then forced him to resign his post. (See Ferenc Nagy, *The Struggle Behind the Iron Curtain*, 1948). Nagy's ouster paved the way for Communist leader Rakosi to consolidate control of government. A new election law was passed by a thoroughly intimidated parliament—by now purged of the troublesome Smallholders—which enabled the Communists to choose the candidates who would run against them. An election law was passed which outlawed the following groups: (1) persons overzealously religious, (2) ex-aristocrats, (3) reactionaries, and (4) persons belonging to the late opposition.

The philosophy guiding the New Order was well expressed by Interior Minister Rajk when he said: "The peaceful and quiet governing of a country is possible only when functional parties do not threaten the unity of the National Assembly." (Michael Florinsky, "Hungary," *Current History*, September, 1947, p. 155). The former Premier, Ferenc Nagy, confessed: "My main fault was that in the beginning I believed in coalition cooperation with the Communists and their sympathizers. I am living proof that you cannot compromise with Communism." (See Nagy's articles in the *Saturday Evening Post*, August 23 and September 6, 1947).

The Soviet Union transformed Hungary into an economic as well as a political colony. Red Army food requisition has permanently injured the peasantry and Hungarian agriculture in general. A trade treaty with Russia provides for Soviet control of the economy through so-called "joint" Russian-Hungarian companies which oversee Hungary's oil, bauxite, minerals, chemicals, power plants, machinery, shipping, air transport, motor transport, automobile manufacture, and agriculture. According to the armistice terms, the Soviet Government received 200 millions in reparations, but it was not stated how the reparations were to be paid, in what materials, or at what assessed value. This enabled the Russians to take whatever they wished, checking it off at low-level prewar prices, an evaluation which automatically increased Hungary's reparation debt by over 100 percent. The United States and Great Britain helped push Hungary into Russian arms by agreeing that the Russians could help themselves to all former German assets, without defining what these were. In addition to helping themselves to all the food they wanted, Soviet military authorities carried away so many goods that no monetary system could possibly have survived the ensuing scarcity. The Soviet Occupation simultaneously printed so much paper money, that the Hungarian *pengo* scarcely had a chance. The Soviet Occupation Army can legally remain in the country until an Austrian peace treaty is signed. This the Soviet Government has shown little desire to accomplish. The Soviet Army of Occupation seized more than half the annual pre-war grain production in less than one year of occupation. The Soviet Union is collecting annually at least one-half of the Hungarian production, and one-third of the Hungarian national income.

RUMANIA

Whereas in Hungary the Russians had been able to create a government, in Rumania they found themselves confronted with an existing anti-Nazi regime. This government, headed by premier Sanatescu, was the result of the coup d'etat engineered by King Michael on August 23rd, 1944. However the incoming Soviet Army brought with it the usual Rumanian Communist emigres, who had spent the war years in Moscow. Soviet policy for Rumania was carried out by the front organization known as the National Democratic Front (NDF). With Soviet Army support, the NDF proceeded to terrorize the population, and forced King Michael to appoint their stooge Groza as Rumania's vice-premier. This was not enough, for Vishinsky soon appeared in Bucharest and told the King that the Communists must be given the Interior ministry as well as the Justice ministry. He also insisted that Groza be made premier. Michael, failing to receive any support from Britain or the United States, capitulated. By March 6, 1945, a new government had been formed, headed by Groza, and with Communists occupying the ministries of Interior, Justice, and Propaganda. In December, the United States and Britain made a half-hearted effort to implement the Yalta pledges regarding basic freedoms and political liberties. But western representatives Clark-Kerr and Harriman proved to be no match for their Russian counterpart Vishinsky, and nothing came of the effort. The United States and Britain ultimately recognized the Groza regime.

Elections, promised for May, 1946, were delayed until November to allow the Communists to make adequate preparations. To set the correct tempo for the election, premier Groza declared that the peasants would be "mercilessly punished" if they did not vote right. Communist leader Emil Bodnares predicted: "We will win, no matter how." (Lehrman, p. 251). Needless to say the Communists won the "election," outlawed the anti-Communist parties, and consolidated their monopoly of political control. As in other Soviet east European satellites, the Communists admitted former Nazis and anti-semites into their ranks, such as Constantin Burducea, Georges Tatarescu, and Lotar Radaceanu.

In 1940 the Soviet Union, with the aid of Nazi Germany, had begun the job of dismembering Rumania. By 1947 the job had been completed, with the tacit consent of the western democracies. According to the armistice terms, the Soviet Government was allowed to requisition all transportation equipment, and has kept it as "war booty." This included practically all Rumania's freighters, locomotives, barges, tugs, autos, and trucks. The Rumanian economy was effectively harnessed to that of the Soviet Union through the establishment of "joint" companies giving the Soviets control over banking, oil, timber, shipping, and aviation. During 1947, the Red Army alone received 10,000 tons of oil each month. Maintenance of the Red Army on Rumanian soil has literally eaten the Rumanian people out of hearth and home. With Russia taking all the grain, Rumania had to import grain for the first time in its history. A bitter joke circulates among the Rumanian peasants as follows: "What is the difference between the Germans and the Russians? The Germans took the eggs and left us the hens; the Russians take the hens and demand we pay them for the eggs the hens would have laid."

BULGARIA

By August, 1944, the Bulgarian Government was asking for an armistice. Bulgarian representatives were in Cairo negotiating with British and American diplomats, inasmuch as Bulgaria had been at war only with the western powers, and no state of war existed between Russia and Bulgaria. The Soviet Government, however, had no intention of allowing Bulgaria to conclude an armistice with the western powers. On September 7th, 1944, the Soviet Union declared war on Bulgaria, and invaded the country. Military control of Bulgaria would lead to a Communist political orientation. The Red Army marched in, followed by the usual group of Communist emigres. The Bulgarian Government was overthrown by a point putsch of the Communists and the Fascist Zveno organization. Colonel Georgiev became the new premier, and he sent an armistice mission to Soviet Marshal Tolbukhin. Georgiev gave the Communists the ministries of Interior and Justice. A front organization was formed called the Fatherland Front, and it proceeded to attack the anti-Communist Agrarian party led by G. M. Dimitrov and Nikola Petkov. Dimitrov, refused asylum by the British mission in Sofia, found refuge in the home of the American Minister, Mr. Barnes.

(See G. M. Dimitrov, "The American Minister Stood By His Guns," *Reader's Digest,* August, 1947, pp. 125-128). Petkov tried to fend off the Communists, but his effort was unsuccessful because he received little or no support from the western powers.

Elections were set for August 1945. As usual, the Communists sought to force the non-Communists to join them in a single slate electoral list. When the Agrarians and Socialists insisted on putting up their own slates of candidates, the Communist radio termed it a "cowardly act against the people." (Lehrman, p. 264). The Fatherland Front saw to it that neither opposition party was free to campaign, and the result was a usual Communist election. In December, 1945, the United States and Great Britain got the U.S.S.R. to promise to "broaden" the Bulgarian Government to include two non-Communist cabinet members. Vishinsky was sent to Sofia to see to it that this took place. Two new faces did, in fact, appear, but they were both from the Fatherland Front. It took the Zveno a long time to realize that it was the prisoner, and not the partner, of the Communists within the Fatherland Front. The Zveno leader Stainov once told the American correspondent Hal Lehrman: "You Americans must be patient with the Russians; you must allow for their peculiar mentality, and win their confidence." It was not much later that Stainov, his usefulness to the Communists having come to an end, was being denounced by the Communist press as a "dirty fascist dog." (Lehrman, pp. 265, 266). The Zveno War Minister, Colonel Veltchev, soon perceived the Communist game, and refused to take orders from the Communists. When they asked him to resign, he refused. The next day the Communists delivered to Veltchev the body of his aide, whose head had been crushed like an eggshell. An official anouncement described it as "suicide by poisoning." Veltchev resigned.

Elections in October, 1946, gave public recognition to the fact that Georgi Dimitrov (no relation to G. M. Dimitrov) was the real power behind the Fatherland Front. A former secretary of the Communist International, Dimitrov was the top Balkan Communist. The usual Communist electoral result having been achieved, Dimitrov appointed himself premier and brought Bulgaria firmly within the family of "people's democracies." In June, 1947, Nikola Petkov, leader of the Agrarian party, was seized, tried in three days, and then executed. Georgi Dimitrov declared: 'If we execute Petkov it will demonstrate how powerless the great democracies are to defend them (the opposition), and how senselessly futile their opposition to Communism has become." Petkov was hanged on September 23, 1947, with the United States and Great Britain standing by and doing nothing.

With Petkov and the last of the opposition out of the way, Bulgaria came to be more and more of a Soviet colony. Occasionally Georgi Dimitrov still had to raise his voice to remind the Bulgarians who was running the country. In February, 1948, when deputy Kota Lulchev dared to question the national budget submitted by Dimitrov, the latter declared, speaking of Lulchev and his friends: "Miserable chatterers. ... You will remember that in this Assembly many times I warned members of Nikola Petkov's group, but they did not listen. They lost their heads and their leader lies under the ground. Reflect on your own actions, lest you suffer the same fate." The budget was passed unanimously. (See G. M. Dimitrov's article, *Saturday Evening Post*, Dec. 6, 1947, p. 28; *San Francisco Chronicle*, March 14, 1948).

The Soviet Occupation denounced "reactionary fascists" and denied them the franchise. Among those so denounced was King Simeon—aged eight years—who was deprived of his throne and future political rights.

ALBANIA

When the Germans evacuated Albania in the autumn of 1944, a Communist group called the National Liberation Front, led by Enver Hoxha, moved into the capital city of Tirana. In November, 1945, Hoxha's regime was recognized by Russia, Britain, and the United States as the provisional government of Albania. But a month later "elections" were held in which Hoxha's Democratic Front, the only party to offer candidates, won all the seats in the Constituent Assembly. This Assembly proceeded to create a "praesidium" which conferred plenary powers on Hoxha as Chief of State. At the same time Soviet Minister Chovakia arrived in Tirana and moved into the residence of the former Italian Governor General.

The Cominform-supported regime of Hoxha and his aide, General Mehmet Shehu, was consolidated at the direct expense of pro-Tito Communists and the much larger anti-Communist groups in Albania. The elimination of the Yugoslavs, who occupied a pre-eminent position in Albania up to the eve of the rupture with the Cominform, was followed by the substitution of military and civilian personnel from the Soviet Union. Yugoslav engineers had built roads, railroads, and factories. A Yugoslav military mission helped to reorganize the Albanian Army. The Yugoslav Government had made substantial loans in money and goods to the Albanian Government. The Soviet Government filled the vacuum left by the Yugoslavs in mid-1948. Soviet Army officers began to arrive on every Soviet ship which touched at the port of Valona. These officers constituted a military mission to Albania, and

Soviet field-grade officers were assigned to the Albanian Army down to and including the battalion level. The Soviet civilian experts who began to arrive in Albania fell into two categories. There were the high party officials who guided the Central Committee of the Albanian Communist Party. It was they who carried out the Cominform purge of 1948. Communist party officials were also given supervisory roles in the principal governmental administrations to insure the loyalty of the government civil servants. The second category of Soviet civilian experts were engineers and technicians whose job was to expand and integrate those sectors of Albania's economy needed by the Soviet Union. More oil wells were drilled, and a pipeline was built to the port of Valona.

By the end of 1950 there were an estimated 3,000 Soviet officers and civilian experts in charge of the Albanian colony. As an outpost of political intrigue and as a headquarters for subversive action against Yugoslavia and Greece, Albania has considerable value to the Cominform.

The disparity between the standard of living of the Soviet missions and the native population is similar to that which existed between colonial administrators and the native population of Africa fifty years ago, except for the fact that the African natives had more to eat than have the Albanians since 1945. In reducing the Albanian economy to suit their own purposes, the Soviet planners have created perhaps the lowest standard of living in Albania that exists throughout all Europe.

Soviet Policy in the "People's Democracies"

Soviet policy for the European satellites is to constantly purge the party ranks, suppress nationalistic feelings, mold satellite economies into that of Soviet Russia's, eradicate religious influences, utilize existing anti-semitic sentiments, and train and equip satellite armies according to Soviet patterns.

One of the least-recognized ambitions of the Soviet dictatorship is to destroy the intellectual life and cultural heritage of the countries it has enslaved. By deporting intellectuals, priests, middle class elements —the educated, literate leadership groups of the population—Russia hopes to create a generation which will be devoid of national patriotic feelings, devoid of any pride in national history, and lacking all desire to be liberated from the Soviet yoke. In Rumania, for example, children must begin studying Russian as the primary language from the age of seven. The Rumanian Army is virtually identical in uniform, arms, and equipment with the Soviet Army.

Russia's aim is to create a United States of eastern Europe, with the satellite economies dedicated to strengthening the Soviet system—a sort of twentieth century mercantilism. Industrialization is being stepped up to Stakhanovite heights. In the realm of agriculture, Soviet policy at first had to move slowly, to take into account the strongly individualistic sentiments of the east European peasantry. However collectivization has been ruthlessly enforced since 1948. The Soviet Union is exploiting countries whose economic and industrial levels were much higher than its own. Soviet policy has accordingly depressed east European standards to the low scale of Russian life.

Recognizing that the strongest anti-Communist influence in eastern Europe has been the Catholic Church, Soviet policy-makers have slowly but surely moved against the Church, with such actions as those taken against Cardinal Mindszenty in Hungary, and the Catholic leadership of Czechoslovakia. In most of these countries the hierarchy of the Church has been virtually wiped out. The Communists have moved more slowly against the Church in areas where it has the greatest following.—i. e., in Poland, Hungary, and Czechoslovakia. Elsewhere they have moved quickly and ruthlessly. When the Communists gained control of eastern Europe during and after World War II, they endeavored to reduce the influence of the Church on the local level, and cut off its communications with the Vatican. Attempts were made to create "national" churches, without success. The heroism of the clergy was just as great when confronted with Soviet terror as when confronted with Nazi terror. The days of the catacombs in Pagan Rome have been relived by the Catholic priests and laypeople of eastern Europe.

Having partially succeeded in cutting off the local churches from their usual channels of spiritual and temporal matters, the Communist states in the satellite areas have sought to substitute themselves as arbiters of such matters. The church organizations have gradually been brought under state control and the day-to-day existence of the clergy made dependent on the state. Communist propaganda against the west and in favor of the Soviet "peace" campaigns is foisted upon the Church. Increasing impediments are put in the way of performance of priestly duties, administering the sacraments, and keeping in close touch with the faithful.

The Soviet satellites have sought to pit the Catholic lay people against their pastors, and also to split parish priests away from their bishops. Some of the purge trials have attempted to discredit the

Church by claiming that the Vatican collaborated with American "imperialism" to aid anti-state agents in satellite nations.

The economic and military integration of east European Communist states, together with the anti-religious and anti-nationalist programs have been accompanied by a series of political purges strongly reminiscent of the Moscow trials in the thirties. In Rumania, Ana Pauker, for a long time the acknowledged political force of that Soviet puppet state, saw her days numbered when she was accused of "crimes against the state" in June, 1952. Her successor to the Rumanian dictatorship was Georghe Gheorghiu-Dej. Hungary's Communist boss, Matyas Rakosi, saw his power position challenged by Laszlo Rajk, leader of the Communist underground during World War II. Rajk was hanged in 1947. The number one Polish Communist when the Cominform was born was Wladyslaw Gomulka, whose portrait was the political on every Polish street corner. However in 1948 he was castigated by the party for "alien opportunistic ideology," lost his job as party secretary, and was put in jail. Bulgaria has seen more changes within the Communist party leadership than any other satellite. First of all Georgi Dimitrov was suspected by Moscow of having Tito-like qualties, and was recalled to Moscow in 1947 for "medical treatment." Shortly thereafter Dimitrov was pronounced dead of a "liver ailment." Dimitrov was succeeded by Vulko Chervenkov, his brother-in-law and former bodyguard. Chervenkov announced his "loyalty to the death" for Stalin. For a time his right hand man was Traicho Kostov. The latter was subsequently attacked as a deviationist, and forced to write a 32,000 word confession. During his trial Kostov repudiated the confession, and was immediately hanged. Perhaps the most dramatic purge of all was carried out in Czechoslovakia in early December, 1952, when the following former leading Czech Communists were put to death: Rudolf Slansky (the power behind Gottwald's coup of 1948), Vladimir Clementis (former Foreign Minister), Ludvik Frejka (author of the Czech five year plan), and Bedrich Geminder and Josef Frank (top ranking Czech party officers). These were but five of eleven ranking Czech Communists who were hanged during the purge.

Although it is true that several thousand refugees from eastern Europe find their way into western Berlin and Vienna every day, it seems to be also true that with the passage of time the Soviet Empire will weld the east European satellites into an integral part of its political, economic, and military system. Existing undergrounds, and the passive but hopeless opposition in these areas have little chance for future freedom, unless and until it comes in the form of liberation by the anti-Soviet coalition.

13

Communism in Germany and Austria

EASTERN GERMANY

In eastern Germany the Soviet Union began to establish, in 1945, a satellite state controlled by Soviet occupation forces and their German Communist servants. It created the "German Democratic Republic" as an attempt to counteract the prestige of the free Federal Republic of western Germany.

The Soviet policy makers set up the east zone puppet state because that was all they could get for the moment. They have continued, however, to show all the signs of still wanting to control all of Germany, which Lenin regarded as the key to control of all Europe. The Soviets showed, in 1948, the extent to which they were willing to go to seize control of the more modest prize of Berlin, that is to say, the western zones of Berlin—the city which lies deep within the Soviet zone of Germany. John Winant, American representative on the European Advisory Commission, had refused to support military requests that the United States insist that the Soviet Government give it a legal path of entry into Berlin.

Inside their zone, the Soviets have sought to wipe out the remains of German culture that stand in the way of communizing the country. Relentlessly they have attacked the churches, the labor unions, the middle classes, and other obstacles standing in their path. They have tried to communize the schools, to control all the arts and amusements of the people, to convert the young men and women, and make the east Germans think that German national interests can only be served by collaboration with the Soviet Union. In these efforts the Soviets and their Communist servants have found some Germans willing to sell out, and some who could be convinced or intimidated by Communist tactics. Yet four-fifths of the Germans behind the Iron Curtain appear to remain anti-Soviet. They obey orders only when they have no alternative. Every day hundreds of east Germans seek refuge in the western zones of Berlin.

The Soviet Union won a diplomatic victory at Potsdam in 1945, just at it won similar victories previously at Teheran and Yalta. It was agreed at Potsdam, by the United States, Great Britain, and the U.S.S.R. to treat Germany as an economic unit. Thus Germany could become self-supporting with free trade between the agricultural east and the industrial west. However the Soviet zone never carried out its end of the bargain. Additionally, the Soviets insisted on taking reparations out of current production. This meant that the United States had to put in a subsidy at one end, while the U.S.S.R. took it out at the other end. Then the United States gave the Soviet Government a set of plates to print the same paper money found in the western zone of the United States. The Soviets proceeded to print all the money they wished, and by simply running the presses they could buy whatever they wanted in western Germany for the cost of the paper and ink.

On July 20, 1946, the United States offered to join the American zone with any one or more other zones in a common economic system. For months the Western Powers urged the Soviet authorities to join in a workable system, especially with a view to controlling inflation. The Soviets refused to cooperate. Finally the Western Powers formed a single economic unit (after initial French intransigeance), with its own currency. Inflation was relieved, and business and industry began to thrive under the "free market" program of Dr. Ludwig Erhard.

The Soviets proceeded to make their own zone into a puppet state, while simultaneously proclaiming it to be a sovereign German state. In November, 1947, a "People's Congress" was created, comprising hand-picked delegates, and pretending to represent the German people. This group, and the Soviet occupation standing behind it, soon made it plain that they stood for unification of Germany, but only under Communist control. The three Western Powers, at long last growing impatient for the political liberty of western Germany, and refusing to allow the Soviets to delay German political independence any longer, decided, in April, 1949, to allow the people of western Germany to establish a free German Government. In east Germany Soviet-type "elections" resulted in creation of the "German Democratic Republic" on October 15, 1950. Superintended by Soviet occupation officials, and by the Soviet secret police, it was clear that a free election would upset Communist control of eastern Germany. In May, 1949 the three Western Powers offered to let the Soviet zone join the newly established Federal Republic of west Germany if the Communist east Germans would allow free speech, free political parties, free elections and independent courts, and if it abolished the political police. The Soviet occupation and the east German Communists turned down this proposal. They launched an extensive propaganda campaign in favor of "unification," a peace treaty, and withdrawal of occupation forces, but with no free elections, and with a purpose of so weakening western

Germany that Soviet control could be extended throughout all Germany.

The Communist attack on the Republic of Korea in 1950, made more urgent the defense of Europe and German participation in that defense. It simultaneously made more extreme the "peace at any price" and neutralist feeling in western Europe. The Soviets therefore stepped up the "unity" propaganda to draw the free Germans of western Germany away from thoughts of defense into a dream of neutrality. Molotov called a meeting of satellite foreign ministers at Prague, out of which came a Soviet proposal opposing arming of Germany, withdrawal of foreign troops, a peace treaty, and a new German government in which east and west Germany would have equal representation. This proposal would have retired American troops beyond the seas, while leaving Soviet troops in nearby Poland; it ignored the armed "militia" of east Germany; it equated east Germany with nineteen millions and a dictatorship to the Federal Republic with forty millions and a free government. German Chancellor Adenauer saw through the ruse, and insisted that free elections must precede any unification of Germany. Since the Communists in east Germany opposed free elections for their zone, there could be no unification of Germany except under Communist terms. Soviet efforts in early 1952 to delay or end any and all proposals for rearmament of western Germany also failed, although Soviet policy-makers no doubt delighted in the French views regarding German rearmament, as well as the anti-Adenauer view of the German Socialist party.

When the Soviets took control of their zone in east Germany, they were bound by the Potsdam Agreement to promote democracy in the area. But they realized that if the east Germans were allowed free and honest elections, the Communist party would receive a small minority of the votes. Therefore the decision was taken to force a "shotgun" wedding between the Marxist parties—Socialist and Communist, and so cripple the remaining non-Communist groups— Christian Democratic and Liberal Democraitc—as to leave the Marxist coalition in control of political affairs. The Socialists were, in the main, opposed to this coalition, but Soviet pressures resulted in the collaboration of several Socialist leaders, including Otto Grotewohl, with the Communists. The united party was established in April, 1946 in Berlin, and called the *Sozialistische Einheitspartei Deutschlands* or German Socialist Unity Party. But this new party(hereinafter referred to as the SED) was no true coalition, but rather a Soviet-controlled organization, and largely Communist in composition. At the end of 1952 a Department of State analysis estimated actual SED strength in eastern Germany at nine percent of the population (*East Germany Under Soviet Control*, U.S. Department of State, 1952, p. 18).

The top levels of the SED resembled those of the Russian Communist party. The SED put its men into every strategic office in the government and in the "mass organizations" that controlled the people. SED officers controlled the youth movement (FDJ), and Democratic Women's Federation, the Consumer Cooperatives, Free German Trade Unions, German-Soviet Friendship Society, Culture League, and the Farmer's Mutual Aid Association.

The east Germans have four spy systems which watch over them: the SED spy system, the FDJ spy system, the Ministry of State Security spy system, and the Russian secret police. The net result is a population which must be very careful what it says and does. The SED spy system was effectively used at the beginning of 1953 to help purge several former leading Communists. On January 4th, the Central Committee of the SED charged that Titoism, Trotskyism and Zionism had been at work among the party leadership. Detailed charges were set forth against Paul Merker, former Politburo member, who was dropped from the party in 1950 on charges of having associated with the mysterious Noel Field. Also cited was Kurt Mueller, former Communist member of the west German Bundestag in Bonn. Mueller had been kidnapped by the Soviets in 1950 after being lured into the eastern zone. Many observers saw in this early 1953 purge a similarity to the anti-semitic purge carried out by Soviet policy in Prague during 1952.

In order to understand how the Soviet authorities operate a puppet government through native officials, it is useful to examine the records of some of the prominent Germans who have headed the east zone Administration, ranging from hardened Communists to opportunists and fellow travelers. These leaders include Walter Ulbricht, Deputy Minister-President of the puppet "German Democratic Republic," Otto Grotewohl, Minister-President, Wilhelm Pieck, President, and Otto Nuschke, Deputy Minister-President.

Ulbricht is perhaps the most important. An old time Communist born in 1893 in Leipzig, his aliases include Ulrich, Leo, Urvich, Sorensen, and Zelle. A Socialist until 1912, he was won over by Lenin in that year, and has worn a goatee and mustache ever since. In 1917 Ulbricht and Wilhelm Pieck were both members of the *Spartakusbund*, along with Rosa Luxembourg and Karl Liebknecht. This organization was the predecessor to the German Communist party. In 1929 Ulbricht was named to the Central Committee of the Comintern. As spokesman for the German Communists in the Reichstag, he defended the policy of collaboration with the Nazis against the Weimar democratic coalition. Again, in 1939, he defended the Hitler-Stalin pact and urged German workers to cooperate with Soviet workers against "British imperialists." Ulbricht appeared to be the number one German Communist in 1945, and has retained that position. As secretary-general of the SED he has the same position in Germany that Stalin had in the Soviet Union.

Grotewohl showed his usefulness to the Soviets as a good orator and a non-party man who obeyed orders. A member of the Socialist party, he collaborated with the Soviet authorities almost as soon as the Red Army entered eastern Germany. Born in 1894, he was in the anti-Nazi underground, and in 1945 at first seemed opposed to union with the Communists. In October, however, he left the Socialist party (which was subsequently outlawed) and joined the new SED, to control several key posts in both the party and the puppet regime. Oftentimes the spokesman for east German authorities, Grotewohl was considered by western observers to be a front for the Soviets in Germany.

Pieck was installed in 1945 as the figurehead of the puppet regime. Together with Ulbricht, he dates back to the founding of the German Communist party. Born in 1876, Pieck has always moved quickly with changing Communist "lines," and thereby survived many purges in the German party. He spent the war years in Moscow, and together with Ulbricht, headed the wartime front "National Committee for Free Germany." He followed the Red Army into Berlin. Although civilian president of the German Democratic Republic, Pieck, like Ulbricht, is a naturalized Soviet citizen. Both men entered their native land in 1945 holding the rank of colonel in the Red Army.

Nuschke was one of the few east German Christian Democrats who collaborated with the Soviet occupation. Born in 1883, he was once described as an "old stubborn Prussian who has always favored a pro-Russian policy" (*East Germany Under Soviet Control*, p. 25). The Soviets cherish Nuschke as a useful "bourgeois front," who, like Grotewohl, give the Soviet satellite regime of east Germany some small semblance of respectability.

The Soviet have made their strongest bid for influence among the youth. The Soviet zone of Germany has its official youth organization, the *Freie Deutsche Jugend* or Free German Youth. This organization stands for "peace and democracy" but only "as exemplified in the Soviet Union." East German parents are urged to send their children at the age of six years to join the Young Pioneers, a sort of cub-scout preparation for the FDJ. Boys and girls may join the FDJ at age fourteen and remain members until the age of twenty-five. The FDJ is affiliated with Communist organizations and fronts in other countries, such as the Soviet Komsomols (youth organization) and the World Federation of Democratic Youth, with headquarters in Paris. In 1951 the FDJ claimed a membership of two million.

The young member of the FDJ finds his time is fully taken up: he must attend endless lectures and classes on the theory and practice of Marxist-Leninist Stalinism; his sports are supervised, and only FDJ members and those belonging to the German Communist unions can become members of the German Sports Organization, which controls all sports, concessions, resort hotels, pleasure trips, and tickets to entertainments.

The FDJ youth must promote the Communist line in his every endeavor. For example, every school class has an FDJ member assigned to it, not only to watch the teacher, but to report what the children say on the playground. For meritorious service, which consists mainly of spying and attending meetings, the FDJ gives badges and money prizes, and there is also the chance of a fat political job for those who catch the eyes of the SED leaders.

Control over east German minds has been attempted by Soviet control of the schools—a state monopoly of education—with all public schools becoming training camps for future Communists. The school system has been called "the most powerful drug in the whole Soviet medicine chest." (*East Germany Under Soviet Control*, p. 41). The purpose of the schools is to make Communists of the children and to train a generation of loyal technicians to take the place of the older ones who have escaped or who cannot be trusted. The Soviets started on the schools as soon they arrived in Germany in 1945. They abolished all private schools and institutions and established a monopoly of education. They abolished parochial schools and religious instruction in the public schools. They continually harassed the remaining religious classes conducted by the churches. Schoolbooks were rewritten and new teachers replaced "unreliable" teachers. The first crop of teachers from the new Communist normal schools graduated in the fall of 1949. One-third of the student's time in these schools is devoted to the science of education on the Soviet pattern. With the passage of time, it was clear that barring liberation from the west, eastern Germany was going to have ever more effective Communist teachers and Communist schools. Another generation would be lost to the western world.

The subjects most favored in the education system are the social sciences, especially history; the German and Russian languages, and the natural sciences. All students must study and accept the "Marxist-Leninist science of society." History starts with the history of the Bolsheviks and goes on to Communist interpretations of past events, current evil doings of the "wicked Americans," and prophecies of the future triumph of Communism. The following questions from an eighth grade examination indicate the extent to which the young east German mind has been contaminated: "What proves that the Soviet Union is our best friend? Why are the imperialists anxious to get more colonies? What causes unemployment in West Germany? Discuss the National Front (a nationalist-inspired Communist organization); Why do progressive workers in west European ports refuse to unload American weapons?"

The Soviet authorities have made strong efforts to mold the minds of the east German population by controlling every kind of entertainment, literature, and the arts. The strict control of all the arts and amusements of the people ranks with control of the schools as an instrument of the police state.

As is true in eastern Europe generally, it is the churches which have put up the greatest resistance to Communism. Hence Soviet authorities in east Germany have found it advisable to avoid all-out war with the Protestant and Catholic churches while endeavoring to undermine their institutional foundations. The Communists have used their propaganda machine to connect the churches with their "peace" campaign. After Bach's High Mass was performed in Leipzig, the closing words "give us peace" were featured in the press as showing that Christianity favors the Communist peace movement. Slowly but surely the eastern regime has been eating away at the power of the churches by gradually restricting their legal rights and by reducing the number of seminaries, buildings, schools, and clergy.

The Soviet masters in east Germany have plenty for the population to do. As under Hitler, there is little unemployment. The typical east German suffers more from long hours, low pay, and bad working conditions than from idleness. The Soviets utilize different methods in controlling farmers, industrial workers, and technicians. Collectivization of agriculture was not the immediate goal; rather have the Soviets sought to make the farmers dependent on the Communist state for their livelihood. The so-called "land reform" program was designed to reward loyal farmers with land taken away from known anti-Communists who were labelled "kulaks." By the end of 1952 it was quite clear, however, that extensive spade work had been done by the Communist regime to prepare the east German farmers for collective farming.

Like the farmers, the wage earners have progressively come under the control of the state. The Communist-controlled Free German Trade Union Federation (FDGB), with more than five million members, includes practically all wage earners except those in the smallest establishments. The most depressed elements in the laboring force are the unfortunates who are forced to work in the uranium mines of Thuringia and Saxony. These mines are operated with the typical Russian disregard for life; cave-ins, explosions, silicosis, and skin diseases take a heavy toll. The bulk of the wage earners in the east zone are in state-owned industries. Here the unions are closely controlled by SED bureaucrats, whose job it is to make the men turn out more work. Social security hand-outs are dependent on the political attitude of the worker, as evinced at shop and union meetings. The main program of the east German government, and therefore of the FDGB is the speed-up program, known in Russia as the Stakhanovite system. A "labor hero" was found in the form of one Adolf Hennecke, who was said to have mined 24.4 cubic meters of coal in an eight hour shift (the normal quota was 6.3 meters). Hennecke was one of many "activists" whose job it was to continually raise work norms, so that each worker would have to work harder to get the same wage. This piece work system is most convenient for speed-up operations; German workers have an old proverb, "*Akkord ist Mord*"—the "piece-work contract is murder."

The propaganda line is that under socialism the workers own the factories, and the more they produce, the better off they are. But many German workers came to realize that what they produced above a bare subsistence was being shipped to the Soviet Union. The activists, who are the Stakhanovites of the system, get higher pay, special rations, tax-free liquor, and even priorities in housing. The mass of workers get correspondingly less. The morale of the workers has not been helped by being jailed for tardiness, or being fired without notice. They have had little enthusiasm for working an extra shift to celebrate the various Soviet holidays, such as Stalin's birthday. They objected to being arrested for complaining about faulty material, or because their paycheck was cut when poor material spoiled their output. They opposed having women sent down into the mines to help their husbands whose paychecks were too small to support the family.

Another vital element in the east German economic system is the technical men—the engineers and managers in industry, and the doctors, lawyers, and other trained men in the professions. At first the regime let these technicians alone. Needing their services badly, it could not initially afford to antagonize them. After the first few years, however, increasing Communist controls and political directives caused defections in the ranks of the technicians. No one knew better than the technical man that the Soviet Union was draining east Germany of goods at low prices, and sending in return raw materials and a few consumer goods at high prices. He realized that the Soviets were interested in east Germany as a colonial territory to be exploited, and as a line of communication with west German businessmen who were willing to smuggle strategic materials through the Iron Curtain.

The two principal secret police organizations in east Germany are the Russian secret police (MVD) and the "People's Police" operated by the east zone Ministry of State Security. The native organization attends to ordinary factory spying, mail and press censorship, and checking of railway passengers, besides the usual work of the uniformed Police. But the Soviets did not trust any part of the native police system, and the MVD therefore controlled its policies, recruiting and training, and spied on its officials and agents. The MVD has also etablished its own complete spy system to watch ordinary citizens. With a network of command posts and secret meeting places throughout the east zone, the MVD solicits information from informers among the population. It also operates it own prisons. Informers are enlisted and held by blackmail.

Outside Germany, General Wilhelm Zaisser is little known. For 18 million east Germans, however, this satellite Minister of State Security and his secret police—the SSD—are the terrible Communist successors of Heinrich Himmler and the Nazi Gestapo. Zaisser lost no time in proving himself to be thorough and ruthless in carrying out Stalin's orders to "purify" eastern Germany. After dragging off some 50,000 unfortunates to prisons, concentration camps, or uranium mines, Zaisser declared: "Hitler's great trouble was that he had no Siberia. We have." (Richard Hanser and Frederic Sondern, "East Germany's Red General," *San Francisco Chronicle,* January 5, 1953). A long-time servant of Moscow, Zaisser has seen service in Spain, China, and other countries as a military organizer, spy, and saboteur. He is the only German Communist to be simultaneously a General in the Soviet Army and a citizen of the U.S.S.R.

When the bloody 1923 "worker's rebellion" broke out in the Ruhr, Zaisser's participation led to his being named the "Red General of the Ruhr." Later he went to Russia and attended Soviet Military schools, returning in 1933 as chief of the Soviet industrial espionage net. As "General Gomez," Zaisser commanded the 13th "Loyalist" (Communist-controlled) Brigade in Spain, and subsequently became chief of all the International Brigades. During World War II, he served as chief of the important Antifa Academy at Krasnogorsk, where he indoctrinated captured German officers in Communism. In 1949, after mapping with Beria and others of the Politburo the construction of the new Soviet

German state, Zaisser went to Berlin to build up the dread SSD.

The "peace law" enacted on December 16, 1950, is designed to scare east Germans into collaboration: penalties range up to the death sentence for "war propaganda" or "scorning the peace movement"— meaning any talk in favor of the western countries and against the Soviet Union. Obeying any order of the Federal Republic (west Germany), listening to American radio broadcasts, or seeing an American movie—all these are now "peace law" crimes. Punishment is centered in the great concentration camps—Buchenwald, Sachsenhausen, Neubrandenburg—taken over from the Nazis. Many prisoners die in these camps, or are sent to almost certain death in the Soviet Union. Behind the prisons and jails where the secret police soften up their victims to confess imaginary crimes and betray their friends, there lies the terror of the work camps of the Soviet Union. No one knows how many German prisoners of war died or are being held in Soviet camps. No one knows how many civilians who have disappeared have been sent to the U.S.S.R. to die.

The most significant part of Soviet operations in east Germany has been creation of "militarized police" or what amounts to a German Army, to be used perhaps the same way the north Koreans and Chinese Communists were used by the Soviet Government in 1950.

In July, 1948, there was a widespread recruiting campaign among remaining German prisoners of war in Russia. The prisoners were carefully screened by Soviet Army officers, to see which of them were ready for military service, and at the same time prepared to accept Communism. Those selected were sent to Germany in August and September, 1948. The recruits included a carefully selected group of former German officers. A leadership was created from German Communists with military training; from Germans who had fought in Spain against General Franco's Nationalist Army; from German officers captured at Stalingrad or elsewhere and indoctrinated by the Soviets. A few are Russians. The entire group largely comprises old Communists, old Nazis, or old soldiers who care more for soldiering than for the independence of a free Germany.

This Communist army in east Germany is called the *Bereitschaften*, or Alerts. It increasingly appeals to Nazi and militarist groups to join up. In November, 1950, the *Bereitschaften* were organized in the form of a skeleton Soviet Army. The typical unit, or *Bereitschaft*, was set up like a Soviet Army mechanized regiment, complete with three combat units of infantry and one of artillery, together with the usual supporting companies and administrative headquarters. There is a system of school units for "political indoctrination and culture," infantry, artillery, engineers, signal corps, armor, and senior officers. Clearly this is not an ordinay police force.

The normal complement of a regular *Bereitschaft* included 371 officers, and 1432 non-commissioned officers and privates. The high proportion of officers was an indication that the force was designed to be expanded by the drafting of common soldiers. In November, 1950, the *Bereitschaften* comprised 51,000 men. Since that time so-called "Air and Sea Police" units have been created—the beginnings of a Navy and Air Force. New recruits were drawn largely from the active Communists in the FDJ and other east zone organizations. In February, 1951, large numbers of Soviet T-34 tanks and artillery were shipped into east Germany.

On October 6, 1952, a large celebration in east Berlin marked the third anniversary of the founding of the east German Communist regime. The Soviets announced that 2612 former Nazis were granted amnesties or reduction of sentences. The objective, obviously, was to enlarge the reserve of men with military experience for use in the east German army. The ceremonies in Berlin were characterized by a visit from Soviet President Nikolai Shvernik, who reviewed units of the east German *Bereitschaften*.

WESTERN GERMANY

Communism was strong in Weimar, Germany because it appeared to a large segment of the working class as a genuine and independent socialist movement. Communism has been weak in the western zones of Germany and in the Federal Republic because it has become increasingly evident that it is a puppet in the hands of a foreign power. Actually, of course, German Communists have always been subservient to Moscow, but this was only clearly perceived by German labor after 1945. Since that time German Communism has received the same fear and hatred as Soviet Communism. If, other than the Communists themselves, there are in Germany some who favor cooperation with the Soviets and their German henchmen in the eastern zone, they do so not out of sympathy for German Communism, but because they want to play off the East against the West, or because they are under an illusion that in a combination of western Germany and the Soviet zone they, the west German industrial leaders or militarists, rather than the Soviet rulers, would come out on top. But the number of such persons has remained relatively small.

German experience with Soviet Communism since 1945 holds it to be responsible for the division of the German nation and for conditions in eastern Germany. Therefore the German Communist party has fared poorly in the elections in western Germany and in the Federal Republic. In the *Land* (state) of North Rhine-Westphalia, which includes the Ruhr, a traditional Communist stronghold in the days of the Weimar Republic, Communist strength declined from 13.7% in 1946 to 7.6% in the 1945 federal elections, to 5% in the 1952 *Land* elections. In the 1949 *Bundestag*, only 15 Communists were elected out of a total parliament of 402 seats, and these were only elected by virtue of the proportional representation electoral system. Since that time the Communist party has been torn by internal schisms, resulting in the expulsion of several parliamentarians from their seats. Communist influence also declined steadily in works councils and in trade unions. By the end of 1952, it appeared that the small Communist faction of western Germany was so isolated and depleted in strength as to be useful only as the vanguard of violence and subversion. In a speech before the Central Committee of the SED in east Berlin (December 5, 1952), Franz Dahlem, member of the Communist Politburo, said that the Communists of free Germany must turn to revolutionary rather than parliamentary methods to overthrow the Adenauer Government. He said that the Government of the Federal Republic "can be overthrown only by a revolutionary struggle by the masses." Dahlem called for mass actions and the use of the general strike, citing Stalin's October statement that peace could not be assured until "imperialism" had been destroyed. The same day east German President Wilhelm Pieck declared: "... only the fall of the Adenauer regime would open the door to German understanding and all-German reunification." (*New York Times*, December 6, 1952).

Perhaps more dangerous than the existing Communist party in western Germany has been the increasing tendency, after the start of the war in Korea, for non-Communist Germans to be lured by neutralist and anti-rearmament dreams. Groups following this general line seem anxious to agree to unification of Germany even if it comes only under Communist aegis.

At the end November, 1952, the deluded and highly articulate advocates of peace-at-any-price formed the All-German People's Party, calling for an united Germany as a "third force" between the Soviet Empire and the western world. This new party appeared to be very weak in numbers, but, by stressing the desirability of unity at any price, it reawakened fears among many Germans that ratification of the treaty system between the Federal Republic and the Western Powers would end all hope of unification. The new party was headed by Dr. Gustave Heinemann, former Lutheran leader in the Christian

Democratic Union, and former cabinet member in the Adenauer Government; its leadership also included Helene Wessel of the Center party, and Hans Bodensteiner, another Bundestag member.

An addition to the Communists and the neutralist groups in western Germany, the continued opposition of the anti-Communist Socialist party to rearmament, and the hopes of many Socialists that German unity can be achieved on close-to-Soviet terms, constitute another factor likely to aid Soviet policy in Germany. Voting on the adherence of the Federal Republic to the defense of western Europe in November and December, 1952, saw the Socialists, Communists, and scattered neo-Nazi and neutralist members voting against the Government majority. The new Socialist leader Ollenhauer seemed to follow a line very similar to that of his predecessor Kurt Schumacher against Adenauer, with emphasis on German nationalism, and a loosening of ties with the United States and the North Atlantic Treaty Organization.

The end of 1952 saw a west German Communist concentration of effort in the industrial heartland of the Ruhr. Repeated acts of sabotage by Soviet agents and native Communists, taken in conjunction with the proximity of the Iron Curtain (only 100 miles to the east), pointed up the threat which was posed by the relatively small number of Communists in western Germany. An estimated 350 Communist agents trickled into western Germany every day during the last months of 1952 to find their way into the vital Ruhr area as propagandists, spies, saboteurs, and instructors. Many of these agents posed as news correspondents, or simply as refugees. Most of them somehow seemed to turn up in the Essen and Dortmund areas, often bringing with them caches of firearms. In 1952 British authorities intercepted an entire truckload of small arms near Kassel.

The shortage of miners in the 143-odd mines of the Ruhr made easier the Communist program of infiltration. One out of each eleven west German miners in the Ruhr area came from eastern Germany. While some of these were *bona fide* refugees, many others were *bona fide* Soviet agents. Additionally, a rather impressive number of Communists in key union and municipal jobs remained from 1945 and 1946 when they were appointed to their jobs by British authorities who then were looking only for anti-Nazis.

In the summer of 1952, I. I. Ilyechev, Soviet Ambassador to East Germany, told Communist leaders that the Cominform had allotted a large sum of money for infiltration of the west German DGB (German Federation of Labor). Shortly thereafter, western intelligence experts found considerable evidence of west German Communists being sent to eastern German schools for training in strike tactics, espionage, and sabotage.

The Soviet penetration of Ruhr unions was made easier by the susceptibility of German Socialist workers to Marxist appeals. By the end of 1952 an estimated 20% of Ruhr shop stewards were Communists who exercised an influence out of proportion to their numbers. The average German worker was little concerned about the party affiliations of a shop steward who championed his economic interest. Furthermore, Socialist opposition to rearmament abetted Communist strike agitation in the Ruhr defense plants.

Communist influence and control among "peace" and neutralist groups in the Ruhr was a matter of increasing concern not only to NATO officials, but to the Federal Republic as well. Bonn Interior Minister Robert Lehr listed 200 Communist front groups in western Germany, most of them in the Ruhr. Communist strength seemed concentrated in Dusseldorf, as well as Essen and Dortmund; it was also apparent in Bremen and Hamburg.

Soviet policy has not been at all niggardly in expending considerable sums of money on "peace" and neutralist feeling in west Germany —money handled deftly and effectively by Frau Grete Thiele of the Bonn Bundestag. The May, 1952 Essen "peace" riots cost the Communists $750,000 to organize. Some of this money was gathered by the cooperation of certain west German businessmen subject to fear of Soviet power and neutralist emotions. Through illegal channels these persons sent iron, steel and machinery to eastern Germany in return for cheaply produced east German consumer goods which were sold in west Germany at a rather sizeable dollar profit. (See Claus Gaedemann, "The Communist Plot to Wreck the Ruhr", *New Leader,* Dec. 29, 1952)

Austria

As was the case in Germany, the Potsdam Agreement provided for a Soviet zone of occupation. This zone of occupation has provided the Soviet Union with an economic and perhaps a military stranglehold on the Austrian Republic, despite domination by the anti-Communist People's Party and Socialist Party. The Communists of Austria polled but five percent of the votes in the 1945 elections. As in Germany the Austrian Communists are regarded as an arm of the Soviet Government. Far better than the French and the Italians, do the German-speaking people recognize the true nature of Communism. The Austrians have seen free people in Vienna kidnapped right under the noses of American and British military forces by Soviet authorities. They have seen

the barbarous might of Soviet power at first hand, and they have shown
how they feel about it in free elections in the two-thirds of Austria
that is free.

Austrian Chancellor Leopold Figl has repeatedly stated that the
U.S.S.R. could prove the sincerity of its concern for a German and
European peace settlement by concluding the long-delayed Austrian
peace treaty. Instead, the Soviet Government had, by mid-1952, frustrated 260 meetings of the representatives of the United States, Britain,
France and Russia by refusing to agree to the many concessions offered
by the Western Powers. The explanation of the tenacity of Russia's
delaying tactics lies partly in her desire to remain in military control
of north-eastern Austria, with troops also stationed in the connecting
countries of Czechoslovakia, Hungary, and Rumania, as well as her
desire to exploit the Austrian economy and prevent the development
of a truly free and independent Austria. Prominent among the reasons
why Austria remains under occupation has been the existence of the
USIA, the Russian initials for "Administration of Soviet Property in
Austria." USIA has proved to be an inexhaustible gold mine to the
Soviet Union, while being for the Austrians a cancer destroying the
economic life of the country, a conspiratorial state within a state—a
means of bribery, sabotage, and terror.

USIA was described by an Austrian observer as "one of the bridal
gifts so rashly bestowed on the glamour-shrouded Soviet Union during
the Potsdam honeymoon." (G.E.R. Gedye, "Why Moscow Sabotages
an Austrian Treaty", New Leader, May 19, 1952). Nobody seems to
have realized the extent to which the loosely-worded Potsdam Declaration was to be distorted by an unscrupulous beneficiary. The Western
Powers failed to stipulate precisely what was to be the administration
and final disposal of genuinely German property in Austria. The result
was that any property on which the Nazis ever laid hands was classified
by the Russians as "German" property. The Western Powers protest,
but do no more.

The Russians seized practically all the rich oilfields of Austria, regardless of their former ownership. Russian abuse of her economic
acquisitions for political purposes has continued since 1945. Not only
does USIA control the rich Zisterdorf oil fields, but it controls heavy
and light industry, metallurgical industries, coal-mining, food-produc-
ing and chemical industries, agriculture, forests, and so forth. In 1950,
USIA pulled off the notorious "scrap deal": USIA agents, with the
help of the Soviet Army, secured vast quantities of war scrap in Vienna
and eastern Austria. Operating through Austrians, the Russians sold
200,000 tons of plundered scrap to Czechoslovakia's war industry

alone. Switzerland took 85,000 tons, paying the Soviets with American cars, chocolate, cigarettes, and other goods. The latter the Soviets then proceeded to sell in USIA stores in Vienna and in the black market at enormous profits.

The Russians began to exploit the oilfields almost immediately after the Occupation began. What was not used by the Soviet Army or sent to Russia was sold to the Austrians, who had to borrow from the United States to get back what was their oil in the first place. Each time the Western Powers propose a new treaty arrangement to the Soviet Union, they have to chalk off an ever growing amount of loss—needlessly incurred at Potsdam.

Although the Austrian Communists are few in number, they have the advantage of a nearby Soviet zone of occupation, and a nearby Soviet Army. Austria's strategic location puts Soviet military forces in a position where they could outflank the American forces in Bavaria, and menace both Italy and Yugoslavia. Soviet policy seems to be in no hurry to abandon the numerous advantages gained by the Potsdam Agreement and the occupation.

Austrian Communists encourage neutralism, anti-western feeling, and constantly seek allies among their Marxist brethren in the Austrian Socialist party. One of these is Karl Waldbrunner, an extremist Socialist, who worked in Russia as an engineer before and during World War II. He became Austrian Ambassador to the Soviet Union in 1945. He has never criticized Soviet policies, and indeed, frequently praised Communist policies. The Communists had little success in trying to form a popular front in the 1949 elections, but were planning more extensive efforts for subsequent elections. They have sought to take advantage of frequent quarrels between the two governing parties—the People's Party and the Socialists. Although both parties have been strongly anti-Communist, their somewhat unnatural alliance, together with the appearance of an ultra-conservative political party in 1949, have resulted in increased political opportunities for the Communists to exploit.

Vienna has been the scene of several Soviet "peace" meetings since 1945, which Austrian Communist leader Ernst Fischer has sought to turn to the advantage of the Soviet cause. Totally disarmed, Austria's capital has been since the end of World War II surrounded by Russian forces five times the strength of the total western forces throughout the country. Every fourth month the Russians take over control of the capital, and do with it what they wish. In December, 1952, a "Peace Congress" was convened in Vienna under the protection of Soviet bayonets. Present were Frederic Joliot-Curie of France, Ilya Ehrenburg of Russia, Pierre Cot of France, and Ivor Montagu of Great Britain, among many others—Communists, fellow travelers, and pacifists who wished peace-at-any price. One of the sponsors of the Congress, Alexei Cepicka of Czechoslovakia, declared: "The peace movement has nothing in common with the ordinary connotations of peace. It would be fatal to confuse the activities of the Peace Partisans with those of sects which refuse to take up arms. Every tendency toward pacifism only aids the enemy. We don't conceal the fact that we are turning out arms—arms of the highest quality. The same is true of the Soviet Union and other countries in our peace camp." (Quoted by G. E. R. Gedye, "Peace Congress in Vienna", *New Leader*, December 15, 1952).

14

Communism in Italy

The Italian Communist party, after 1945, became the largest Communist party in Europe numerically. Up to 1947 it held key positions in several ministries and furnished Italy with important and influential public officials both inside and outside the country. Until 1951 Communist mayors ruled Turin, Genoa, Venice, Bologna, and Florence. The Communists controlled the Italian General Confederation of Labor; they reached millions of Italians through their active and widely-read press.

From the very first, Italian Communists have been servile to Moscow. On January 21, 1921, a minority of the Italian Socialist party decided to split off and form the Communist party. Other Socialists had previously broken away to form the Fascist party, among them Benito Mussolini. The Italian Socialists had been very sympathetic to the Russian Bolsheviks, and had, indeed, joined the Third International in 1919. However, when the Comintern sent an order to the 1921 Socialist Congress, only 57,000 out of 169,000 Socialists present voted to secede from the party and form the Communist party. The message to the Congress from Zinoviev, Lenin, Bela Kun, and Bukharin bluntly announced: ". . . before knowing what will be the majority opinion at your congress [we declare that] those who refuse to accept the separation from the reformists violate an essential order of the Communist International, and, by that alone, place themselves outside it." (Quoted by Aldo Garosci in *Communism in Western Europe*, jointly authored with Mario Einaudi and Jean-Marie Domenach, Cornell University Press, 1951, p. 159). In short, the Italian Communist party was formed under the orders of the Communist International operating as the agency of the Russian Bolshevik party and the Soviet Government.

In March, 1922, the Communists opposed joint action with the democratic parties against Fascism: "Another hypothesis is that the government will invite the proletariat to participate in an armed struggle against the assault of the right. This invitation can only be a trap. . . . In consequence, no 'loyalty' should be proclaimed or practiced in respect to such a government." (*Ibid.*, p. 161). The Communists showed their contempt for democratic government when their organ *Ordine Nuovo* (August 11, 1922) told the Fascist leader Giunta: "We have the honor to inform you that we think even less than you do of parliamentary rights and duties. In seeing them torn to bits we have even more to gain than you."

By 1926 the Fascists had consolidated control of Italian Government, and the Communists, together with other non-Fascists, were relieved of their parliamentary seats. In the fall of that year the Communist leaders Gramsci, Terracini, Roveda, and Scoccimarro were arrested and subsequently sentenced to jail terms averaging twenty-three years. However it was not until July, 1935, when the Dimitrov report to the Comintern decreed the new united front anti-Fascist line, that the Italian and other continental Communists sought common action with other groups against Fascism. This action came to an end with the Hitler-Stalin pact, but was resumed in June, 1941, when Germany turned on its Russian partner.

During the Fascist period in Italy, the Italian Communists built up an underground organization which functioned partly in France. With the advent of the Hitler-Stalin pact, many Communist leaders went to Moscow, to return in the fall of 1941 to begin establishing propaganda groups in Milan and Turin. By April, 1943, important steps had been taken to re-establish Communist cadres in Italy. The party leadership was molded in the underground and in prison. With the exception of Palmiro Togliatti, Luigi Longo, and Mario Montagnana, the bulk of the Communist leaders spent long years in jail, during which time they developed hardened cadres and attracted many who came to seek ever more extreme solutions to their predicament.

Toward the end of 1942 and in the spring of 1943, the returning Communist factions led strikes in Turin and Milan. This, together with the exodus from jail of many Communists after the Badoglio coup d'etat of July 25th, led to increasing Communist control among the workers. Entire Fascist unions were taken over intact by Communists, and most notably by Giovanni Roveda, the Communist union boss. The bureaucratic structure erected by Fascist corporatism was practically taken over lock, stock, and barrel by the Communist party.

When Togliatti returned from Russia in April, 1944, he brought with him instructions from Moscow that the Italian Communists were to collaborate with the Christian Democrats, Socialists, the Action party and other groups comprising the Committee of National Liberation. But the Communists were never able to realize their goal of taking over the Committee and transforming it into a ready-made Communist regime, as they had done in eastern Europe. Although they took part in the governments from April, 1944 to May, 1947, they were never able to obtain the cabinet posts with decisive power over the state apparatus. This was partly due to the vitality of the non-Communists, and also to the fact that the Allied Control Commission for Italy was an effective tripartite group, with the American and British representatives able to thwart Communist designs. Togliatti did for a time gain control of the Ministry of Justice, but the Communists never entered the ministries of Foreign Affairs, Interior, and Defense.

The failure to gain control of Italian Government is attributable to many factors. The formation of the Marxist People's Democratic Front in 1948, in which the Communists persuaded most Socialists to join them in a supreme effort against De Gasperi, only solidified the anti-Communist factions behind De Gasperi, and forced the Church to take its most explicit stand on the Communist issue, a stand which caused many Italians to think twice before voting Communist. The Communist-led violence throughout Italy in July, 1948, came as a shock to many persons, who for the first time realized that the Communists were willing to resort to violence should they fail in their legal efforts to gain power. The discovery of large arms caches in northern Italy, and apparent collusion with Tito stiffened anti-Communist feeling in Italy. Then too, the foreign policy attitudes of the Communists hurt their cause considerably. First and foremost, Togliatti's ties with Moscow made his party appear less Italian than the others. Until the summer of 1948 Cominform policy dictated that Istria and Trieste should go to Tito. Therefore the Italian Communists were put in the awkward position of having to support Yugoslavia on an issue in which most Italians felt strongly in favor of a return of Italian rule to the area. Here was a clear cut case of the Communists taking dictation from abroad contrary to Italian national policy which they claimed to defend. This issue and others indicated to most Italians that the Communists were nothing but instruments of Soviet interests. Another factor was the Communist campaign against the Marshall Plan. This campaign found little support in a country so much in need of aid.

The organization of the Italian Communist party is a typical Communist organization. Moscow determined during the years of World War II that the post-war leader was to be Palmiro Togliatti, alias Ercoli, alias Mario Correnti. When he returned from Moscow in 1944 he abruptly changed the party line, which at that time opposed collaboration with King Victor Emmanuel, as well as cooperation with the Committee of National Liberation. Togliatti assumed the key position of secretary-general of the party. An early associate of Gramsci's, Togliatti became a member of the Executive Committee of the Third International in 1934, retaining the position until 1943, when this organization changed its outward appearance. Togliatti had gained the trust of the Moscow leadership during the Spanish civil war, when the International put him at the "disposal" of the Spanish Communists and the "Loyalist" regime. With the help of Luigi Longo, Togliatti helped the Spanish Communists capture the Popular Front, which very nearly won permanent control of Spain.

After Togliatti, in the Italian Communist leadership, come Pietro Secchia and Luigi Longo. Considered shorter-tempered than Togliatti, they have long records as able organizers. Longo was a leader of the Communist-controlled International Brigades in Spain, where he developed considerable military acumen. In addition to these, the party directorate, as constituted in 1948, included Giorgio Amendola, Girolamo Li Causi, Celeste Negarville, Teresa Noce, Agostino Novella, Giancarlo Pajetta, Giuseppe Rossi, Giovanni Roveda, Mauro Scoccimarro, Emilio Sereni, and Velio Spano. By 1951 Rossi had been dropped, and the following were added: Arturo Colombi, Giuseppe di Vittorio, Edoardo d'Onofrio, Ruggero Grieco, Umberto Terracini, and Rita Montagnana. The majority of these leaders, including Togliatti, Secchia, and Longo are of Piedmontese origin. Only a minority are of working class origin; most of them come from the elements of the population closer to the *petit bourgeoisie*. In addition to their positions on the party directorate, di Vittorio heads the General Confederation of Italian Labor, and d'Onofrio heads the men's federation of the party. Terracini represents what some observers consider to be a possible "Titoist" element in the party.

Although the majority of the leadership stems back to the early days of Italian Communism, its following is largely of post-World War II vintage. At Florence, on October 3, 1944, Togliatti made it clear that Moscow wished a large mass party appealing to all Italians, rather than a small nucleus of professional revolutionaries. Later he said: "A party that is truly a people's party is present wherever the people meet and are active, in the factories, the fields, the offices, the ships, the unions, the cooperatives. But the people are first of all at home where the women are, and the women are the ones who set the tone of family life. As long as we do not succeed in establishing ourselves in the homes, in the markets, wherever the life of most of the people goes on in its elementary forms, we shall not be able to say we have succeeded in establishing a people's party." (Quoted by Garosci, p. 199). Particular success was achieved among the youth, and to a lesser degree, among the women.

The Italian Communists claimed 1,700,000 dues paying members in 1945, and 2,580,000 in April, 1951. The homogeneity and zeal of this large number, however, cannot be compared to the small nucleus of dedicated Communists which numbered but 50,000 in 1921.

Many are Communists only in name; many simply vote Communist as a protest against an ill, real or imagined. Other factors are involved in the size of the party, nevertheless. On August 31, 1947, the party secretariat announced: "To spur the membership campaign, the party has decided to reduce the price of the 1947 card. For all who join the party after September 1, the price will be reduced to ten lire." This sum represented half the price of a newspaper. The proceeds from this sale of party cards, together with the income from party newspapers, books, and magazine subscriptions, represents most of the financial strength obtained from inside Italy. Party members come largely from northern Italy and Rome, with gains made in southern Italy only since the end of 1947, and these almost entirely from the poorest peasants, called the *braccianti.*

The size of the Italian Communist party is also attributable to the fact that in 1946 the official party daily *Unita* played down the atheistic aspect of Communism, and implied that Catholics could join the party without hurt to their religion. In 1948 Luigi Longo made it clear, however, that the party could no longer tolerate religious-minded members. At about the same time the Church took a firm stand on the irreconcileability between Catholicism and Communism. Still another factor in the size of the party is the fact that since April 15, 1949, the Communist Youth Federation was revived in an effect to challenge the strong Catholic youth groups throughout the country.

Top party workers, editors of *Il Unita,* and the union bosses, are paid salaries by the party; many of these do, nevertheless, draw some income from other sources. The party leadership has established an elaborate system of "education" within the party—more properly labelled propaganda. Beginning with the lowly Communist cell, elementary propaganda courses are designed to instill in every member a rudimentary knowledge of Marxism as interpreted by Stalin, as well as the current party "line." Each month information is sent down to cell leaders telling them the things to be stressed during the following month. In this way the overall party's propaganda is synchronized. Correspondence courses also characterize party "education" on the basic level. Beyond the cell are section schools, and then federation schools, the latter two types with special instructors. On the national level there exist several party schools in which the higher party members receive detailed and important information. These national party schools were established in Bologna, Milan, and Rome, with courses of from three to six months duration. Rome is the scene also of a school for women, and the seminar for advanced studies.

The party machinery is a large-scale operation which tends towards a bureaucracy. A personal record must be kept of each member, down to the cell level. These records are detailed, and are kept up-to-date. Aldo Garosci has said that "the Communist party has a more complex and up-to-date personnel file system than an army." (*Ibid.*, p. 205).

The party press is extensive and powerful. The official party organ *Unita,* published in Rome, has regional editions in Milan, Turin, and Genoa, with an estimated circulation of 500,000 copies— the only self-supporting newspaper among all the political parties. Communist-controlled papers include *Milano-Sera, Progresso* (Bologna), *Corriere* (Florence), and *Paese* and *Paese-Sera* of Rome. Communist weeklies include *Vie Nuove, Calendario del popolo,* and the youth magazine *Gioventu nuova.* The party also publishes a theoretical monthly called *Rinascita,* edited by secretary-general Togliatti. Then there exist the Communist publishing houses which turn out a flood of books and pamphlets: *Centro Diffusione Stampa, Rinascita, Milano-Sera,* and the *Edizioni Sociali.*

Most sinister of all the party organizations are the para-military groups. These organizations showed considerable strength in 1948, and their only match was the highly-trained police of the Minister of Interior and units of the Italian Army. Large arms caches have been found, consisting of weapons and ammunition seized by Communist underground members during World War II, some material from Tito's Yugoslavia received prior to 1948, and some Russian armaments. Information on these para-military organizations is scarce, but the fanaticism and efficiency of its officers is beyond question. There was serious concern during 1948 lest the Communists would resort to arms after failing at the ballot box. From all appearances, the unofficial leader of the Communist armed units has been the militant Luigi Longo, whose experiences in Spain were extensive.

Italian Communists control many organizations not officially in the party. Most important of these is the Italian General Confederation of Labor. Founded in 1944, the Confederation originally included Christian Democrats and independent Socialists. However, the supremacy of the Communists was quite complete; their union organizer di Vittorio ran the union pretty much as he saw fit. A former colleague of Longo's with the Spanish Communists, di Vittorio completely overshadowed his Socialist and Christian Democratic associates. By 1948 it became apparent to the non-Communists that the Confederation was being used by the Communist party for the goal of a Communist Italy.

Accordingly the Christian Democrats and the independent Socialists left the union to form their own independent federations.

Other national mass organizations controlled by the Communists include the National League of Cooperatives (headed by the Communist deputy Giulio Cerreti), the National Association of Italian Partisans, and such "front" organizations as the Partisans of Peace, the Labor Front, the Land Constituent Assembly, the Cultural Alliance, and the League of Democratic Communes.

Communist strength in Italy has been greatly enhanced by virtue of the fact that most Italian Socialists have sold out to their Marxist brethren. Their behavior was quite similar to those of east-European Socialists and unlike that of most German Socialists and many French Socialists. The national elections of 1946 saw the Socialists still an independent party, which polled 21% of the popular vote as compared to 19% for the Communists. Since that Italian Socialism has almost completely been reduced to an appendage of the Communist party.

The Italian Socialists had, from the very start, been quite sympathetic to the Bolshevik revolution, and had even joined the Third International in 1919. Large numbers of Socialists swung over to the Communists, although by 1946 there were still more Socialist voters than Communist voters. The story of the capitulation of Italian Socialism to Soviet Communism properly begins in 1942, when its leadership consisted of Pietro Nenni and Giuseppe Saragat. Working through Nenni, the Communists gradually tied the Socialists to themselves, by infiltration of their own personnel, through formal pacts calling for joint action and joint party orders, and through the very dynamics of a disciplined, militant party operating against a loosely organized, wavering, and fragmentized opposition. Nenni approved the drift to Communism, whereas Saragat favored an autonomous Socialist grouping. The 1946 Socialist Congress in Florence voted as follows on relations with the Communists: 338,000 voted for alliance with Communism; 300,000 voted for autonomous status; 83,000 voted for an independent, anti-Communist position. Nenni was retained as party leader, with the independent Socialist Ivan Matteo Lombardo as the number two man. The show of Socialist strength in the 1946 elections resulted in redoubled Communist efforts to capture the entire Socialist apparatus. These efforts proved successful. Togliatti declared, on November 1, 1946, that a joint struggle for power by the Communists and Socialists was forthcoming.

Faced with the choice of capitulation to the Communists or anti-Communism, most Socialists followed the Marxist inclination. Municipal elections in November reflected the new Communist strength and

Socialist weakness. Early in 1947 Saragat decided upon an independent course, and formed the Italian Socialist Worker's party. Pietro Nenni took the bulk of the Socialists with him into the arms of the Communists.

In the 1948 elections, the Nenni Socialists accepted a joint electoral list with the Communists in the so-called Popular Front. This joint list worked to the advantage of the Communists who, through their greater control of the use of the preferential votes, saw to it that the Socialist members of parliament would be fewer than the Communists, and that those few would be orthodox.

Italian Socialism has thus become an auxiliary of Soviet policy in Italy. The party became, after 1946, a base of recruitment and development for the Communist party; more important, it enabled many Socialists to preserve a fiction of autonomy, while simultaneously enhancing the strength, extent, and flexibility of Soviet power in Italy. Many Italians were permitted to serve the Communists without actually becoming party members.

In the 1946 elections, the Communists, running on their own separate lists, received 4,358,000 votes (19%). Two years later the combined Communist-Nenni Socialist vote, as found in the Popular Front, was 8,137,000 (31%). In the municipal elections of May and June 1951, the combined percentage rose to almost 37%.

The strength of the Communist party is primarily in central Italy, secondarily in northern Italy, and weakest in southern areas. The central part of Italy comprises fairly prosperous to weak agriculture, flourishing handicrafts and a not highly developed industry. The 1948 elections reflected losses in the industrial north, and gains in the agrarian south. With the Communist absorption of the Socialists, Communism became the only practical alternative to Christian Democracy for Italian voters. There being no practical democratic alternative to the Christian Democrats, Italy seemed destined to be split into two totally irreconcilable camps.

The Communists appealed to anti-religious groups, neutralist groups, and the always fruitful intellectuals. Soviet policy sought to extend the Communist-controlled base either in the hopes of ultimately receiving the votes of a majority of Italians, or with a view to successfully manipulating the para-military forces in conjunction with a military effort through Austria or Yugoslavia.

Among the many Soviet sympathizers in the Italian academic world are found such persons as Marchesi, Cantimori, de Martino, Luporini, Banfi, and della Volpe. Anti-American and neutralist groups found their champion in the person of the redoubtable Nenni. As deputy-chairman of the "World Peace Council", Nenni paid a visit to Stalin in July, 1952, to receive a Stalin Peace Prize. After a one month visit, Nenni returned to Italy to sound the tocsin of neutrality; "An Italy that found in neutrality the conscience of her internal unity and her international interests would meet most open and cordial sympathy in the Soviet Union." (*Avanti*, August 3, 1952).

15

Communism in France

Soviet policy for France is carried out by a militant, well-organized French Communist party. Its history begins in 1921, but the tradition it has utilized is much older. In France, Leninism was built upon a movement which was undoubtedly the most class-conscious and tumultuous of all Europe.

The insurrection of 1848 and the 1871 Commune were the most notable stages of a bitter and bloody struggle which aided Karl Marx in the development of his doctrine. The first and second Internationals, as predecessors to the Comintern (Third International) and the Cominform, had their roots in French revolutionary history. The United Socialist party (S.F.I.O., or French Section of the Worker's International) was a combination of Marxian Socialists and home-grown French Socialism. The victory of the Bolshevik revolution, however, forced the inevitable showdown between the two factions of the party. After World War I the European Socialists were confused and divided. Their pacifist and opportunistic policies had largely failed, and many of their followers and some leaders were becoming "bourgeois". Therefore the Bolshevik revolution with its attendant success, led many Socialists to conclude that the only clear and sure path for them to follow was the path blazed by Moscow. The French Socialist Congress of December 29, 1920, voted 3208-1033 to join Lenin's new Communist International. The defeated minority remained as the French Socialist party (S.F.I.O.), retaining to this date the label "section of the worker's international."

The new French section of the Communist International wasted no time in achieving prominence. In the early 'twenties it campaigned in the name of anti-colonialism for the Moroccans rebelling against the French. Presiding over the Communist Committee of Action for the Moroccan wars was Maurice Thorez, who was swiftly promoted by the Soviets to the French Central Committee in 1924, and to the French party politburo a year later. In 1923 the party had its first big clash with the French government by opposing French occupation of the Ruhr. Premier Poincaré raided the offices of the Communist organ L'Humanite, as well as Communist union headquarters, and arrested a number of Communist leaders including Marcel Cachin.

During the 'twenties, the Communist party followed a rigid, orthodox policy of non-cooperation with other parties, harsh discipline, and the creation of a new union, the Communist General Confederation of United Labor (CGTU), apart from the Socialist-dominated General Confederation of Labor (CGT). As a result of this policy there developed vicious internal struggles for party leadership between three groups: the rigid Marxian theorists who talked way above the masses, recently converted Socialists still thinking confused home-spun humanitarian thoughts, and practical opportunistic Leninists, led by Thorez. When Moscow gave Thorez the leadership in 1930, he denounced his predecessors as men who "completely disdained the daily realities, forgetting that politics is the art of the possible." (Quoted by Andre Laguerre, "French Communism," *Life*, January 29, 1951, p. 101).

In 1928 the French Communist party received over one million votes and won thirteen seats in the Chamber of Deputies; in 1932 it had declined to 800,000 votes and ten seats. But during this period the party overcame its internal divisions and became a strong organization whose trained militants cast fear into the hearts of French governmental leaders. At the end of 1932 the party comprised only 25,000 members; by the end of 1936 party membership had risen to 390,000. The huge increase was due to the policy of the united front, as laid down by Dimitrov in 1935, although actually begun in France in 1934. Thorez sought "anti-fascist" alliances with the Socialists, "progressive" Christians, and France's traditionally anti-clerical farm vote. The election of 1936 was a victory for the Communist party, which won 1,488,000 votes and 72 seats in the Chamber of Deputies. As a member of the Popular Front together with Socialists and Radical Socialists, Thorez made his famous wheedling overtune: "Catholic, worker, employe, artisan, peasant, we hold out the hand to you . . ." (*loc. cit.*). The French Communists appeared for the first time not as a party of foreign agitators under Moscow direction, but as a French party, participating in the anti-Fascist struggle, sharing in French patriotism against Germany as partner in a coalition including two parties which claimed to be the only true inheritors of the French revolution.

Communist distrust of the Socialists was too great to allow participation in a government where it would not have the majority. The Communists, therefore, remained outside the cabinet and led the workers into an ever greater hostility to the government. In line with Moscow directives, the Communist leadership was driven into a nearly isolated position, while striving desperately to retain anti-fascist alliances. The Nazi-Soviet pact caught Thorez and his colleagues out on the end of the anti-fascist limb, and the entry of Soviet troops into Poland as allies of Hitler proved to be too sudden a reversal of policy. The war that had been described by Thorez originally as a just defense against fascist aggression, suddenly became a war thrust upon the people of Germany and Russia by the French and British imperialists. The party lost many adherents, and Premier Daladier dissolved it in September, 1939, and arrested many of its leaders. Thorez escaped, by deserting his army unit and flying to Moscow; his assistant Jacques Duclos disappeared into the underground, to work for a time against his own country as part of the Hitler-Stalin pact strategy. When German troops entered Paris in May, 1940, Stalin sent a telegram congratulating Hitler on his military success. This came as a further blow to Communist strength in France.

The policy of the Communists until June 1941 was one of lying low, and using the Soviet-German friendship to help create a "worker's and peasant's government" to conclude a satisfactory arrangement with the German occupation. (See A. Rossi, *Physiologie du parti communiste francais*, Paris, 1949). It was not until June 22, 1941, when Hitler's troops attacked Russia, that the Communists completely and unequivocally entered the resistance, to launch a new era in which the party, because of the new "patriotic" line, was again able to rally to its banners large masses of followers.

The resistance era marked the rebirth of the party. With the defense of the Soviet Fatherland against Nazism as their supreme goal, Communists throughout Europe arose to a man and fought in the resistance without stint. From its underground and resistance cadres, together with the prestige gained from its performance, the post World War II French Communist party emerged as a mass party, whose position was even further enhanced by the post-war status of the Soviet Union. Communists dominated many of the resistance groups, which they transformed into quasi-political groups; Communists were represented on all the committees of liberation. The party seized a daily newspaper in each department of France, and party membership soared to over 500,000 by March, 1945. With the Communist International ostensibly dissolved, the French Communists could plausibly pose as an authentic French political grouping, with nothing but the nation's interests at heart. It was obvious that in 1945 five million men and women who voted Communist included a majority who felt that the post-war party was something new and different from the pre-war model.

The Communists dominated the drafting of the first post-war constitution, with the acquiescence of the Socialists. This draft constitution was rejected by the French people, however, who followed the advice of De Gaulle and the largely Catholic *Mouvement Republicain Populaire* (MRP) instead. However the second attempt at a constitution saw MRP compromise with the Communists, with the result that it was approved by a slim majority of combined Communists, Socialists, and some followers of the MRP. At the general elections for the first National Assembly under the newly approved constitution, the Communists polled 5,489,000 votes (28.4%) to win the largest single bloc of seats in the Assembly, closely followed by the MRP (26%). Until May of 1947 the Communists were represented in French governments together with the MRP and the Socialists. During the period 1945-1947, the party "followed a tactic, both subtle and dangerous, which consisted in masquerading as a government party while retaining a monopoly of revolutionary hope and action." (Raymond Aron, *Le Grand Schisme*, Paris, 1948, p. 190). The Communists played a double game of working for their own interests and those of the Soviet Union, while remaining simultaneously in the government. This game came to a climax when the Communists voted against military aid to anti-Communist forces in Indo-China, and then tried to remain in a government whose budget its deputies voted against. This violation of the constitution resulted in President Auriol terminating the functions of the Communist cabinet ministers.

In September, 1947, a conference of nine European Communist parties convened in Warsaw. The Soviet chairman Zhdanov, also a leading member of the Soviet politburo until his later death, announced the founding of the Cominform—successor to the Comintern—to guide the various Communist parties in the increasingly hot "cold war." Thorez and Togliatti represented France and Italy, respectively, and brought back with them the new "hard" line. Thorez referred to the Marshall Plan as "an attempt by warmongering American capitalists to enslave Europe." (*L'Humanite*, October 31, 1947). In November a central strike committee, dominated by the Communists, inaugurated a series of violent and bloody strikes throughout France, in what appeared to be an experiment to see how near to overthrowing the Republic the new Communist policy could come. These strikes awakened some Frenchmen to the true nature of the Communist party in France. Catholic and Socialist factions within the Communist-dominated General Confederation of Labor broke away to form their own unions.

The anti-government policy, adopted since 1947, included opposition to the Marshall Plan and Atlantic Pact, opposition to the war in Indo-China, opposition to the UN effort in Korea, and support of the Soviet "peace" program. In the 1951 national elections the Communists lost 450,000 voters, and declined percentage-wise from 28.6% to 26.5%. Nevertheless they polled 900,000 more votes than their nearest rival, the Gaullist Rally of the French People (RPF), and placed the second largest bloc of deputies (103) in the new National Assembly. Communism was still a major force in France which Soviet policy could continue to use as a major weapon in its arsenal for world revolution.

By 1952 the prime objective of the Communists was to prevent France from becoming an effective partner in the North Atlantic Treaty Organization, and prevent German rearmament by playing upon traditional nationalistic anti-German French sentiment. Whatever success this policy has had is attributable to the Big Five of the French Communist party. These include Maurice Thorez, Jacques Duclos, Auguste Lecoeur, Etienne Fajon, and Benoit Frachon. Thorez, the long-time leader, left France for Moscow in 1950 for medical treatment, and had not returned by the end of 1952, even though the newspaper *Ce Soir* ecstatically announced on September 3, 1952: "After having recovered his health and strength in the great country of socialism, in the country of Stalin whom we assure of our infinite gratitude, Maurice Thorez is preparing his return to France to resume his place as our head in the great fight for bread, liberty, national independence, and peace." At the same time Duclos announced his appeal for a new "united front" against the Schuman Plan, NATO, and German rearmament. This appeared to indicate a change away from the isolated position in which the party found itself after 1947.

During Thorez' absence, the party was efficiently ruled by Duclos. Born in 1896, he is considered the party's master tactician. A good debater, Duclos combines "insolent aplomb and genial cynicism with a talent for irony and invective." (Laguerre, *op. cit.*, p. 102). Leader of the parliamentary Communist bloc, Duclos maintains an absolute discipline over his cohorts. His deputies, like all paid Communist of-ficeholders, retain but little more than $1,000 of their annual salary. The balance, totalling more than three-quarters of a million dollars annually, is reportedly handed over to the *Banque Commerciale pour l'Europe du Nord* in Paris, which is controlled by Soviet capital. This bank handles all Communist transactions in France. Duclos also controls all mass campaigns, such as the "peace" campaign, as well as the party's vast propaganda machine.

Auguste Lecoeur was born in 1911, and was developed by Thorez to ultimately succeed to the party leadership. He is in charge of the party machine proper, from the departmental federations down to the cells which he seeks to organize in every office and plant. Etienne Fajon is five years older than Lecoeur; he heads the dreaded Ideo-logical Section and the Central Commissions of Cadres. An intractable doctrinaire, he checks up on every party activity and reports directly to Moscow through the Cominform, to which he is attached as one of the French representatives. The last of the Big Five is Benoit Frachon, who guides the party's labor operations. Born in 1895, his toughness and organizing ability were largely responsible for the Communists gaining control of the General Confederation of Labor. This provides the Cominform with what amounts to a stranglehold in most of the strategic French industries: mining, metals, railroads, gas and electricity.

Two leading French Communists, Andre Marty and Charles Tillon, lost their high standing in the party hierarchy in September, 1952, because they disagreed with the new tactic of a united front. Both were well-known for their liking of strikes, violence, and coups. Both had taken leading roles in resistance groups, and Marty had worked with other leading Communists in Spain, fighting against the Nationalist forces of General Franco. It was also a fact that neither Marty nor Tillon had ever gotten along well with Thorez, who may have ordered their purging from his Moscow vantage point.

At the end of June, 1952, the French Communists received orders to stop frightening "liberal" and bourgeois groups with violent tactics, and to form temporary alliances with neutralist and peace-at-any-price elements. That this was but a temporary tactic was shown when the fellow-traveller Pierre Cot was scolded by Auguste Lecoeur for suggesting that the "peaceful coexistence" thesis should be permanently adopted both in foreign policy and domestic matters. Lecoeur pointed out that such a move would be tantamount to renunciation of the class war doctrine. (*L'Humanité*, September 5, 1952).

One of the vehicles for the new "peace" line was a newly created organization called "Fighting Democracy." Formed on July 17, 1952, it was headed by a man thought formerly to be anti-Communist—the Socialist labor leader Leon Jouhaux. Winner of a Nobel Peace prize in 1951, Jouhaux apparently was willing to front for the men running the new group because peace meant more to him than liberty—peace a la Neville Chamberlain. A prime mover behind the front was Louis Dolivet, editor of the widely read *United Nations World* until 1951, when the United States Government refused him re-entry into the country. Born in Bessarabia in 1902, his real name was Ludovic Brecher or Iliceanu—nobody seems positive since he has used so many aliases. Other names used by him include Udeanu and D'Olivet. Expelled from Rumania as a Soviet agent, Dolivet subsequently worked in Switzerland and France for the Soviet Government. He was trained in the art of organizing front groups by the grand master of

the Trojan horse strategy, Willi Muenzenberg, and worked also for
the Swiss Communist Leon Nicole. Organizer of such fronts as the
Congress Against War, the World Committee Against War and Fascism, and the Universal Rally for Peace, Dolivet was an ideal man to
lead French dupes and "intellectuals" into Fighting Democracy. In
1934 Dolivet made a trip to Moscow, where he became friendly with
Olaf Ashberg, a Swedish banker who financed many Communist fronts
in the 1930's, and Pierre Cot, former French Air Minister and fellow
traveller. Ashberg and Cot were useful to Dolivet when, after the
fall of France, he fled to New York and helped found *Free World,* later
the *United Nations World.* Dolivet and Cot helped sponsor Henry
Wallace's trip to France after the war, a trip heavily exploited by the
Communists. In 1946 Dolivet applied for American citizenship, but
was turned down, due to his Communist affiliations.

Dolivet's assistant, Henri Laugier, took the post of secretary-general
of Fighting Democracy. Formerly Assistant Secretary General of the
United Nations, Laugier was a signer of "peace" petitions appearing
in *L'Humanité,* prominent in *Les Amis de l'U.R.S.S.,* and active in the
Stalinist-dominated France Forever group during World War II. As
a member of the Legion of Honor, professor of physiology at the Sor-
bonne, former key member of the French Foreign Office and the UN,
Laugier was an ideal choice to help lead French intellectuals into the
new front. (See Robert Pascal, "Red Agents Launch New Front,"
New Leader, September 15, 1952).

Many prominent French men and women have collaborated with
the Communists in their "peace" campaign and previous tactics. These
include the existentialists Jean Paul Sartre and Maurice Merleau-Ponty,
the physicist Frederic Joliot Curie and his wife Irene, artist Pablo
Picasso, Yves Farge, Louis Aragon, Paul Eluard, and Jean Boulier. In
addition to these rather obvious Soviet partisans, French Communism
occasionally receives a helping hand from quite respectable and influential sources in France. For example, the widely read newspaper
Le Monde published a false report on the defense of France allegedly
written by American Admiral Fechteler, which led to considerable
anti-American feeling. Edited by Hubert Beuve-Mery, *Le Monde* frequently takes on a neutralist and even anti-American tone. One of its
foreign correspondents is Robert Buillain, charged by General Wil-
loughby with supplying secret information to the Soviet spy ring of
Richard Sorge. (See Candide, "X-Rays on Le Monde," *Freeman,*
December 1, 1952).

Although Soviet policy for France seems to have temporarily
abandoned the violent and militant tactics characterizing the period

1947-1952, there is no doubt that the para-military strength of the party lies behind the scenes to be used again at the appropriate moment. Significantly, the rioting which took place at the end of May 1952 was presaged by an article appearing in *Cahiers du Communisme*, intructional organ of the party's Central Committee, and written by Francois Billoux, member of the French Communist politburo. Billoux reaffirmed the class struggle doctrine and ordered wide-spread violence against American military aid to France and the defense of Europe. On May 28th, Jacques Duclos led a massive and bloody riot in Paris protesting the arrival of General Ridgeway as new NATO Commander. Duclos was arrested when he was discovered giving orders to the rioters and hiding loaded pistols and a blackjack in his car. Charged with an attempt against the state's internal security and with leading a forbidden demonstration, Duclos was released from jail several weeks later by the French Appeals Tribunal, headed by a notorious fellow traveler.

Raids by the police uncovered arms caches in many places and hundreds were arrested. However, Communist headquarters in Paris were forewarned of possible investigation; when the police arrived, they discovered newly burned party documents. Police also found evidence of an espionage ring at the French naval base of Toulon.

On July 17, 1952, the Paris newspaper *Figaro* printed excerpts from Duclos' notebook, which was seized during the Paris riots. These notes said in part: "The French Army fights a war in Vietnam, in Korea, assassinates in Tunisia, fights against workers on strike. It is integrated into a European Army. There cannot be a question of defending an army which serves imperialist designs. We work for the certain defeat of that army in Vietnam, in Korea, in Tunisia, and we fight against preparations for a third world war."

Communist military policy has been served by the creation of a training center of militants in the Parisian suburb of Viroflay. Only ten minutes drive from the Supreme Headquarters of the Allied Powers in Europe, this Moscow academy for propaganda, subversion, and military training is located in a two-storied French chateau surrounded by walls, thick hedges and barbed wire. "Director of Studies" here is Victor Michaud, member of the party politburo and also member of the National Assembly. Michaud also edits the journal *Cahiers du Communisme*. At Viroflay carefully selected candidates take courses in military strategy and tactics, anti-NATO activities, riot and strike techniques, and the principles of world revolution.

In seeking to establish the reasons for Communist strength in France, it is a grave error to adopt the oversimplified formula "poverty causes

Communism." Poverty, is of course exploited by Communism. But to say that it is the sole cause is to overlook the fact that Communists have never won a free election giving them control of government, as well as the fact that where Communists are in power, the worst kind of poverty and misery reigns. In Czechoslovakia the Communists took over in spite of that country's great social and economic achievements. On the other hand Turkey, with a low standard of living, as well as Spain, Ireland, and others, are all strongholds of anti-Communism. As Irving Brown, European representative of the American Federation of Labor has pointed out, the crude "economic determinism" argument ignores the non-economic, ideological factors which play considerable roles in France and the rest of Europe. The Communist hard core, he said "which will constitute the real menace to France in time of crisis, remains unaffected by all improvements in the economic and social position of the worker." (Irving Brown, "Europe 1952," *New Leader*, October 13, 1952).

Another explanation of French Communist appeal, that of Jean-Marie Domenach, is the "feeling that European capitalism is doomed, a feeling that leads non-Communists to a sort of inertia. . . . without a revival of European hope which can find outside of Communism its objectives and the will to realize them, the French Communist party will continue, with its ups and downs, to be a powerful force, because it is intrinsically and . . . physiologically connected with the European crisis whose symptoms France, as always, displays most violently." Nevertheless says Domenach, "The present policy of the U.S.S.R. can only accentuate the decline of the French Communist party. This decline, however, will not go very far and will leave the party well above its prewar position." (Einaudi, Domenach, and Garosci, *Communism in Western Europe*, Cornell University Press, 1951, pp. 150, 151.).

16

Communism in Spain, Britain
and Other European Countries

Soviet policy for Spain has been aimed at gaining control of the government by trojan horse strategy from within (as in 1934 and 1936) or seeing to it that the geopolitical and military importance of Spain is denied to any anti-Soviet coalition.

The establishment of the Spanish Republic in 1931, which was to a considerable degree the work of pressure groups including Communists, opened the door to possible Communist control of Spain. Working through the Marxian Socialists, the neo-Marxian Republic Action party of Manuel Azana, some of the Progressive Republicans led by Zamora, and several important unions, including the Anarcho-Syndicalists, the Communists gradually extended their influence in the Republic. The Socialist party dominated the drafting of the 1931 constitution, which substantially weakened the two anti-Marxist elements of Spain—the Army and the Church. Remarkably similar to this document was the constitution drawn up by the French Marxists in early 1946; it too was characterized by an all-powerful, unicameral legislature and a weak executive.

During 1932 and most of 1933 the Spanish government was headed by Manuel Azana, and it was more and more oriented along Marxist lines. The majority Socialist party slowly but surely swung to the revolutionary approach, and away from moderation. A Socialist Manifesto dated July 17, 1932 declared: "The revolutionary movement is not yet over." On January 11, 1933, left-wing extremists murdered three Civil Guardists at Casas Viejas. The increasingly pro-Soviet tone of the Azana regime led the Progressive Republican and Radical parties to desert the government and join the opposition.

The first and last free election Spain ever had was held in October, 1933, and resulted in a victory for the anti-Marxist coalition of the center and right. Largo Cabellero, self-styled Lenin of Spain, and Socialist leader, immediately urged the left to regain control of the government by force. Socialists, Communists, and Anarco-Syndicalists led riots and strikes which helped prevent the appointment of the anti-Communist Gil Robles as premier, with the result that the milder Lerroux was made head of the cabinet. Leftist violence culminated with the derailment of the Barcelona-Seville express on December 8, 1933, causing nineteen dead. Marxist militias and youth groups led by Caballero were formed "for the defense of the republic." They soon found a comparable opposition in the newly organized *Falange Espanola,* led by Jose Antonio de Rivera.

In September, 1934, Caballero again threatened the government with revolt in an effort to prevent Robles from entering the cabinet (Salvador de Madariaga, *Spain,* Creative Age Press, 1943, pp. 330, 331). Shortly thereafter Robles joined the cabinet, and two further members of his parliamentary group, the *Accion Popular* came with him. This was a perfectly normal and parliamentary move, but it displeased the left, which raised the standard of revolt. Marxist leaders Caballero, Azana, and Companys led Socialist, Communist, and Republican Action revolutionaries, together with anarchist elements, in a rebellion against the Republic. French and Russian ships landed ammunition (E. A. Peers, *The Spanish Tragedy,* Oxford University Press, 1936, p. 159). The First Soviet Republic of Spain was proclaimed, with its seat in Oviedo, Asturias. Currency and stamps were issued bearing the hammer and sickle insignia. With the rebellion of 1934 the left lost every shred of moral authority to condemn the rebellion of 1936.

There can be no question as to who instigated the 1934 revolt: this was Soviet intervention in Spain two years ahead that of any other foreign power. The Soviet organ *Communist International* boasted on November 5, 1934; "The workers of Asturias fought for Soviet power under the leadership of the Communist party." The report of the Seventh World Congress of the Comintern in October 1935 analyzed the Soviet failure and instructed the Spanish representative Garcia as to future action.

Having failed by direct method actions, the Communists and their allies decided to form a united front on the political level, and infiltrate Spanish government using the trojan horse strategy outlined by Dimitrov at the Comintern Congress. The Popular Front was formed, consisting of Communists, Socialists, the Republican Action party of Azana, and the Anarcho-Syndicalists. The Front put considerable pressure to bear on President Zamora to dissolve the Cortes and hold new elections. This Zamora did on January 7, 1936, in violation of parliamentary custom that the leader of the largest party in the Cortes (Robles) be first given a chance to form his own cabinet. The election date was set for February 15, 1936. Amid an atmosphere of terror and violence instigated by the left, the center-rightist coalition won 5,051,935 votes, to 4,356,579 votes for the Popular Front (some leftists claimed it was 4,910,817 for the anti-Marxists and 4,206,155 for the Front). It was clear, then, that the anti-Marxist coalition had won the popular vote, but the matter of who won the most seats in the new Cortes was disputed. Due to the peculiarities of the electoral system, it was possible for a party or coalition polling a minority of the popular vote to gain a majority of the seats in parliament. Azana, leader of the Popular Front, claimed that the Front had won 258 Cortes seats, as opposed to 214 seats for the right-center coalition. In the face of violent protests from the latter, President Zamora asked Azana to take over the premiership. Zamora later claimed, however, that the Popular Front had only won 200 seats. (*Journal de Geneve*, January 17, 1937). Azana then proceeded to appoint a commission to "verify" the election, with the result that forty more anti-Marxists were deprived of their seats, and replaced by members of the Popular Front, some of whom had not even run for office in the first place.

The "election" of 1936 was the death blow struck at the Spanish Republic not by Fascism, as some have held, but by the partisans of Soviet power. Constitutional government and parliamentarism was dying, and the left admitted as much. Following the seizure of power by the Popular Front, the Marxist daily *Claridad* commented: "We are approaching the ultimate implications of our electoral triumph. Shall we return to legality as the Rightists demand? To what legality? We know no law but that of revolution." These sentiments were echoed in the Socialist monthly *Leviatan*: "Peace and concord are chimerical and no less chimerical is a policy of conciliation or of the center. Either revolution or counter-revolution. There is no middle course."

From February 15, 1936, the Marxist-incited mob ruled Madrid. Centrists and rightists were attacked and their press destroyed. Churches were sacked or fired, and church-goers assaulted. Azana's "government" either could not or would not keep order.

Bela Kun, the old Hungarian Communist leader, together with Soviet and other agents began arriving in Spain in the middle of March, 1936. (See *London Times*, April 14, 1936, and *Le Matin* of Paris, March 22, 1936). On April 20th a party of Russian Communists passed through Paris on their way to Spain, and were granted every courtesy by the Popular Front ambassador there. Soviet strategists held a meeting in Valencia on May 16th, attended by Soviet ambassador Marcel Rosenberg, Bela Kun, a certain Codoliva, alias Medina (representing the Comintern), Largo Caballero, and the Stalinite Socialist Alvarez del Vayo. It was planned to transform the Popular Front into a Communist-dominated regime capable of holding the Iberian peninsula in the interests of Soviet power. A coup to achieve this end was scheduled for July 25th. (Arthur Lovejoy, *World War in Spain,* 1939, p. 176).

Meanwhile the Popular Front succeeded in ousting Zamora as President and replaced him with Azana. The Socialist Prieto was first appointed premier, but was shortly succeeded by the Gallegan leftist Quiroga. Caballero remained outside the government, biding his time, and training his militia. Violence shook the country. A lieutenant of the Civil Guard was murdered by leftist groups on April 14th. The rightists retaliated by killing the leftist leader Castillo. Falangistas challenged Caballero's milita in the streets of Madrid.

A few courageous anti-Communists remained in the parliament to try to return constitutionalism and bring the Azana regime to its senses. Robles and Calvo Sotelo made speech after speech (See *Parliamentary Record,* June 16 - July 13, 1936) demanding restoration of public order, and listing the number of people killed, buildings and churches fired, and other terrorist activities. The rest of Europe saw what was happening in Spain and most moderate organs of the press agreed with Sotelo and Robles that the Spanish Republic was dead and that Marxist terror ruled. (See the *Manchester Guardian,* May 8, 1936, and the *London Times,* June 6, 1936).

The Marxist coalition did not intend to allow free speech in the Cortes much longer. When Sotelo again admonished the Azana regime on July 7th for its failure to keep order and listed some of the damage done by Caballero's militia while the police and fire departments stood by doing nothing, the Communist parliamentary leader Dolores Iburrari arose and cried out: "That is your last speech Senor Sotelo." On the night of July 12th the government police arrived at Sotelo's house, and although he had parliamentary immunity; they shoved him in police lorry number 17, "worked him over," and dumped his body at one of Madrid's outlying cemeteries early the next morning. Sotelo's death was the spark that set off the Nationalist revolution which commenced on July 17th. His murder, threatened by a government deputy and carried out by the government police, was a signal that there was no longer room for an opposition party, and that only force could assert the will of the majority as expressed on February 15th. The Popular Front had seized power and could not be ousted by parliamentary means. The constitution was dead; the Republic was a thing of the past.

The revolt was led by Generals Sanjurjo, Mola, and Franco. While the Spanish Army remained loyal to its leaders almost to a man, about half the navy and half the air force went over to the Azana regime. The Carlists, the Falange, and most of the adherents of the center-rightist coalition majority of February joined the Nationalist cause. Within a week, before the Nationalists received any foreign aid whatsoever, half of Spain was in Nationalist hands.

The Spanish Army, led by General Franco in the south and General Mola in the north (Sanjurjo was killed in a plane accident) could easily have taken Madrid had it not been for the intervention of international Communism in the form of the International Brigades of Luigi Longo, Andre Marty, Klement Gottwald, and others. These brigades began to arrive in Madrid on November 8, 1936. (Salvador de Madariaga states: "The purely national phase of the civil war begins on July 17th and ends on November 8, 1936, with the appearance of the International Brigades in Madrid"). Actually Communist military aid had appeared even earlier, for the fellow-travelling French Minister for Air, Pierre Cot, had arranged in August for 100 war planes to be flown to Spain.

Dr. Maranon, "Father of the Spanish Republic," declared: "The Loyalist [Popular Front] regime has become entirely Communist. A liberal has nothing in common with such a regime. . . . I never saw a greater absurdity than that the people should call the Reds loyal and the Nationalists rebels. How can you call the people loyal who disregarded all law and assassinated Calvo Sotelo, the leader of the opposition, because they saw in him a danger to their Soviet plans?" (*Revue de Paris*, December 15, 1937). Many other Spanish republicans, including Radical leader Lerroux and Ramon de Ayala, uttered similar sentiments. Winston Churchill declared: "The hideous series of nightly butcheries have robbed the Madrid Government of the lineaments of a civilized power." (*London Evening Standard*, October 2, 1936).

Communist leader Andres Nin boasted on September 4, 1936: "The Government no longer exists, we are the government." Some hopeful moderate Socialists like Indalecio Prieto tried to remain in the regime, but soon discovered that the Soviet military mission of General Goriev and the local Communists (aided by the International Brigades) were running the government. By the end of 1936 the pro-Soviet group in the government, led by del Vayo and Juan Negrin had gained the upper hand, expelling Caballero, who had begun to display independent Marxist attitudes. The Spanish historian de Madariaga comments: "The chief agent of the Soviet Trojan Horse policy in Spain was Alvarez del Vayo, the stronger and more efficient for his remaining officially a Socialist. His trips to Moscow began in 1930." (de Madariaga, *op. cit.*, p. 368). Louis Araquistain, former Republican Ambassador to Paris, confirmed this when he said: "Communism was to blame for the Republican disaster in Spain, and the responsibility of Alvarez del

Vayo, instrument of the Communist party, is one of the greatest." (*New York Times*, May 19, 1939; Del Vayo is an editor of New York's liberal *Nation* magazine). The most damning evidence of Communist control of the "Loyalist" regime comes from Indalecio Prieto, Socialist Minister of Defense until 1938, who published his report to the Socialist party in 1938 in the form of a publication entitled *How and Why I Left The Ministry of Defense*. This revealing document, published in Paris, states in part: "Caballero learned that Foreign Minister del Vayo appointed hundreds of political commissars in the Republican army—almost all Communists; from the first moment the Communists were the most privileged part of the Republican army. . . . Because I refused to take orders from Moscow, Juan Negrin expelled me from the Government." (Quoted by de Madariaga, *op. cit.*, pp. 471, 472). A very interesting letter from Stalin to Caballero, dated December 21, 1936, is yet another piece in the Spanish Soviet operation. This letter is reproduced in de Madariaga's book, page 472. The Communist-dominated government in Madrid further sold out the Spanish birthright by sending 530 million dollars worth of Spanish gold to Russia. This gold left Cartagena on October 25, 1936, and arrived in Odessa on November 17, 1936. The Soviet Government announced that it had found "new mines behind the Urals." The new mines were the boxes of the Bank of Spain. (*Ibid.*, p. 390).

The Spanish "civil war" lasted for three years. The Spanish Army, with the aid of German and Italian forces, defeated the Communist International Brigades and Marxist and Anarcho-Syndicalist militias. Originally located in Burgos, the Nationalist Government liberated Madrid in the early spring of 1939 and was almost immediately recognized by everybody except the Soviet Union. Indeed many states had recognized the Burgos regime as the legal government much earlier, beginning with Guatemala's recognition on November 8, 1936.

The Nationalist Government of General Franco was neutral during World War II. Following the end of that war, however, international Communism renewed the attack in two ways: first, by an attack on Spain in the United Nations organization, and secondly, actual guerrilla-type activities by emigre rebels in France and their French Communist allies. Communist Poland and other Soviet mouthpieces tried to distract UN attention away from Soviet activities in Iran and eastern Europe, by claiming that Spain was a threat to world peace. The UN found no evidence to support this charge, but did vote to boycott Spain diplomatically. This vote represented a distinct victory for Soviet Russia, and was not reversed until 1949. Since that time most states have returned ambassadors to Madrid, and the United States made arrangements with the Spanish Government to use Spanish aid and naval bases as part of the defense of the European continent against Communist aggression. In December, 1952, Spain offered the UN troops for the Korean fighting.

For some time Communist guerrilla training schools in southern France sought to develop a threat to Spain through the use of French Communist raiders and emigre Communists from Spain. This threat was never great, and seemed practically ended by 1952.

GREAT BRITAIN

From the Communist viewpoint, Great Britain is the epitomy of decadent capital-imperialism which must be destroyed. Since 1945, however, Russia has sought to turn Britain against the United States by encouraging the long-sought for rivalry alluded to by Stalin in his speech to the 19th Congress of the Russian Communist party, when he declared that there could be no peace until the leading "imperialist" powers were destroyed—in wars against one another.

As the cold war in Europe became more intense in 1947, Soviet policy sought to encourage neutralist and anti-American feelings among Britishers. Warnings were issued that close ties to America might well result in Great Britain becoming the 49th state. British Communists and fellow travellers sought to put fear into the hearts of Britishers on the basis that American defensive plans for Europe which included American air bases in Britain, would antagonize Russia into bombing Britain. These persons tried to emphasize that the global struggle was one in which Britain should at least remain neutral. When the Korean war started, pro-Soviet elements in Britain pictured General MacArthur as a war-monger who had aggressive designs on them. Appeasement efforts by India were applauded, and, of course, British recognition of Communist China was used as an important argument for not prosecuting the Korean war vigorously.

Communist influence in Britain has not been inconsiderable. British Marxists formed the Democratic Federation back in 1881. Three years later they changed the name to the Social Democratic Federation in emulation of Socialist parties in other countries. Led for a time by Henry M. Hyndman, the movement soon fell into bitter factionalism. The strongest element then formed the British Socialist party, nucleus of the later Communist party, which was created on August 1, 1920, under the leadership of the veteran radical Sylvia Pankhurst. Meantime Hyndman and some of his friends joined the Labor party. Pro-Communist and pro-Marxist influence—including Fabians—have remained in the left wing of the Labor party since its inception in 1906. Leading members of the Fabian Society such as Sidney and Beatrice Webb and George Bernard Shaw, although disassociating themselves from certain aspects of Marxist doctrine, were generally quite sympathetic to what they called the Soviet "experiment."

Another early pro-Communist element in the Labor party, Sir Oswald Mosely, has in recent years been a vigorous proponent of Fascism. In 1930 a left wing Laborite, Mosely received the support of the Independent Labor Party in advocating a controlled economy to deal with the economic crisis of that time. Mosley's program was only narrowly defeated at the Labor conference at Llandudno in October, 1930, but he was elected to the party executive. In that same year the Independent Labor party reaffirmed its position as "an independent Socialist organization, making its distinct contribution to Labor party policy and having its distinct position within the party." In 1931 the ILP elected only five members to Parliament, the Communsts none, and Labor only 46 (as compared to 289 in the previous election).

The Labor party took a stand against both Fascism and Communism in 1932, and the ILP seceded from the Labor party. Communist overtures to Labor for joint action were unavailing. The 1935 elections saw one Communist member elected (William Gallacher). The Communists and their allies continued to exert pressure on the Labor party for a united front according to the dictates of International Communism as interpreted by Georgi Dimitrov at the 1935 World Congress of the Comintern. The first success in Britain was an agreement in January, 1937, for joint action between the Communist party, the ILP, and the Socialist League. This represented real progress for the Communists inasmuch as the Socialist League was a part of the Labor party and the League included such men as Sir Stafford Cripps, Aneurin Bevan, John Strachey, Harold Laski, and H. N. Brailsford among its leadership. Condemning common action with the Communists and the ILP, the Labor party expelled the Socialist League and ousted Cripps, Bevan, Sir Charles Trevelyan, and G. R. Strauss. Bevan and Strauss returned to the Labor party after Russia attacked Finland in 1939; Cripps was re-admitted somewhat later.

In 1945 the Communist party elected two members to Parliament out of twenty-one candidates, and received 100,000 votes. In 1950 the party put up 100 candidates and polled 92,000 votes, but failed to elect a single member. In 1951, all ten Communist candidates were defeated, and the party polled but 22,000 votes. The Korean war apparently made many Britishers realize that the Communists were not just another political party to the left of Labor. Another explanation of the low Communist vote in 1951 must also be attributed to the fact that the Communists slackened their efforts and even campaigned on the slogan: "For a Labor majority and a Communist group in Parliament." Communist leaders counted on Aneurin Bevan's anti-rearmament and anti-American left wing Labor faction to do their work for them. (*New York Times,* October 23, 1951). Bevan's book *In Place of Fear* was prominently displayed along-side works of Stalin, Lenin, and Marx at the 22nd Communist party Congress held in London in April, 1952. A campaign to wean the Labor party away from its "right wing leadership" was the keynote of the meeting. The Battersea Town Hall was decorated with a banner inscribed: "Labor-Communist Unity Action Will Smash Toryism." Harry Pollitt, general secretary of the party urged east-west trade, reduced rearmaments, withdrawal from Korea, Malaya, and Egypt, and the "throwing off of America's domination of Britain." (*New York Times,* April 12, 1952). R. Palme Dutt presided in the absence of William Gallacher, who was in Australia. Mr. Dutt announced the party membership at 35,000.

One area in which British Communists and Soviet policy have made some penetration has been in the union movement, and specifically in local units of the Transport and General Worker's Union, Britain's largest. A study was made by Dr. Joseph Goldstein of Communist Arthur Deakin's local union as a case history of Communist infiltration and domination. There, he found, the Communists moved in with a hard core of loyal supporters. Average attendance at union meetings was 27 out of a membership of 1,000. Five Communists and two fellow travelers were able to ultimately dominate these meetings by volunteering their services for distasteful jobs and staying late until only thirteen union members were left. Then they had their majority and voted in their program. Dr. Goldstein found that less than one percent of the membership was responsible for proposing all resolutions in an average year. That was how a small minority was able to speak and act for a large local union with a constantly-changing membership. It is a technique that the Communists know is almost foolproof because of the lack of interest by rank and file members in what goes on inside their unions. Deakin's local also had interesting ways of "rigging" union elections through the distribution of ballots by a Communist convener of shop stewards and by arranging to have the ballots counted by a group of stewards dominated by the Communists. When national union officers instructed the local union to get rid of the Communists, the latter went through an elaborate "resignation" ceremony, but remained in the party and in their union jobs nevertheless. ("Communism in Labor Unions," *U. S. News and World Report,* July 25, 1952).

When Stalin's heir apparent, G. M. Malenkov, told the 19th Congress of the Russian Communist party in October, 1952, that the time had come to return to the united front tactics in Europe, British Communist leader Harry Pollitt emphasized the necessity of boring within unions dealing with military production. Some success was achieved in the Amalgamated Engineering (Machinists) Union, whose 725,000 members were almost exclusively employed on armament production. Wal Hannington, well-known Communist labor organizer appeared as an AEU organizer in the north London area—a district where big airplane plants were located. In the National Union of Mineworkers the Communist minority led by Abe Moffat, the Scottish mine leader, declared that miners will "not cut coal in any war against their socialist brothers of the Soviet Union." One of Communism's greatest allies is Arthur Horner, secretary of the National Union of Mineworkers. His position is the most important post in British industry held by an avowed Communist.

Many events have occurred since 1945 to shake the confidence of Britishers that there is little or nothing to fear from Communism at home. Many of them had tended to look upon American concern with Communism as "hysteria." It was therefore acutely embarrassing when Britain learned the details of the Klaus Fuchs atomic spy ring and of the operations of Dr. Allan Nunn May, the first of Britain's atomic traitors. Still another British atomic scientist, Dr. Bruno Pontecorvo, disappeared in 1950 with important secrets to Soviet-controlled territory in central Europe. In the summer of 1951, two top members of the British Foreign Office, Donald Duart MacLean and Guy Francis de Moncy Burgess, disappeared somewhere in France in an apparently voluntary trip to Soviet-controlled territory. Their dramatic flight brought on demands that Britain's loyalty set-up, which has no loyalty oath requirement and allows Communists to hold "non-sensitive" jobs, be overhauled. (See article by Gilbert Bailey, *New York Times,* June 17, 1951).

In June, 1952, a British Foreign Office radio operator William M. Marshall, was jailed on a charge of passing on "highly secret and confidential information" on three occasions to the second secretary of the Soviet Embassy in London. Previously employed by the Foreign Office in Iron Curtain countries, Marshall reportedly "knew the whereabouts of secret Allied radio stations in Europe and their call signs and wave lengths," among other things. The Soviet diplomat who received the information, Pavel Kuznetsov, was ordered expelled from Britain. A somewhat similar case occurred in early December, when a British soldier, Tony Ernest Dewick, was convicted of plotting to hand over military secrets to a foreign power with the aid of the Young Communist League, of which he was a member.

One of the most articulate advocates of Soviet policy in Britain has been the Dean of Canterbury, Dr. Hewlett Johnson. When he returned from Communist China in the summer of 1952 full of stories of American "germ warfare" in Korea, seven Anglican clergymen sat on the same platform with Johnson as he addressed over 1000 persons at a meeting sponsored by the Britain-China Friendship Association. His pro-Soviet clergymen allies include Rev. Stanley Evans and Rev. Bryn Thomas. (Douglas Hyde, "The Red Dean's Clerical Comrades," *America*, September 6, 1952).

The most important ally of Soviet Communism in Britain, however, is Aneurin Bevan. Although occasionally insisting that he is anti-Communist, Bevan's speeches and actions betray the Henry Wallace of 1948. Here are some of his statements which have given pleasure and delight to the Communists: "The dangers of Communism, if dangers there are, come not from military plans but from the failure to redress wrongs that exist in western society. . . . I say to my American friends that their economic and fiscal policies are doing more damage to western Europe than Stalin can ever do." (Quoted by Salvador de Madariaga in "Open Letter to Mr. Bevan," *Manchester Guardian Weekly*, March 27, 1952). Statements expressed by Bevan in his book *In Place of Fear*, published in London in April 1952, were widely and effectively used by the Communists: "In so far as I can be said to have had a political training at all it has been in Marxism. . . . The picture of the Russian worker held down by a ruthless dictatorship is false. The scale of rearmament urged upon the democracies by the United States is a source not of strength but of weakness." (Quoted by Clifton Daniel, *New York Times*, April 4, 1952).

Bevan's pro-Communist allies in the Labor party include Michael Foot, Ian Mikardo, Richard Crossman, and Tom Driberg. The Bevan wing of the party elected six members of the Labor National Executive Committee of 26 in September, 1952. These included Bevan, Mrs. Barbara Castle, Driberg, Mikardo, Crossman, and Harold Wilson; James Griffiths, also on the Committee, was considered friendly to Bevan. A month later 82 Labor parliamentarians voted for Bevan as Labor's deputy chieftan, as opposed to 194 votes for Herbert Morrison. This election indicated a rise of Bevan's strength in the party.

The Communists play up Bevan's anti-American speeches and actions for all they are worth. Animosity toward and even violence against American service men stationed in Britain as part of the European defense force are actively promoted. American Air Force General Francis Griswold declared on November 29th, 1952: "Communists are exploiting . . . an organized 'Yank, go home' campaign that is being echoed by certain nationalist elements."

Most serious from the point of view of American-British relations is the rise of anti-American feeling in clearly non-Communist areas. The previously referred to propaganda against General MacArthur, and unfair reporting from Korea, has strengthened Communist points of view. Then too, certain "respectable" British publications have given British readers the impression that American courts are cruel to pro-Communists or Communists. Geoffrey Crowther, writing in the July 26, 1952 issue of the London *Economist,* made this remarkable charge: "It is also an unfortunate fact that nobody who is tried in the United States . . . on any charge which suggests, however remotely, disloyalty, can expect at this moment to have a fair trial."

Soviet policy could be the only gainer of increasingly anti-American nationalist and left-wing Labor elements in Britain, who seem bent on making Stalin's dream come true—that the United States and Great Britain would ultimately come to blows, as the prelude to the collapse of imperialism, and the victory of Soviet-type Socialism. (See Colm Brogan, "Our British Critics," *Freeman,* September 8, 1952.)

SWEDEN

The Swedish Communist party had an announced membership of 35,000 in 1950. Founded in 1921, Swedish Communists reached the height of their power in 1946 when they polled 372,424 votes. In the 1950 election they polled 187,707 (five percent of the total). In Stockholm the Communists controlled 17 seats in a city council of 100; they lost twelve of these seats in 1950. In Gothenburg they dropped from fifteen to nine seats, out of a total of 60. Communists lost all their seats in the city council of Malmo, third largest Swedish city.

Prior to 1935 Swedish Communists violently attacked all non-Communists. At the 1934 party Congress Sven Linderot, Swedish Communist leader, declared: "Social Democracy which infuses the minds of the workers with social-fascist ideology and keeps them from fighting fascism, is thereby acting in support of fascism. As Stalin has said, it is the twin brother of fascism." (Paul Bjork, *Swedish Social Democracy Looks at Communism,* ECA Special Mission to Sweden publication, Stockholm, 1950, p. 10). This policy came to a close with Dim-itrov's speech in 1935 advocating a united front with Socialists, "liberals," and others against Fascism. Policy changed again in 1939 when the Communist daily *Ny Dag* rejoiced over the Hitler-Stalin pact and Communists watched pro-Nazi groups jail Swedish citizens who put Sweden first.

After June 22, 1941, Swedish Communism became much stronger as the government and the people enthused over Russia's behavior. One leading non-Communist paper invited Russia's leading propa-gandist, Ilya Ehrenburg, to become a regular contributor. In the first post-war elections, the Communists polled 11 percent of the total vote. Their prestige remained high until the Czech coup d'etat of 1948. Elections in that year saw a decline to 6.3% of the total vote. Com-munist strategy thereafter was concentrated on building strength in certain areas such as Stockholm, Gothenburg, Vasternorrland, and Norrland, and left the rest of the country pretty much alone. A special pocket of Communist power was developed in Norrbotten, along Sweden's northern frontier. Indeed the Communists, long in-fluential in Norrbotten, increased their strength there between 1944 and 1948, whereas they declined everywhere else. Communist leaders could even go so far as to assert that they would not defend Swedish territory in the event of a Soviet attack. (*Ibid.*, p. 40).

Most widely publicized of all Swedish Communist maneuvers was the so-called Stockholm Peace Appeal. In November, 1949, the Comin-form ordered the "peace" campaign. Immediately the Swedish Com-munist publication *Var Tid* proclaimed: "When the pressure of the reaction and the imperialists to make preparations for a third war and to involve Sweden in the American bloc is exercised with all conceiv-able means, the effect of confining the class struggle only to economic demands would be to leave the working class unarmed on the most important front, the struggle for peace." (*Ibid.*, p. 4). Communist leader Hilding Hagberg declared that the Socialist Government "does not strive for any socialist reforms; its stabilization policy prepares the way for crisis, fascism, and war." (*Loc. cit.*). A Stockholm restaurant was the scene of the launching of the world-wide "peace" campaign, which in essence demanded that the free world remain peaceful while Soviet Russia marched forward unimpeded.

Soviet policy in Sweden attempts to pose Communism as being favorable to Swedish neutrality. The primary effort, of course, is to prevent any Swedish rapprochement with the NATO. Swedish neu-trality was becoming more difficult all the time to maintain, and was based on certain misconceptions of the nature of the world struggle.

One aspect of this misconception was manifested by the Swedish Trade Minister and former professor in the United States, Gunnar Myrdal. In 1946 Myrdal returned home to Sweden convinced of an American depression which might inflict unemployment in Sweden. He concluded, therefore, a five year long term credit agreement with Soviet Russia, according to which Russia could spend 200 millions dollars in purchases of Swedish manufacturing products. He felt that this device would assure Sweden's markets, and therefore the jobs of her workers. He hoped also that the agreement would improve Swedish-Soviet relations. But Myrdal's dire prediction of capitalistic depression and better relations with Russia proved incorrect. For his thanks Soviet Russia began to label Sweden a "warmonger" in 1950.

Sweden has learned the hard way that lenient treatment of Communists—the tendency to regard them as a harmless group of ideological dissenters—helps nobody but the Communists. In line with this attitude, the Communist leader Hilding Hagberg was named to the Royal Investigating Commission for Defense in 1945, giving the Communists access to Sweden's top national defense secrets. No loyalty screening of applicants was attempted. All this was quickly changed when the dramatic story of Soviet espionage in Sweden broke out in the summer of 1952. The story starts in 1928 when one of the conspirators, Ernest Hilding Andersson, joined a Communist youth organization in Stockholm. A few years later he joined the Swedish navy, and influenced his fellow sailors with a Communist periodical appropriately entitled *The Torpedo*. In 1940 Andersson became a petty officer, and by 1950 had completed courses in radio, electronics, and radar. His advancement in the Royal Navy was paralleled by advancement in the Communist party. In 1946 a reporter of the Communist *Ny Dag* introduced Andersson to Konstantin Vinogradov, a secretary in the Soviet Embassy. After a two years friendship the Soviet "diplomat" turned him over to his first official contact, Victor Anizimov of the Tass News Agency in Stockholm. Anizimov gave Andersson a thorough training in the techniques of espionage.

In November, 1949, Andersson was given his first assignment: a complete report on the defense set-up in the Stockholm naval base, including security measures designed to protect key points against sabotage and seizure. This assignment was easily accomplished. He then turned over to Soviet authorities complete information about the east coast naval base of Karlskrona. Later he gave the Soviets important data from Lappland, especially about the air and naval base at Lulea and the Boden Fortress (key to Sweden's northern defenses). On September 21, 1951, however, Andersson was caught in the act of turning over secret information to a Soviet Military Attache named Orlov in Karlskrona. Another spy, Johan Fritiof Enbom, admitted turning over to Soviet authorities military secrets for ten years. He said it was his duty to "smooth the Red army's path to liberate Sweden from the dreaded western occupation." (*Time*, June 30, 1952, p. 32). Two other Swedes were involved in the spy ring: Fingal Larsson and Arthur Karlsson. A Polish Communist Military Attache was notified in July, 1952 that his presence in Sweden was no longer desirable. He had been caught photographing secret airfields reserved for wartime use only.

Sweden's attempt at neutrality was further taxed in June, 1952, when an unarmed Army transport plane, flying between Stockholm and the Soviet-occupied island of Hiiumaa in the Baltic, was shot down by Soviet fire. Three days later a Swedish Catalina flying boat was searching the area for survivors, and it was attacked by Russian jet fighters and shot down. The crew was picked up by a German ship, and returned to Stockholm to describe the wanton Soviet attack over international waters. The Swedish reaction was a quick and angry one. Thousands of Swedes demonstrated outside the Russian Embassy, and Swedish Air Force planes were told to continue the search for the first plane and to shoot on sight anybody who might try to interfere.

Norway, Denmark, and Finland

In 1919 the Norwegian Labor party resolved to sever all ties with the Second International (Socialist) and to affiliate with the new Third International (Communist). In 1921 a faction of the Labor party broke away from Comintern discipline to form the Social Democratic party. The Labor party proved difficult to manage, however, and the Comintern during 1922 and 1923 had to send Bukharin and Karl Radek to Norway to keep it in line. Towards the end of 1923, an attempt on the part of the Comintern, acting through the German Communist Edwin Hornle, to end Labor party wavering once and for all was defeated by the Labor party Congress by a vote of 169-103. The minority stayed loyal to Stalin and became the Communist party. The Labor party remained Marxist in character, and became the largest Norwegian worker's party, followed by the Social Democrats, and then the Communists. In 1927 the Labor and Social Democratic parties merged, and the Labor party has dominated Norwegian politics since that date.

The Communists polled only six percent of the vote in the 1952 elections, but remained a threat because a disproportionate amount of Communist strength and effort remained concentrated in sparsely settled northern Norway.

Soviet policy towards Denmark takes into consideration that country's strategic geographic location between the Baltic and North Seas. Soviet control of Denmark would mean sealing off the Baltic Sea, endangering Allied shipping in the North Sea, and establishment of a springboard for attack on England or the Low Countries. Danish Communists reached their height of pre-war strength in 1939 when they received 41,000 votes and won three seats in the parliament. They did almost six times as well after World War II, and in the elections of 1950 received 94,468 votes to gain seven seats in the parliament. This compared with 813,512 votes for the victorious Social Democrats, who controlled 59 seats.

During the Hitler-Stalin pact, Danish Communists were free to do as they wished. Not until June 22, 1941 did the Communists join the rest of the population in the resistance. After the war Communist leader Aksel Larsen was invited into the Danish cabinet, along with his colleague Alfred Jensen. In the 1945 elections the Communists received 255,236 votes and eighteen seats in the parliament. The Communists had made a real dent in the Social Democratic ranks. The Communists were so much encouraged that they sought to swallow up the Socialists through a united front technique. This effort failed, and Communism was meantime partly discredited in the eyes of the Danes when Russia seized the island of Bornholm and held it until the Danes promised not to let any other power use it for military purposes.

Soviet power menaces Denmark primarily from the island base of Ruegen, which neutralizes Bornholm. Soviet military units in east Germany are only one hundred miles from the Danish frontier. Here is the real danger. To the NATO powers on the other hand, it became increasingly clear that the defense of Scandinavia depended fundamentally on the successful defense of strategic Denmark.

Finland lies in the hands of the Russian bear, who can close his fist any time he sees fit. Soviet power exercised an economic stranglehold over Finland after World War II, and made it impossible for Finland to have any freedom of action internationally. Invaded by Soviet Russia in 1939-1940, Finland was treated very shabbily by the Allies, who considered her a Nazi satellite and saddled her with slavery to Soviet Communism. At the mid-century Russia controlled the military approaches to Finland. The great Soviet base at Porkkala dominates Helsinski, which it adjoins. The Soviets seized the northern Finnish territory of Petsamo during World War II, as well as considerable territory along the frontier. So terrible is the fear of Russia, that a Finnish businessman was impelled to say: "We are not beside the Iron Curtain, we are beneath it and wondering when it will fall."

The 1951 parliamentary elections saw the Communists win 43 seats, trailing the Social Democrats with 53 and the Agrarians with 44. Three years previously the non-Communist parties miraculously prevented a Czech-style coup d'etat engineered by Interior Minister Leino. Since that time the Communist organizations, known as the Finnish People's Democratic League (SKDL) has survived only due to the support it receives from the Soviets. The Communists do retain considerable influence in the unions, controlling eight out of thirty-nine unions attached to the Central Federation of Trade Unions. In 1947-1948 when the Communists wielded much more power than after the Leino coup backfired, they instigated many wildcat strikes, but the labor situation subsequently became stabilized. The Communists polled 389,000 votes in the 1951 elections, behind the Social Democrats and Agrarians who received well over 400,000 each.

The Soviets apparently feel that as long as they can control Finland economically and through the constant military threat, and so long as Finland cannot join the western coalition, there is little need in going through with a conquest that might cost a good deal more than it would gain.

The Low Countries and Switzerland

Communism has never been a factor in the political situation of the Low Countries. The majority of Marxists joined the Socialist parties of Belgium and the Netherlands, which have gradually developed along anti-Communist lines. It is true that right after World War II the Communist parties of the Low Countries showed some voting strength, to the tune of about ten percent of the vote. The Dutch Communists polled 502,000 votes in 1946, 382,000 in 1948, and 328,000 in 1952. The same declining ratio appeared in Belgium. In Belgium, however, the Socialists invited the Communists and Liberals into a two year postwar coalition as the better alternative to allowing the Social Christian party to govern the country. From 1948 to 1952 the latter controlled the government while the Marxists and Liberals were in the opposition —except for periods when the Socialists joined the government. In the Netherlands the Communists retain a following in the Hague, Amsterdam, and Rotterdam. In Belgium the Communists have their strength in Brussels, Antwerp, and in the French-speaking Walloon country, which is the Socialist stronghold. Percentage-wise, the Communist parties in the Low Countries dropped to about five percent of the popular vote in the 1952 elections.

Soviet policy for the Low Countries was bent on encouraging industrial slowdowns, shortening the conscription, and building neutralist feeling and apathy toward the NATO.

Switzerland in a sense might well be called the cradle of Communism, since Lenin and Engels laid their plans for the first successful revolutions in Zurich. It was from Switzerland that the German General Staff physically transported Communism in the form of Lenin and his chief lieutenants to Russia, in the spring of 1917. Yet Communism has never been a serious political factor in the country, and Soviet policy has largely been interested in Switzerland only as a neutral ground from which to operate spy rings and infiltrate international organizations located there. Most Marxists in the country are Socialist; the Communist party, banned from 1940 to 1944, was revived in the latter year as the Swiss Labor party. It polled 3.6% of the vote in 1947, and 2.6% in 1951.

Switzerland has her "Red Dean" of Canterbury in the form of Professor Andre Bonnard, wealthy Greek scholar. Bonnard was the head of the Swiss branch of the Soviet-controlled World Peace Partisans. He was arrested in July, 1952, as he left for the East Berlin Peace Meeting where he proposed to show that the United States was dropping bugs on the Chinese Communists, and to prove that the International Red Cross was a tool in the hands of "warmongers" in America, Britain, and Switzerland.

17

Communism in Latin America and Canada

Soviet policy in Latin America plays on the extremes of wealth and poverty, economic distress, and above all, on nationalism. The anti-Yanqui, anti-imperialist approach has been the regular Leninist-Stalinist tactic for "backward" areas. Local Communist operations have been directly supported by the Soviet Union—most blatantly by Soviet Ambassador Constantin Oumansky when he went to Mexico at the end of World War II. The Communist uprising in Colombia in 1948 during General Marshall's visit to that country was timed to show how quickly and effectively Communist para-military groups could spring into action. Throughout all of Latin America, Soviet policy seeks allies in its hate-America campaign, and usually finds these allies—both among Marxist elements and extreme nationalist groups who don't look too closely at the sort of people they associate with. Soviet Communism has had considerable successes in Guatemala, and to a lesser degree in Mexico, Brazil, Chile and elsewhere.

GUATEMALA

In 1944 the regime of Jorge Ubica was overthrown in a revolt in which the Communists played an important role. Coming at a time when the Soviet Union and Communism in general held a relatively high place in the hearts of many, and also at a time when there existed some anti-American feeling based on attacks upon the United Fruit Company, Communist leader Jose Manuel Fortuny found his job somewhat easier than it normally might have been. The president of the new revolutionary government was Juan Jose Arevalo, an educator and social reformer who styled himself a "spiritual socialist." He worked with the Communists and other revolutionary groups which included Spanish Communist emigres. He encouraged Communist organization of the unions, and attacks on the U. S.-owned United Fruit Company. Fortuny was one of the authors of the new constitution which contained quite a few Marxian overtones.

In 1950 Arevalo was succeeded by Jacobo Arbenz, who continued the policy of coddling the Communists and bringing them into the government. Arbenz and other government officials made it a point to attend and praise Communist and pro-Communist meetings. Anti-

Communist meetings were either ignored by the government or suppressed. In July, 1951, the Arbenz government tried to force the nuns who were teaching in an orphan asylum to leave; when a spontaneous anti-government demonstration ensued, the police intervened and fired into the crowd, killing four persons and injuring sixty-one. A wounded student declared: "Guatemala is the only country west of the Iron Curtain where anti-Communist demonstrations are shot at by police."

Representatives of the opposition are absent from most of the important congressional committees including the key agrarian reform committee. Arbenz and his colleagues have given every aid and encouragement to Vicente Lombardo Toledano's Communist Confederation of Labor, and to the French Communist Louis Saillant, who helped organize Guatemala's unions. Local Communists Fortuny and Victor M. Gutierrez have been showered with official favors and their influence in government has been steadily extended.

Despite statements from some government quarters that the Arbenz regime is a friend of the democratic west, it is a fact that the two government newspapers never have had anything good to say about United States aid to the Republic of Korea. On the contrary, Soviet propaganda about American bugs being dropped on the hapless Chinese Communists is given full and free play in these government organs. The president of the Guatemalan Congress, Roberto Fuentes Alvarado, who is anti-American and anti-Catholic, was a delegate to the Soviet "Peace" Congress held in Vienna in December, 1952.

Most observers seem to think that President Arbenz is not himself a Communist, but rather a tool of the Communists. Carlos Simmons, one of the youthful leaders of the anti-Communist National Civic Committee said; "The President is not a Communist, he is a leftist, but he cannot do anything against the Communists because he is afraid." Towards the end of 1952, there was evidence of increased Communist strength in Guatemala. On November 22, 1952, three new cabinet ministers were appointed, all of them more favorable to Communism than their predecessors. The new Foreign Minister, Paul Osegueda, long affiliated with pro-Communist causes, was charged with having been selected by the Cominform to head Latin American Communism in 1953. (*New York Times*, May 20, 1952, and *San Francisco Examiner*, November 23, 1952).

MEXICO

Guatemala's neighbor to the north, Mexico, has seen considerable Communist activity in the past. It was from Mexico City that Soviet

Ambassador Oumansky guided Latin American Communism for some time, and from Mexico City that Vicente Lombardo Toledano extended his Communist Confederation of Labor throughout much of Latin America.

Communist strength in Mexico was at its height during the administration of President Lazaro Cardenas, 1934-1940. In 1940 a schism developed in the party with the result that there broke away from the orthodox Communist party two groups—first, the *Partido de Obreras y Campesinos,* and later the *Partido Popular* of Toledano. But it soon became apparent that the policies of these two Communist factions were little different from those of the official *Partido Communista de Mexico.* They all supported the "peace policies" of the Soviet Union, bleated violently against "Yankee imperialism," and shouted enthusiastically about "socialist construction" in the U.S.S.R., the "people's democracies" of eastern Europe, and the "New China." They denounced Tito in chorus, and acted very much as though they were one party. Of the three Communist groups, Toledano's seemed to be the strongest, as well as the most favored in Moscow. Toledano was a member of the Government's official Institutional Revolutionary Party (PRI) until 1948, and retained the closest contacts with governmental leaders. His leadership of the Latin American Worker's Federation and status as vice-president of the Communist-controlled World Federation of Trade Unions made him easily the most prominent Stalinite in Mexico.

As the 1952 elections approached, the various leftist parties began to withdraw their own presidential candidates, attempting to form a coalition in support of General Miguel Henriquez Guzman, the strongest challenger to Adolfo Ruiz Cortines, candidate of the PRI. On May Day Communists rioted in the streets of Mexico City in an effort to draw attention to themselves and perhaps gain public sympathy when their leaders were arrested——Dionisio Encina, David Alfaro Siquieros, and others. Two persons were killed in the violence, and many injured, with the result that many Mexicans, including the anti-Communist Confederation of Mexican Workers, demanded that the Communists be outlawed.

A month before the election there appeared to be some bad feeling between Encina's official Communist party, and the better known faction led by Toledano. The Communist pary had originally thrown its support to Toledano's *Partido Popular,* and then had instructed him to seek a coalition with General Guzman, leader of the Federation of People's Parties. When protracted negotiations for the coalition broke down, Encina publicly denounced Toledano for the failure. Encina claimed that chances for defeating the government candidate Cortines were dimmed by parties and candidates who placed their own selfish interests above those of "defeating the Government, Yankee imperialism and its policies of war, national colonization and oppression of our people." (*New York Times*, June 9, 1952). In reply, Toledano's number one lieutenant in the *Partido Popular*, General Octavio Vejar Vasquez, former Minister of Education, charged that the Communists were jeopardizing left-wing unity with wild statements which would "lessen the prestige and normal authority" of the better known faction of Toledano.

The election saw Cortines of the PRI win in a landslide victory. Guzman's chances for a serious challenge had been shattered when Toledano decided to run on his own ticket without Communist support. No sooner were the elections over, than the Encina Communists again came out in support of unity around the person of Guzman. The Communists declared that the "democratic opposition has the obligation to group its forces around the triumphant (sic) candidate General Henriquez Guzman." They further demanded a "fight to the end for the victory obtained, mobilization of the masses to force the Government to accept the victory and convene the people to fight against the Government fraud." (*New York Times*, July 12, 1952). Guzman seemed to join in the Communist threat of rebellion when he stated on October 2nd, 1952: "I am at the will of the people and shall do what the people order."

In the event that the Encina and Toledano groups could form an effective coalition with the Guzman forces—in which the Communists would call the tune, there might ensue real trouble for the Cortines Government. Even with the political complexion of Mexico changing towards the right, Communists still retained some influence in certain government circles, notably in the Education Ministry formerly controlled by General Vasquez. This ministry subsidized for some time the Fund for Popular Culture, which was Communist-controlled and devoted itself to the publication of Communist literature. A similar situation existed in the Ministry of Finance, where the Fund for Popular Economics was used by Communists for their own propaganda.

One of the most interesting figures in Mexican Communist circles has been the artist Diego Rivera, twice expelled from the party, who, in November, 1952, asked readmission into Stalin's Mexican fifth column. Rivera coupled his plea to be taken back with an appeal to "all intellectuals of Mexico and the entire world to join the ranks of the only party fighting for human rights, the victory of socialism and peace." For a time a Trotskyite, who had invited Trotsky to live in his house shortly before Trotsky was assassinated by the Soviet MVD (secret police), Rivera was fond of painting murals showing American aggressors dropping bugs on poor innocent Chinese Communist women and children.

Mexican Stalinites showed their power in February, 1952, when they joined ranks to condemn forthcoming Mexican-American negotiations for a military aid agreement. The Marxist painter Siquieros painted a mural showing President Truman shackling the wrists of an armed Mexican peasant on his knees. In his other hand President Truman was holding a thick wad of money. This mural was reproduced widely in the leftist press as part of an anti-American aid agitation. At the same time the "National Council for Peace" published a protest against the projected American aid which was signed by Mexico's fellow travelling intellectuals. The protest appeared as an advertisement in many Mexican papers, paid for by the Communists and Toledano's Popular party. Signers of the protest included Enrique Gonzalez Martinez (poet and writer), Eulalia Guzman (historian), Gabriel Figueroa (movie cameraman), and Emilio Fernandez (film director). They denounced the aid program as a "menace to the free exercise of national sovereignty and to the development and betterment of our country." (*New York Times*, February 11, 1952).

The Communist and fellow traveller campaign proved so successful that President Aleman's regime decided to end the talks with the United States on the military aid program. Communist circles were quick to rejoice, one organ stating that Mexican rejection of American aid constituted "one of the most serious defeats inflicted on the oppressive war diplomacy of the United States in Mexico and Latin America."

BRAZIL

The Soviet fifth column in Brazil has been led for some years by Luiz Carlos Prestes, considered by many observers to be the top Soviet agent in all of South America. Using nationalism as a weapon, Prestes has succeeded in arousing certain anti-American prejudices, and has placed important Communists and fellow travellers in the armed forces and elsewhere in Brazilian public life.

Although the Communist party was outlawed in 1947, it has not been thwarted by the Brazilian Government, especially since the return to power of Getulio Vargas. Communists are free to do pretty much as they please, and their newspapers and other publications appear regularly on the newsstands, notably their principal organ *Im-*

prensa Popular. In 1952 there were twenty-two Communist dailies and thirty-five weeklies published in Brazil.

One of the most sensational stories of Communist infiltration into the armed forces began in March, 1952, when the Brazilian military hero General Euclides Zenobio da Costa, who had led the Brazilian Expeditionary Forces in Italy during World War II, submitted his resignation to President Vargas in protest at the official eye-winking at Communist and pro-Communist activities in the government and in the army, led by War Minister General Estillac Leal. Nothing happened for several days, but on March 26th, Vargas made a typical "compromise" by dismissing both Zenobio and Leal from their posts. The story, however, was far from over. The scene shifted to the Military Club of Brazil, ostensibly a social and benevolent organization, but actually frequently involved in politics. There an election for the presidency of the club aroused national interest. General Estillac Leal became one of the candidates, with strong Communist and fellow traveller support. Bitterly anti-American, Estillac claimed the United States was trying to steal Brazil's natural resources for the benefit of its "war economy." In opposition to the Communist faction led by Estillac was the "Democratic Crusade," standing for close military and economic collaboration with the United States in defense of the western hemisphere and in favor of strong measures against Communism in Brazil. This faction was led by General Alcides Etchegoyen, and included the Brazilian Chief of Staff and many of the nation's most distinguished military officers. During the campaign General Estillac charged that his opponent was favoring a policy of "entreguismo," a coined word frequently used by the Communists meaning a policy of handing over Brazilian natural resources and sovereignty to foreign interests. General Etchegoyen immediately demanded that Estillac either prove his charge or withdraw as a candidate.

On May 22nd, 1952, the election was held, with the result that the anti-Communist candidate Etchegoyen won a landslide victory—gaining 8,288 votes to 4,469 cast for Estillac. The Military Club's official organ *Revista Militar,* which had printed stories influenced by the Estillac faction derogatory to the United States war effort in Korea, began to take on a tone much more friendly to the United States.

Still another scandal broke in July, 1952, when it was discovered that the government attorney in charge of investigating Communism in the armed forces had himself been affiliated with Communist causes dating back to 1929. This man was Amador Cisneiros do Amaral, listed in police files as a Communist (*Correio da Manha,* July 12, 1952). This disclosure indicated that the struggle to weed Communist influences out of the army was by no means ended. In addition to General Estillac, the leading Communists and pro-Communists were identified as Colonel Olimpio Ferraz de Carvalho, Lieutenant Hilton Bergmann, and Major Humberto de Andrade, former editor of the *Revista Militar.*

The man Brazilian Communists hate the most is Carlos Lacerda, editor of the anti-Communist newspaper *Tribuna da Imprensa.* Lacerda publicized Communist and pro-Communist activity day after day, with photostated evidence of Stalin's supporters in the Brazilian Foreign Office. Listing names, dates, and places, Lacerda cited four consuls, two *charge d'affaires* and three home office functionaries as Communists. The chief offender, he said, was career diplomat Orlando Leite Ribeiro, "a personal friend of Communist leader Luiz Carlos Prestes." The *Tribuna* claimed that after Leite Ribeiro became chief of the foreign ministry's administration, many Communists and fellow travellers found their way into key posts and received quick promotions. When one of the accused, Normelio Ramos, replied that he was no Communist, Lacerda printed proof that Ramos was a party member and listed his party card number.

The regime of Getulio Vargas had frequently been attacked by the *Tribuna,* but the campaign of its editor had produced enough proof to make it politically unwise to ignore Lacerda's charges. Several foreign office bureaucrats were dismissed, and an investigation was begun. (*Time,* July 21, 1952).

Brazilian Communists have been effective in mobilizing nationalistic feelings into anti-American directions by claiming that Brazil's tremendous potential oil and rubber resources were going to be exploited by the United States. Communist-led demonstrations took place on April 21, 1952, to celebrate "The Day of Petroleum and of National Independence," devoted to attacks on "Yankee Imperialism." The Communist organ *Imprensa Popular* announced the formation of "The Center for the Study and Defense of Petroleum." Communists claimed that Brazil was being ignored while America made loans to many countries who had contributed nothing to the Allied effort in World War II. When Secretary of State Acheson visited Brazil in July, 1952, the Communists dubbed him "the foreign minister of bacteriological warfare" and claimed that he had come to take Brazil's oil and force Brazil to send troops to Korea.

CHILE

Since the formation of the Chilean Popular Front in 1936, the Communists have played a crucial role in the political life of Chile. Communists have come closer there than anywhere else in the western hemisphere (aside from Guatemala) to controlling a national government. Communist support of Gabriel Gonzalez Videla in 1946 helped him gain the presidency. He then proceeded to appoint three Communists to the cabinet. In 1952 Communist support of Carlos Ibanez helped him gain the presidency in similar circumstances.

In the years 1937 to 1946 the Communists achieved considerable political power and prestige. Carlos Contreras Labarca, architect of the party's successes, outshone his more celebrated counterpart in Brazil—Carlos Prestes. In 1947 the Chilean Communists rose to their greatest heights in polling 16% of the vote in municipal elections. By this time they had gained a position of predominance in the most strategic labor unions (copper, nitrate and coal).

The founder of the Chilean Communist party was Luis Recabarren. For years he tramped up and down the northern deserts and the central valley of Chile preaching hatred of the landlords, foreign capitalists, and the Church. He incited bloody riots and strikes which led to his banishment from the country. There is some evidence that Recabarren met Lenin while he was in Europe in 1908, at the meeting of the International Socialist Bureau in Brussels. In 1922 the Socialist Labor party of Recabarren joined the Comintern, and shortly thereafter Recabarren went to Soviet Russia to attend the Fourth World Congress of the Comintern. His party changed its name to the Communist party, and remained thenceforth in the closest possible touch with Moscow headquarters.

Except for repression during the first Ibanez regime (1927-1931) the Communists were given full and free play in Chile until 1948. Their most successful period stemmed from the united front tactic as practiced since 1935. Previous to this time the revolutionary and anti-religious attitude of the party leadership had antagonized many who otherwise might have been attracted. After 1935 the policy was one of appearing to defend Chilean nationhood from landlord and foreign capitalist oppression. The 1935 Popular Front with the Socialist and Radical parties won the Communists many friends previously unfriendly. The Communists supported the Socialist and Radical presidential candidate for the 1938 elections, Aguirre Cerda, who narrowly won against the conservative candidate. It was the first time that the Communists were partners in a victorious coalition in Chilean history. Membership in the Popular Front brought the Communists many opportunities for infiltration into societies and groups from which they had previously been isolated. Communists began to overshadow Socialists in the Chilean Worker's Confederation, and by 1941 the Communists had more than doubled their congressional representation—from six deputies in 1937 to 16 in 1941. President Aguirre vetoed a Conservative-Liberal bill which would have outlawed the Communist party.

The fruitful united front policy came to an end with the Hitler-Stalin pact, when the Communists betrayed their Russia-first convictions and shocked their Socialist and Radical allies. However the international situation after June 22, 1941, favored a return to the Popular Front, which is what happened in Chile. The Communists successfully formed a broad united bloc in support of the United Nations and against the Axis. To preserve harmony in the coalition the Communists gave up the candidacy of Gonzalez Videla in 1942 to support the Radical candidate Juan Antonio Rios, as did the Socialists. Rios was elected, and the Communists were so encouraged that they invited the Socialists to join them in a single Marxist party in 1944—an invitation which the Socialists rejected. However Communist inroads into the Socialist party were so successful that by 1946 large groups of Socialists had swung into the Communist camp, and Communist influence among the unions was predominant.

Not only did the Communists profit from divisions among the Socialists, but also from the inability of the Conservatives and Liberals to agree on a presidential candidate in 1946. With the conservative elements presenting two candidates, the Communists joined with the Radicals to support the candidacy of their old friend Videla. The Socialists nominated their own candidate, who polled only 12,000 votes.

Radical-Communist candidate Gonzalez Videla polled 192,000 votes, followed by Cruz Coke (Conservative) with 142,000, and Alessandri (Liberal) with 131,000. It was estimated that the Communists threw as many as 50,000 votes to the new president. Because Gonzalez failed to carry a majority of the votes cast, the election was referred to Congress which finally designated Gonzalez president after the Communists had threatened to "carry the defense of their victory at the polls to its extreme consequences." (*El Siglo,* Santiago, September 26, 1946). When the Communist leader Carlos Conteras Labarca was invited into Gonzalez's cabinet in 1946, he was replaced as party leader by Racardo Fonseaca.

Meantime Conteras Labarca represented Chile at the United Nations Conference at San Francisco. Other Communists in the cabinet were Victor Conteras Tapia (Minister of Public Lands and Colonization) and Miguel Concha (Minister of Agriculture). The participation of Communists in the cabinet naturally antagonized large elements of the population, which, together with increasing Soviet aggression throughout the world, forced President Gonzalez in 1947 to remove the Communists—but only when three Liberal ministers also agreed to withdraw. The President praised the Communist ministers for their "sincerity . . . patriotism and honesty." (*El Mercurio*, Santiago, April 17, 1947). For the moment the President was able to retain the support of the Communists in parliament, but the Communist leaders were maintaining that "there was another way out of the crisis." (*El Siglo*, Santiago, April 17, 1947). This threat materialized in the bloody and violent strikes in June involving Santiago bus drivers, and the even more sanguine October bloodshed among the coal miners in Lota and Coronel. By August the President, with the support of large sectors of all the other parties, began to retaliate. Communist leaders were imprisoned and their news organs suppressed. In September, 1948, Congress outlawed Communist activity under any name whatsoever.

In November, 1948, Communist and anti-administration nationalists were arrested on charges of plotting to overthrow the government. Among the nationalists was former president Ibanez, who had been exiled to Argentina, where he was welcomed by the Peronista press. A year later a riot in Santiago—largely Communist organized—resulted in further bloodshed. These, coming on top of similar violence in copper and nitrate mining towns three months previously, were indications of the length to which the Communists were willing to go against their former political allies.

In 1952 the Communists made a political comeback. After promising to support the Socialist presidential candidate Salvadore Allende, Communist leaders received instructions from Brazilian comrade Prestes on August 12th to throw their weight behind the former nationalistic dictator, General Carlos Ibanez. Ibanez campaigned on anti-Yanqui imperialism slogans, and hinted that he might lift the ban on the Communists and restore normal relations with Soviet Russia. On September 8th, 1952, Ibanez was elected president with the support of nationalist and Communist groups, primarily the former. After the election Ibanez disavowed rumors that he was going to be hostile to the United States. He did, however, say that Communists "will enjoy all the guarantees that a democratic regime offers as long as they remain within the law." (*New York Times*, September 10, 1952).

In foreign policy the Chilean Communists have long made plain that they "have the obligation of defending the Soviet Union against all attacks" (Andres Escobar, *Las Finanzas del Partido*, Santiago, 1940, p. 4). Champions of recognition of Soviet Russia in 1944, they bitterly opposed the diplomatic break of 1947. President Gonzalez had said that "the events which disturbed public tranquillity of Chile . . . were caused by the instigations of international Communism exercised through Chilean groups . . . directed by the Union of Soviet Socialist Republics." (*El Mercurio*, Santiago, October 22, 1947). It was a fact that Soviet agents Eudocio Ravines and Vittorio Codovilla, among others, visited their Chilean brethren; it was claimed that these two directed the Chilean comrades in accord with Moscow directives. (*La Nacion*, Santiago, April 30, 1948, pp. 6, 7.).

The Chilean Communists have long been the best organized and most disciplined of all Chilean political factions. As allies of President Ibanez they might prove to be again a serious factor in Chilean national life. (For an excellent discussion see S. Cole Blasier, "Chile, A Communist Battleground," *Political Science Quarterly*, vol. LXV, no. 3, pp. 353-375).

CUBA

For many years Cuba was considered to be the center of Soviet operations for Latin American Communism. The return to power of General Fulgencio Batista in early March, 1952, changed all that, however.

In its earlier stages Cuban Communism comprised principally foreigners; it was not until 1930 that some success was had in enlisting native Cubans in Stalin's cause. By the mid-'thirties the Communists rose to some prominence when they supported the presidency of General Batista. In 1938 they became a legal political party. The rise of Communist influence paralleled the rise of the General Confederation of Cuban Workers which the Communists came to control. Communist leaders posed as the only friend of the exploited sugar plantation workers against the "foreign oppressors."

In the 1944 elections, the Cuban Communists polled 120,000 votes (six percent of the total), a gain of 39,000 over the 1940 tally. Three Communist senators and six representatives were sent to the new Congress to represent Soviet policy. One observer, commenting on the election, pointed out that it was not the numerical strength of the Communists that mattered, but rather "it is the extraordinary ability to utilize a minority position to infiltrate; to occupy key positions and create the appearance of power even though that power is merely that of a minority exceptionally well-organized against a majority which has devoted itself primarily to bewailing its tragedy and deploring the rise of Communism." (Richard Pattee, "Communism in Cuba," *Catholic World*, December, 1946).

Cuban Communists followed the example of their American brethren in 1944 and changed their name—to the Popular Socialist party. The hammer and sickle emblem was abandoned in favor of the machete, and the party membership was gradually increased to 120,000. Although the Communists supported Batista against Grau San Martin in the 1944 presidential elections, they curried favor with San Martin when he was elected, with a huge pro-San Martin rally in Havana on July 4, 1944. Communist influence remained important under Grau's regime, and until 1952, under the leadership of such men as Julio Blas Roca, Juan Martinello, Lazaro Pena, and Fabio Grobart.

Soviet policy for Cuba was most effective after diplomatic relations were established in 1942. A huge Soviet Legation moved into a luxuriously furnished estate in the exclusive Vedado section of Havana. It was believed that the Legation was the central clearing house for propaganda throughout the Caribbean area and into other parts of Latin America, for Cuban Communists were often sent on "tours" of other countries to carry out Soviet propaganda missions. In addition to the Legation, two other vehicles of Soviet policy were the newspaper *Hoy*, with a circulation of about 25,000, and the $100,000 modern radio station *Mil Diez*. Until its suppression in 1950, *Hoy* was the only Havana paper with a special edition reaching the provinces on the same day of publication. The Communists also published *Cuba and the U.S.S.R.*, a counterpart of the American *Soviet Russia Today*. The radio station probably reached more Cubans than all other Soviet media. Until it was silenced in 1950 it presented Soviet-slanted "news," Marxian "education" programs, Russian language programs, and attempted to accustom Cubans to celebrate Soviet national holidays. The party also maintained an indoctrination school for the workers and their children, a theatre for Soviet films and other entertainment, and a Cuban-Soviet Institute of Cultural Interchange. Chief source of financial support was union dues and revenue from Communist publications, insurance companies, bookshops, and the radio station.

The Soviet star in Cuba began its decline in 1947 when Grau San Martin's Labor Minister maneuvered the Communists out of the labor confederation; the Communist radio and publications were subsequently closed. In August, 1950, the government of President Socarras launched an all-out anti-Communist campaign, and closed down the newspaper *Hoy*. The Soviet aggression in Korea served to accentuate the Communist decline in the country.

At the beginning of March, 1952, the old Cuban politician Fulgencio Batista staged a coup d'etat and returned in triumph to power. He immediately made it clear that the official anti-Communist program was to continue, and even be intensified. When two Soviet couriers attempted to land in Havana from Mexico, on March 31, 1952, Batista told them to go back to Mexico. On April 3rd the Soviet Government broke off diplomatic relations with Cuba.

It appeared that the era of Soviet influence in Cuba was over with, at least for the time being. Furthermore, Batista was known to be most hostile to the Communist-dominated regime in Guatemala, and friendly to its most vigorous opponents. (See article by H. Hart Phillips in *New York Times*, April 6, 1952, p. 22).

OTHER LATIN AMERICAN COUNTRIES

Of the remaining Latin American Countries, Communism seemed to be most influential, in 1952, in Bolivia. The revolutionary government of President Victor Paz Estensorro included three Communist cabinet members—Juan Lechin, German Butron, and Walter Guevara Arce.

Estensorro is leader of the National Revolutionary party (MNR), and was finance minister in the regime of Colonel Gualberto Villarroel in 1946 when it was overthrown and Villarroel was hanged from a lamp post. Estensorro fled to Argentina, where he received asylum for six years. Early in April, 1952, a bloody revolt instigated by the MNR overthrew the existing regime, and Estensorro returned in triumph with the blessing of Peron. The revolt was in part inspired by trade unionists led by the Communist Juan Lechin, who urged an anti-American program, as well as nationalization of the Bolivian tin industry. Communist aid to Estensorro was rewarded by three cabinet posts for the Communists. Observers pointed out that should Bolivian tin be denied the United States by a Communist-influenced Bolivian government, it would leave only Communist-threatened Malaya and Indonesia as sources of tin. (Letter to *New York Times* by Arturo Cano, dated May 15, 1952).

Juan Lechin, Minister for Mines and Petroleum announced on May 2nd, 1952: "Iran has given us an example that when the workers mass in defense of their interests, there is no power human or divine that can resist them." His Communist-controlled publication *Rebellion* stated on the same day: "We, with all the workers of the world, will continue the revolutionary struggle until final victory." The paper also attacked "a band of FBI spies which functions under the direction of the American Embassy." Lechin's extremist measures and his power in the labor unions appeared to be one of the dominant forces in the new government. (*New York Times*, May 3, 1952, by Edward A. Morrow). On the other hand vice-president Hernan Siles Zuazo declared that Lechin's Communist faction would not dominate the government, which, he said, would seek "only to maintain our own national and international independence—independence from Moscow, Buenos Aires, and Washington."

Communism in Venezuela, Colombia, and Argentina has not been important. Communists did take part in the 1948 anti-American violence in Colombia, but seem to have lost influence since that time. But in these countries, as well as in other Latin American states, there did seem to be a tendency after 1950 for Communist groups to ally themselves with Peronista-minded nationalists in the common anti-Yankee imperialism line.

CANADA

Communist strength manifested itself most dramatically in Canada at the end of World War II when the Soviet espionage ring of Soviet Minister Zabotin was exposed. This involved the scientist Nunn-May (released from jail in Britain in 1952), and the two Canadian Communist leaders Sam Rose and Fred Carr. Soviet cipher clerk Gouzenko tipped off Canadian officials and asked for asylum. The subsequent revelations shook the usually complacent Canadians into a realization that the Soviet operation was effective and dangerous even in their country.

In August, 1951, it was revealed that Communist-controlled unions in Canada had a strong hold on strategic mining and electrical manufacturing companies engaged in vital defense work. These unions were expelled from the CIO in 1950 for being Communist-dominated; they are the Mine, Mill and Smelter Workers Union, and the United Electrical, Radio, and Machine Worker's Union, both of which subsequently obtained contracts in Canada with companies engaged in radar manufacturing and atomic research. The head of one of Canada's largest unions, the Labor Congress of Canada, was charged by both the CIO and the AFL with being over-tolerant of Communists in his midst. This man was Percy Bengough, leader of 450,000 unionists in Canada. (See article by Louis Stark, New York Times, August 13, 1951).

One of the persons most prominent in exposing the Soviet espionage ring in 1946 was Royal Canadian Mounted Police Superintendent John Leopold, who had once spent seven years as an undercover agent in the Canadian Communist (Labor) party. In the fall of 1952 he attacked those who displayed apathy and ignorance of the Communist problem in Canada, and said: "You can't gauge a potential fifth column in terms of numerical strength. The Communists have stripped away their dead wood and are more dangerous now than ever."

18

Communism in the United States

The Soviet Union considers the United States its greatest enemy. To the forces of international Communism, the United States is the citadel of capitalism and imperialism, and as such, it presents the foremost obstacle to the establishment of Soviet power throughout the globe. The goal of Soviet policy, which is the establishment of a world U.S.-S.R., cannot be achieved until the United States is transformed through war or revolution into a Soviet Republic.

Ever since the United States replaced Great Britain as the leading world power, Soviet policy-makers have made long-range plans to weaken America diplomatically and from within. Both Stalin and Malenkov, in their speeches to the 19th Congress of the Russian Communist party in October, 1952, made it clear that until the United States and other leading "imperialist" states are destroyed, there can be no peace (*New York Times,* October 4, 1952). In spite of occasional and soothing Soviet statements preaching policies of peaceful coexistence, Soviet policy towards America remains in fact one of unrelenting hostility—a hostility readily apparent to students of the Soviet *Mein Kampf.* The mainstream of Stalin's writings and those of his colleagues and predecessor is rich with language making it abundantly clear that in the long run it will be a Soviet world or a world without the Soviets.

Naturally, during periods such as occurred between June 22, 1941, and the end of World War II, Soviet tactics dictate temporary rapprochement with any available ally. When the Soviet base of operations itself is threatened, every effort must be made to secure and safeguard that base without which world revolution would be impossible. Thus, Soviet tactics dictated Communist support of American aid to China against Japan in order to prevent the latter from becoming a threat to Soviet penetration into the Far East, but the termination of such aid was insisted upon when Japan was defeated. The same tactics urged support of Tito from 1943 to 1948, and the reverse thereafter; use of the atomic bomb in 1945, but not after 1950; American intervention in Europe between 1942 and 1945 but not after that date, and so on.

Communism has promoted hostility toward the United States not only in industrially advanced countries like Britain, Germany, France, and Japan, but also in backward and colonial or semi-colonial areas—

as in Asia, the Middle East, and Latin America. Beyond this, Moscow has directed American Communism to disrupt the American economy and divide Americans against their fellow citizens: Protestants and Catholics against Jews, Protestants against Catholics, whites against Negroes, labor against management, etc. The "Hate America" campaign, which so distressed American Ambassador George Kennan in 1952 has become a characteristic of the Soviet and Communist press. For misguided Americans who have insisted upon "getting along" with Russia through diplomatic concessions and offers of economic aid, it has been particularly distressing that the Soviet leadership has shown no propensity to reciprocate. Whereas it took many Americans a considerable time to get over the 1941-1945 "honeymoon" period with Soviet Russia, it took Soviet policy-makers no time at all to resume their long-range attack on the United States. It was not until the Soviet coup in Czechoslovakia in 1948, the war in Greece, the Berlin blockade, and finally the Korean war, that an overwhelming majority of the American people finally realized that no matter how peaceful their intentions might be towards international Communism, peace was unattainable as long as Soviet Russia persisted in carrying out its *Mein Kampf* through wars and revolutions. Indeed it became increasingly clear that peaceful coexistence was impossible between Soviet Russia and the United States and that only the establishment of a new Russian regime could lead to long-range peace; this through no choice of the United States, but due to the inexorable dialectics of Soviet Communism.

Soviet policy towards the United States operates on the diplomatic and psychological warfare level in Washington, at the United Nations, and in the capitals of the world. It operates on a "cold-war" basis when French Communists dump American military supplies into the water at Bordeaux and Oran, when east German police kidnap Americans in Berlin, when violence breaks out in Colombia during the visit of the American Defense Secretary, etc. Finally, Soviet policy operates ultimately on the direct military level, as when Soviet fighter planes shoot down unarmed American transports or when the Soviet leadership directs satellite armies in Korea and Indo-China against western and anti-Communist forces at little loss to the Soviet Union.

The efforts of international Communism within the United States have aimed at infiltrating into government, education, industry, and the mass media—radio, publishing, and television. Communist "front" organizations have been formed to influence public policy along lines favorable to Soviet Communism. Most important, perhaps, have been the activities of Soviet agents working with American Communists and fellow-travelers to direct American foreign policy into a pro-Communist orientation or at least one not opposed to concrete Soviet goals. These activities have included theft of atomic secrets, sabotage, and espionage. The most notorious cases of Communist activity have involved *Amerasia* magazine, the Institute of Pacific Relations, infiltration into the UN, the Hiss affair, and the leading American Communist leaders prosecuted under the Smith and McCarran Acts.

Prior to examining certain of these cases, an understanding of the Communist party in the United States and its legal status is necessary.

THE COMMUNIST PARTY, U.S.A.

In seeking to compel the Communist Party of the United States to register with the Department of Justice in accordance with the Internal Security Act of 1950 (commonly known as the McCarran Act), the Attorney General submitted to the Subversive Activities Control Board on November 22, 1950, a petition worth citing at length here because it makes crystal clear that American Communists—like Communists the world over—are operating solely as tools of Soviet policy:

"The Attorney General respectfully represents to the Subversive Activities Control Board that the Communist party of the United States of America was required under Section 7 (A), (C), and (D) of the Internal Security Act of 1950 to register and file a registration statement with the Attorney General on or before October 23, 1950, as a Communist-action organization and it failed to do so and continues to fail to do so. Pursuant to Section 13 (A) of the Act, therefore, the Attorney General petitions this Board for an order, after appropriate proceedings, directing the Communist party of the United States of America to register with the Attorney General as a Communist-action organization in the manner required by the Act, and directing further that if the organization fails to comply with the board's order, each section, branch, fraction, or cell of the organization shall register as a Communist-action organization. . . . The Attorney General alleges the following facts, based on information and belief relating to the character of the Communist party of the United States as measured by the standards specified in the Act:

"Commencing in or about 1919, and continuing to the date of the filing of this petition, except for the period of the Communist Political Association from May, 1944 to July, 1945, there has existed in the United States an organization known from time to time by various names, which is now known as the Communist party of the United States of America. . . . This organization has been composed of large numbers of members and affiliates who function through state, county, city, and other units, which are subject to the supervision and control of the Communist party. . . . the Communist party has been and is substantially controlled by the Government and Communist party of the Soviet Union, and by the foreign organization being known at various times as the Communist International (Comintern) and the Communist Information Bureau (Cominform).

"Throughout its existence the Communist party has operated and continues to operate primarily to advance the objectives of the world Communist movement. The organization always has been a participant in the world Communist movement, which has its home base in the Soviet Union.

"The policies of the organization have been formulated and carried out and its activities have been performed pursuant to the "correct" Marxist-Leninist position as set forth in directives, interpretations, publications, and other communications issued by Stalin, the Communist party of the Soviet Union, the Communist International, the Communist movement, all for the purpose of effectuating the policies of the Government of the Soviet Union and the organization of the world Communist movement.

"In 1921 the Communist party, which had become a member of the Communist International, agreed to be bound by the twenty-one conditions for membership in the Communist International. Among the conditions which the organization accepted was the principle that all resolutions of the Communist International and its executive committee were binding on the Communist party. The Communist International has maintained its representatives in the United States for the purpose of directing and supervising the activities and the conduct of the leaders of that organization. The representatives of the Communist International have been empowered to serve on the organization's committees, to preside at meetings of the Communist party and to cast the deciding vote.

"The young Communists in the United States functioned through an organization known as the Young Communist League, the youth organization of the Communist party. The Young Communist League was a section of the Young Communist International . . . directed and controlled by the Communist International.

"In or about 1929, there developed a serious factional dispute within the Communist party. The controversy was submitted to a committee of the Communist International at Moscow for resolution and was finally settled by Stalin's direction to the American Communist leaders who appeared before him that the minority faction had the approval of himself and the Communist International and would henceforth control the organization. As a result, the leaders of the majority faction were expelled from the organization.

"Since September, 1928, the Communist party has been guided to the 'correct' Marxist-Leninist position by the Program of the Communist International which was adopted at the Sixth Congress of the Communist International held on September 1, 1928, in Moscow, and which was published in the United States by Worker's Library Publishers, an organ of the Communist party. The Communist party officially adopted and subscribed to that program and continues to adhere to it. Similarly in 1939, the Communist party, together with the Communist parties of other countries, was supplied with the most recent Marxist-Leninist manual, the *History of the Communist party of the Soviet Union*, which was prepared for use as a guide to action with the active participation of Stalin and was authorized by the Central Committee of the Communist party of the Soviet Union. This manual and other similar publications of the organization have been published in the United States by International Publishers, an organ of the Communist party. Other Marxist-Leninist publications which the organization has used and continues to use as guides to action include *Foundations of Leninism* by Stalin; *State and Revolution* and *Imperialism,* by Lenin; *The Communist Manifesto* by Marx and Engels; *Problems of Leninism* by Stalin; *The Communist,* and its successor, *Political Affairs;* the *Daily Worker* and the *Worker;* and such compilations of Marxist-Leninist writings as *Strategy and Tactics, Theory of the Proletarian Revolution,* and *Dictatorship of the Proletariat.*

"In November, 1940, the Communist party voted to disaffiliate the Communist International for the avowed purpose of removing itself from the terms of the so-called Voorhis Act, but in fact the organization continued to uphold the principles of the Communist International, and the Communist International continued its direction and supervision over the organization through its resident representatives in the United States. In 1943, when the Government of the Soviet Union was militarily allied with the Government of the United States and other capitalist democracies in the conduct of World War II, the Communist International was formally dissolved. Shortly thereafter, in the spring of 1944, the Communist Party similarly dissolved itself and the leaders of the Communist party created a Communist Political Association.

"With the end of hostilities in Europe in 1945, the Communist party was instructed by the leaders of the world Communist movement, including Jacques Duclos, a leader of the French Communist party and former member of the executive committee of the Communist International, and Dmitri Manuilsky, a leader of the Communist party of the

Soviet Union and former general secretary of the Communist International, to reestablish itself in the United States for the purpose of again carrying forward the program and activities to which it had adhered from 1919 to 1944. In July, 1945, the Communist party was reconstituted in accordance with the directions which it had received.

"In 1947 the Communist Information Bureau was established as the organization for the world Communist movement and as a successor to the Communist International. Because of the terms of the Voorhis Act and the Foreign Agents Registration Act, the Communist party found it inexpedient to become a formal member of the Communist Information Bureau, but it has affiliated with that organization of the world Communist movement, and it has conformed its policies and activities to the policies and activities of the Communist Information Bureau.

"Throughout its existence the Communist party has never knowingly deviated from the views and policies of the Government and Communist party of the Soviet Union, the Communist International, the Communist Information Bureau, and other leaders of the world Communist movement. Whenever such views and policies have conflicted with the position taken by the Government of the United States, the Communist party has opposed the position of the United States.

"Except when the United States and the Soviet Union were potential or actual military allies, the Communist party has consistently expressed the view that the United States is an imperialistic power bent on instigating wars for world domination, and that the Soviet Union and other Communist nations are the only true democracies which seek to preserve peace."

That the vacillating views of American Communists have slavishly followed the zig-zags of Soviet policy was made plain by the Attorney General:

"The Communist party advocated opposition to the League of Nations while the Soviet Union opposed such organization, and when the Soviet Union reversed its position the Communist party supported the League of Nations.

"The Communist party endorsed and justified the trial and execution of a large number of prominent Russian military and political leaders by the Soviet Union in the 'purge' of 1937.

"The Communist party supported and justified the position of the Soviet Union in the Russo-Finnish war in 1939. It supported and justified the territorial expansion of the Soviet Union through the conquest of Polish territory in 1939, and the absorption of Latvia, Estonia, and Lithuania in 1940.

"Commencing in or about 1935, the Communist party softened its previous attacks against democratic capitalism to advocate a program of united front action to combat fascism and nazism in accordance with the changed policy of the Communist International.

"When on August 23, 1939, the Hitler-Stalin pact was consummated, the Communist party overlooked its opposition to fascism and nazism and supported the Hitler-Stalin pact. During the period from the signing of the Hitler-Stalin pact to June 21, 1941, the Communist party characterized the war between western European states and Germany and Italy as an 'unjust' imperialist war which Communists could not support and affirmatively sought to prevent American aid from being given to the western European nations.

"Coincident with the German attack on the Soviet Union on June 22, 1941, the Communist party abruptly reversed its position by characterizing the war as a 'just' war against fascism requiring the support of all Communists and demanded that the United States give full assistance to the nations opposing Nazi Germany and Italy. Once the Soviet Union was engaged in the war, the Communist party abandoned its attacks on the Government and institutions of the United States and its traditional disruptive tactics in favor of a policy of cooperation with all forces directly or indirectly aiding the Soviet Union in its war effort. In accordance with this policy, the Communist party expressed its approval of the dissolution of the Communist International in 1943, and the Communist party itself was dissolved in May, 1944.

"With the termination of hostilities in Europe in 1945, the Communist party, in accordance with the instructions from the leaders of the World Communist movement, was reconstituted in July, 1945, for the purpose of returning to the views, policies and activities which it had followed prior to May, 1944.

"In 1946 the Communist party supported the demands of the Soviet Union upon Turkey for revision of the Montreux Convention so as to give the Soviet Union a voice in the control of the Dardenelles.

"In the period following the termination of hostilities in World War II the Communist party consistently supported the policies and tactics of the Soviet Union, the world Communist movement and the Communist parties in Bulgaria, Rumania, Hungary, Albania, and Poland in their efforts to obtain control of the governments of these countries and, since the success of such efforts, the Communist party has vigorously supported the conduct and policies of those Communist Governments. The Communist party supported and justified the Communist destruction of the democratic Government of Czechoslovakia and has continued to support the Communist Government which replaced the Czech-oslovakian democracy.

"The Communist party supported the coalition of the Chinese Communists with the Nationalist Government of China during World War II and thereafter supported the Chinese Communists in their violent revolution against the legal Government of China. (It) supported the violent revolutionary efforts of the Communist guerrillas in Greece and similarly supported . . . efforts of the Communists in Indo-China, Burma, and the Phillipines. (It) supported the Communist efforts to prevent the successful establishment and maintenance of the Government of Western Germany and supported the Soviet blockade of Berlin in 1948.

"Since the end of World War II the Communist party has opposed those facets of American foreign policy which it regards as inimical to the interests of the Soviet Union and the world Communist movement such as the Truman Doctrine, the Marshall Plan and the resultant program of the Economic Cooperation Administration, the North Atlantic Pact, the Military Assistance Program for the Atlantic Pact nations. It has supported and justified the stifling of internal opposition to the various Cominform Governments through repressive measures against religious and political leaders such as Cardinal Mindszenty and Nicola Petkov, and through widespread programs of religious oppression.

"The Communist party supported the Communist Government of Yugoslavia when that Government collaborated with the Soviet Union and the Cominform, and it has opposed and condemned the Yugoslavian Government since its defection from the Soviet Union and the Cominform. (It) opposed and condemned the position taken by the United States in its opposition to the Communists in the Italian elections of 1948 and charged American policy in Italy with leading to the attempted assassination of Togliatti, the Italian Communist leader.

"From the time the scheme was first launched by the Communist Information Bureau, the Communist party has rendered unqualified support to the "peace" campaign of the World Partisans of Peace and its Stockholm Peace Petition.

"It has consistently supported the Communist Government of North Korea both before and after that Government's violent invasion of the Republic of Korea, and has opposed the United States and the United Nations in defending the Republic of Korea; and it now supports the intervention of the Chinese Communists in the Korean conflict."

The Justice Department highlighted the nature of the relationship between the American Communist party and the Soviet Government in these words:

"The Communist party now receives and from time to time in the past has received financial aid, from or at the direction of the Government and Communist party of the Soviet Union, the Communist International and the Communist Information Bureau. Communist party publications, in effect, have been subsidized by receiving pre-paid cable information from Communist sources; the Communist party has received quantities of propaganda materials without cost for sale at a profit.

"Communist party members attending Communist training schools in the Soviet Union have received transportation and living expenses for attending such schools. Such members traveling in the Soviet Union and other Communist nations for the purpose of orientation, attending Communist meetings or observing the operation of Communist governments have received transportation expenses and salaries while engaged on such missions.

"The Communist party regularly reports and has reported to the Government and Communist party of the Soviet Union, and to the Communist International and the Communist Information Bureau, and has sent members and representatives to the Soviet Union and other foreign countries for instructions and training in the principles, policies, strategy and tactics of the world Communist movement. Representatives of the Communist party reported its programs and internal activities to the Communist International through its world congresses held in Moscow and through its executive committee and Presidium, on both of which American Communists served, and reviewed instructions in the principles, policies, strategy and tactics of the world Communist movement. Until travel abroad was rendered impossible by World War II, the Communist party sent members and representatives to the Soviet Union from time to time to report the activities of the Communist party and to transmit to the Communist party instructions in the principles, policies, strategy and tactics of the world Communist movement. It further reported its program and activities to the Soviet Government, the Communist party of the Soviet Union and to the Communist International through representatives of the Communist International within the United States. Until travel abroad was rendered impossible by World War II, the Communist party sent members and representatives to the Lenin Institute and other schools and classes held in the Soviet Union, and to Spain during the Spanish Civil War for instruction and training in the principles, policies, strategy and tactics of the world Communist movement.

"After the Communist International was dissolved in 1943, the Communist party continued to report its policies and activities to the lead-

ers of the world Communist movement. Thus, the contents of a vital
document on the organization's affairs, which was suppressed by it in
the United States, were transmitted abroad during the war by means
unknown and were made known to Jacques Duclos, general secretary
of the Communist party of France and former member of the Executive
Committee of the International. The Communist party continues to report to the Government and Communist party of the Soviet Union and
the Communist Information Bureau by publishing in Communist party
publications important statements, convention reports and speeches.
Such matters are subsequently commented upon by such publications
as the Soviet Union's *Pravda* and the Cominform's *For A Lasting
Peace, A People's Democracy* which indicate when corrections of policy
are necessary.

"From the inception of the organization to the date of the filing of
this petition, the principal leaders of the Communist party have been
and are subject to and recognize the disciplinary power of the Soviet
Government, the Communist Information Bureau and other spokesmen
of the world Communist movement.

"This power has been exercised principally through the Communist
doctrine of 'democratic centralism' which binds all Communists to ex-
ecute the decisions of the leaders of the world Communist movement.
When leaders of the organization have failed to obey the decisions of
Stalin, the Communist International and other spokesmen for the world
Communist movement, they have been expelled or otherwise censured.

"It was in recognition of the disciplinary power exercised by the
Government and Communist party of the Soviet Union and the Communist International that leaders of the Communist party were assigned by the Communist International as its representatives in such places
as China, Germany, Latin America, India and Great Britain.

"For the purpose of expediting and promoting its objectives and con-
cealing its foreign direction, domination and control, the Communist
party from its inception has adopted a multitude of clandestine practices. While the degree of secrecy has varied from time to time, there
has been strict adherence to the practice of secrecy during the period
from July, 1945, to the time of filing of this petition.

"The means by which the organization has sought to cloak itself in
secrecy includes the following:

"The practice of having both open and concealed members; the
policy of refusing to disclose to courts and other Governmental agencies
having a right to such information the facts concerning the membership
and operations of the organization; the practice during periods of strict
secrecy of destroying or secreting existing records and of not keeping

membership records and of not issuing membership cards; the use of protective language in the organization's constitution to mask the organization's real objectives; and the use of words in the organization's terminology which have one meaning to the uninitiated and completely different meaning to members of the organization; the practice of identifying members by party names, numbers and symbols; the use of code words, couriers, confidential mailing addresses and other similar devices; the practice of resorting to false swearing where deemed expedient; the practice of having secret meetings limited to trusted members; the reduction of the size of important committees so as to limit the number of persons who have access to vital information; the division of the membership into groups of no more than five so as to protect the identity of other members of the organization; the practice of assembling materials and devising plans for the underground operation of the organization; and the practice of instructing members who are not openly known as such to refuse to disclose their membership in the organization and of instructing all members of the organization to refuse to disclose the identity of other members of the organization.

"From 1919 to the date of the filing of this petition, the leaders of the Communist party and a substantial number of its members have considered the allegiance they owe the United States as being subordinate to their loyalty and obligations to the Government of the Soviet Union. The Government of the Soviet Union has been and is regarded as the only fatherland of the world Communist movement, which all Communists are obliged to support and defend under all circumstances.

"The Red Flag has been and is recognized as the flag to which Communists owe primary allegiance. In the exent of a war between the Soviet Union and any other nation, it is the recognized duty of all American Communists to support and defend the Soviet Union. In the event of war between the Soviet Union and the United States, the Communists in the United States have obliged themselves to act to defeat the military efforts of the United States and to aid and support the Soviet Union. The Communist party teaches its members that in such event they must act to foment a civil war in the United States as a means for impairing the nation's military effort and for establishing a Soviet America having a dictatorship of the proletariat such as exists in the Soviet Union.

"At the Seventh World Congress of the Communist International, the delegates from the Communist party, including some of the present leaders of the organization, took an oath to 'Comrade Stalin, Our Leader,' pledging their complete support and assuring him that they would be faithful to the end.

"To the leaders and members of the Communist party, patriotism means solidarity with and support of the Soviet Union." (*New York Times,* November 23, 1950).

In October, 1949, about a year before the Justice Department took the above position, the eleven top leaders of the Communist party were convicted of violating the Alien Registration Act (popularly known as the Smith Act) after the longest trial in American criminal history. The relevant parts of the statute under which the indictments were drawn were as follows: "It shall be unlawful for any person to knowingly or willfully advocate . . . or . . . teach the duty, (or) necessity, . . . of over-throwing or destroying any government in the United States by force or violence. . . . to organize . . . any society, group, or assembly of persons who teach, (or) advocate, . . . the overthrow or destruction of any government in the United States by force and violence." The indict-ment stated that the leaders in question—William Z. Foster, Eugene Dennis (alias Francis X. Waldron), John B. Williamson, Jacob Stachel, Robert G. Thompson, Benjamin J. Davis Jr., Henry Winston, John Gates (alias Israel Regenstreif), Irving Potash, Gilbert Green, Carl Winter, and Gus Hall (alias Arno Gust Halberg) "unlawfully will-fully, and knowingly, did conspire with each other and with divers other persons . . . to organize as the Communist party of the United States of America a society, group and assembly of persons who teach and advocate the overthrow and destruction of the United States by force and violence." The beginning of the conspiracy was placed at June 2, 1945, when the wartime Communist Political Association re-organized as the Communist party, "a society, group, and assembly of persons dedicated to the Marxist-Leninist principles of the overthrow and destruction of the Government of the United States by force and violence." Subsequent Communist top-level meetings on June 18, 1945 and July 26th were also listed as part of the conspiracy, as were the formation of Communist clubs, district and state units, recruitment organizations, publications, and study classes—all of which advocated principles of Marxism-Leninism calling for the necessity of overthrow-ing and destroying the United States by force and violence. (For text of Judge Medina's charge to the jury see *New York Times,* October 14, 1949).

Evidence against the Communist leaders came from their writings and those of Stalin and other foreign Communists, from testimony given by former Communists, from FBI men who served as Commu-nists, and from the many inconsistencies and contradictions made by the Communist leaders themselves when they testified in their own be-half. The jury (and the Supreme Court later on) agreed that these men were not only teaching the doctrine of war and revolution, but actually preparing to utilize such doctrines against the United States.

Although the Communist party today officially numbers but 30,000 members, it continues to lead several hundred thousand secret members and countless gullibles by making great outcries about "peace," the Korean war, and the "threat" of West Germany. The *New York Times* recently reported that Communists retain "important strongholds on the west coast waterfront, in the vital radar and electronics industry, in the copper, lead, and zinc mines and smelters, and in communications." The party therefore remains important and dangerous as the vanguard of large numbers of dupes, sympathizers, and peace-at-any-price elements. (*New York Times,* January 25, 1953).

Communist effectiveness should also be measured in terms of the activities of Soviet agents and their American counterparts in the United States. Sober review of these activities should give pause for thought as to whether or not the battle here at home is won.

The Amerasia Case

Nathaniel Weyl calls the *Amerasia* case "one of the gravest breaches of security in the wartime history of the United States." Certain American officials funneled hundreds of classified reports including top-secret papers to *Amerasia,* a Communist-controlled magazine seeking to influence American policies affecting the Far East area. Apparently due to the political climate prevailing in 1945, however, prosecution of this case by the Justice Department was lacking in vigor; four of those arrested in this connection were never indicted and the remaining two escaped with trivial fines.

Amerasia magazine succeeded the blatantly Communist *China Today* in early 1937, but the latter's editors—Frederick Vanderbilt Field, Philip J. Jaffe and Ch'ao-ting Chi—remained to direct *Amerasia.* Owen Lattimore, another *Amerasia* editor, exercised considerable influence there as well as in organs of the Institute of Pacific Relations (which he also edited), disseminating his views on Asia via the U. S. Government, the universities, and Asian experts and scholars. Housed in adjoining buildings in New York, *Amerasia* and the IPR were linked by interlocking executive personnel. Entire *Amerasia* articles were wired to Moscow by *Tass,* the Soviet news agency, prior to publication. The Chinese Communists were pictured as agrarian democrats desirous of freeing China from "imperialist" designs. As World War II engulfed Asia, important American policy-makers in Washington used *Amerasia* and the publications of the Institute of Pacific Relations as basic guides.

Early in 1945 officials of the U. S. Office of Strategic Services discovered that secret information was finding its way into the editorial
offices of *Amerasia*. On March 11th OSS Security Officer Frank Bielaski
led a raid on the *Amerasia* premises and discovered many hundreds of
government documents, most of them marked "secret" or "top-secret."
Included were detailed military plans for the bombing of Japan which,
if turned over to the Soviet Government by *Amerasia's* Communist editors, would have been of considerable value (Russia was still tied to
Japan by treaty obligations). Several days later the FBI seized 1700
government documents in the possession of *Amerasia's* editorial staff.
At about the same time editor Philip Jaffe was seen by the FBI to enter
the Soviet consulate in New York and meet with both Earl Browder
and the Chinese Communist representative to the San Francisco UN
conference.

FBI surveillance uncovered two government sources of the classified
documents—Emmanuel Larsen of the State Department, and Lieu-
tenant Andrew Roth of Naval Intelligence (and formerly of *Amerasia*).
Also implicated were Kate Mitchell, an editor of *Amerasia*, Mark Gayn,
a Soviet-educated free lance writer, and, most important of all, John
Stewart Service, career diplomat. Editor Jaffe also received informa-
tion on China policy from President Roosevelt via the writer Edgar
Snow—information not even known to Acting Secretary of State
Joseph Grew. (See Nathaniel Weyl, *The Battle Against Disloyalty*,
Crowell, 1951, p. 230).

After observing Service meet Jaffe several times in Washington hotels
and pass on to him government documents, the FBI arrested Jaffe,
Gayn, Mitchell, Larsen, Roth, and Service, on charges of espionage.
However, the prosecution was half-hearted and lacking in vigor. The
Justice Department claimed that some of the evidence had been ob-
tained by questionable methods. The result was that only Jaffe and
Larsen were punished—by fines of $2500 and $500 respectively.

It was not until the evidence of the Senate Internal Security Com-
mittee began to reach the public in 1951 that further action was taken.
This, in conjunction with revealing information on the case contributed
by Frederick Woltman and the magazine *Plain Talk*, led the Loyalty
Review Board to term Service a "doubtful security risk"; Larsen and
Roth had meantime left government employment and *Amerasia* folded.

The Institute of Pacific Relations

On July 2, 1952, the Senate Internal Security Subcommittee reported
its findings on the Institute of Pacific Relations and its relation to sub-

version and internal security. This followed an eighteen month study of IPR files and testimony from sixty-six witnesses.

Established in 1925 to disseminate information about the Pacific area, the IPR had branches not only in the United States, but in France, Britain, Russia, Japan, China, and other countries. Most of the Institute's financial support came from America especially from such persons as the wealthy Communist Frederick V. Field. For many years the IPR and its publications held virtually a monopoly in the field of Far East information. Government agencies, universities, and writers relied on the IPR for practically all their information on the islands and countries of the Pacific.

The Senate subcommittee concluded that the IPR was "considered by the American Communist party and by Soviet officials as an instrument of Communist policy, propaganda, and military intelligence;" that Owen Lattimore was "a conscious, articulate instrument of the Soviet conspiracy"; that over a period of years "John Carter Vincent was the principal fulcrum of IPR pressures in the State Department;" and that the IPR "possessed close organic relationships with the State Department through interchange of personnel, attendance of State Department officials at IPR conferences, constant exchange of information, and social contacts."

In the summer of 1941 two of the three most effective leaders of IPR entered new fields. Frederick V. Field became the head of the Communist-directed American Peace Mobilization and Owen Lattimore was appointed FDR's personal emissary to Chiang Kai-shek. Phillip Jessup and Edward C. Carter remained to run the IPR. On June 18, 1941, while the Hitler-Stalin pact was still in effect, Lattimore and Carter lunched in Washington with Soviet Ambassador Oumansky after Lattimore learned through Presidential Advisor Lauchlin Currie (his close friend) that he had been appointed to the Chungking post. From that time onwards, efforts were made in the Far East to dissuade Japan from adventures against Russia and to encourage an adamant American stand behind China, leaving Japan with the opportunity to attack southwards—ultimately against the United States. Closely connected with these efforts was the Soviet spy ring of Richard Sorge and his Japanese IPR associates Hotsumi Ozaki and Kinkazu Saionji. Involved in the latter ring also were Agnes Smedley and Gunther Stein (the IPR correspondent in Chungking). In Washington, not only did Currie oppose any agreement with Japan, but Harry Dexter White, Under-Secretary of the Treasury, used his influence to oppose the efforts of Ambassador Grew to keep the peace. Currie and White were later named by

Elizabeth Bentley and Whittaker Chambers as members of a Soviet espionage ring in Washington. After Pearl Harbor, Lattimore returned to Washington where he used Currie's office in the State Department Building and took care of Currie's highly sensitive and important mail. In October, 1942, he arranged a meeting between Under-Secretary of State Sumner Welles and Communist leader Earl Browder, resulting in a communique implying equality between the Chinese Government and the Communist rebels.

In December, 1942, the IPR arranged a conference at Mont Tremblant, Canada, which was jointly organized with the State Department. Those in charge were Currie, Alger Hiss, Joseph Barnes, Phillip Jessup and Edward Carter. During the following year, IPR writers and propagandists did much to influence American thinking and policy. These included Maxwell S. Stewart, Lawrence K. Rosinger, and T. A. Bisson. Their writings were widely circulated in governmental quarters with the aid of Professor John K. Fairbank, John Carter Vincent, and others. Rosinger, identified as a Communist by three witnesses, refused to say whether or not he was a Communist; his book *The State of Asia* was published in 1950 under IPR auspices. Bisson had been a close friend and associate of Jaffe and Lattimore in trips to Communist China, in the Communist-dominated magazines *China Today* and *Amerasia,* and in the publications of the IPR. Bisson also frequently used the pen name Frederick Spencer, which happened to be Frederick V. Field's name in the Communist party. After serving in Japan from 1945 to 1947, Bisson obtained a teaching post at the University of California with the aid of a grant from the Carnegie Foundation.

During the period 1941-1945, the IPR and its members and friends in government sought to pressure policy in behalf of the Chinese Communists through the dispatches of foreign service officers John P. Davies, Jr. and John Stewart Service, the Henry Wallace mission to China, and the Marshall mission to China. Davis and Service sent dispatch after dispatch back to Washington praising the "democratic nature" of the Chinese Communists, damning the National Government, and urging a coalition in which the Communists found a satisfactory place. On November 15, 1944, Davies wrote: "A coalition Chinese Government in which the Communists find a satisfactory place is the solution of this impasse most desirable to us." The Wallace mission to China laid the ground for treating the National Government and the Communist rebels as equals in a contest decided by the United States. Wallace insisted that Chiang Kai-shek come to terms with Stalin relative to a new power balance in Asia. His subsequent book,

Soviet Asia Mission, was largely written by Andrew Steiger, author of articles contributed to the *Daily Worker* (Wallace was at this time Vice-President of the United States).

During this period, and prior to the Marshall mission to China, the Soviet line for China began to change, with increasing emphasis on the "agrarian reformers" and the need of a coalition government in China including the Communists. This new line was reflected by articles written by Vladimir Rogoff, the Soviet agent, and T. A. Bisson. In January, 1944 Rogoff visited New York and held a secret conference with John Carter Vincent, Owen Lattimore, and others. A Washington conference with Alger Hiss and Lauchlin Currie was vetoed at the last minute by Rogoff for security reasons.

Lattimore's visit to the White House in June, 1945, together with the influence of John Carter Vincent, tended to result in a hostile American attitude toward Nationalist China and a friendly disposition toward the "agrarian democrats." In December General Marshall went to China armed with policy instructions drawn up by Vincent and Secretary of State Byrnes. At a time when Chiang's divisions were chasing Communist armies northward, General Marshall put heavy pressure on him to take Communists into the Government or suffer the consequences of curtailed American military aid. Chiang, who understood Communism far better than his American advisers (Wedemeyer and Chennault excepted), refused to comply. The result was a Marshall-inspired action cutting off the flow of military supplies to Nationalist China from the spring of 1946 to the summer of 1947. Subsequent American aid to the forces of Free China consisted partly of American equipment which had rotted on Pacific islands for years and ammunition that would not fit the bores of Nationalist rifles.

Col. L. B. Moody, U.S. ordnance expert in China, agreed with Admirals Berkey and Cooke that Nationalist armies began to lose after 1947 because of the year-long embargo, and the old story of "too little too late." All told, Chinese armies received less than one-third the amount of arms against Communism than did the Greeks and the Turks in a comparable period. (See chart in Freda Utley, *The China Story,* Regnery, p. 47). Even after the 1948 China Aid Act, shipments were delayed; when some guns finally reached Chiang's armies, they were found to be without bolts and hence useless. During this same period Soviet aid via Manchuria to the Communists continued without interruption.

By October, 1949, it was clear that the Republic of China had lost the mainland of China. In that month the State Department called a meeting of Asian "experts" (most of them influenced by the IPR) to get advice as to what to do next. The majority of these "experts," led by Lattimore and L. K. Rosinger, urged recognition of Communist China, a move ultimately blocked by the influence of Senator Vandenberg.

The results of the Senate investigation in this connection were only just beginning to be seen as the new Administration took office in January, 1953. John Carter Vincent followed the path of John Stewart Service when he was declared a doubtful security risk by the Loyalty Review Board. Lattimore was indicted on seven counts of perjury, and the spotlight of publicity was put on persons like Rosinger who refused to say whether or not they were Communists. This did not prevent Rosinger from receiving approximately $8,500 in grants from the Rockefeller Foundation between 1950 and 1951. The IPR sore continued to run as blood flowed in the hills of central Korea.

The Fuchs-Rosenberg Case

There can be little doubt that Emile Julius Klaus Fuchs was the most successful spy in history. As director of the chief atomic research center in England and one of the outstanding intellects in theoretical physics, Fuchs was one of the best informed physicists both on the atom bomb and the projected hydrogen bomb. Between 1943 and 1947 Fuchs transmitted enough information to his Soviet superiors to advance Soviet atomic development by at least twelve months. It may well be that Soviet confidence, bolstered by Fuch's atomic information, was so high in 1950 as to encourage the risk of all-out war in Korea.

Fuchs came to Britain from Germany as a known Communist and yet was assigned to atomic research. In 1944 he came to the United States and went to Los Alamos, where the atomic bomb was actually built. To make matters worse, his immediate superior was Dr. Hans Bethe, chief pioneer in the theory of the H-bomb. The key man in Fuch's spy ring was Harry Gold, a Philadelphia research chemist. As was the case with other ring members, none knew Fuch's real name and he did not know theirs. Gold received his assignments from two Russians in New York who sent him to Los Alamos to get information from Fuchs for transmission to the Soviet Union. Cooperating with Gold were David Greenglass and Julius and Ethel Rosenberg (the latter were party members of some duration). All three went to Los Alamos to help the Soviet cause.

In 1949 Fuchs was arrested in Britain. Not long after he identified Harry Gold (whose name he had not known but whose photograph he recognized) as his courier, Gold confessed he had worked under the direction of Soviet consular officials in New York. His confession

drew attention to Greenglass and the Rosenbergs. The former had supplied the Rosenbergs with atomic information until the fall of 1945,
when he told Julius Rosenberg he would not go back to Los
Alamos to continue supplying information. A subsequent business quar-
rel led to the situation in the 1951 trial wherein Greenglass, together
with Gold, turned state's evidence and told a story which marked the
Rosenbergs as among the most dangerous espionage agents of our time.
It developed that Rosenberg was the one who gave orders to Greenglass, paid him for his services, and once ordered him to Prague via
Mexico, when he learned that Gold had confessed.

In March, 1951, the jury found Gold, Greenglass, the Rosenbergs,
and Morton Sobell guilty. However only the Rosenbergs received the
death penalty, inasmuch as Gold and Greenglass had helped the prosecution.

The Alger Hiss Case

On July 31, 1948, Elizabeth Bentley told the House Un-American
Activities Committee an amazing story of Communist espionage, listing many prominent persons in American public life. In an attempt to
check the veracity of this story, other witnesses were called, including
an editor of *Time* magazine—another former Communist—Whittaker
Chambers. On August 3rd, he testified that he had been a party member between 1934 and 1947, assigned to work with a Communist spy
ring within the United States Government. Chambers named many of
the same persons mentioned by Miss Bentley, including Alger and
Donald Hiss of the State Department; Lee Pressman, former General
Counsel of the CIO; Nathan Witt, former Labor Department attorney;
Henry Collins of the State Department; and Harry Dexter White, an
Assistant Secretary of the Treasury when he left office.

Alger Hiss had played a prominent role in the State Department,
climaxing his official career as presidential adviser at the momentous
Yalta Conference, and as major domo at the San Francisco UN Conference. In the middle of 1948 Hiss left the State Department to become
president of the Carnegie Endowment for International Peace. On
August 5, 1948, Hiss told the House Committee that he had never been
a Communist and that he had never known Whittaker Chambers, even
when shown a picture of the latter. Most of the Committee's members
were so impressed by his testimony that they felt he must be telling
the truth and the case was almost dropped. However Rep. Richard
Nixon, (now Vice President of the United States) and Committee
Counsel Robert Stripling had doubts about Hiss. At their insistence

the Committee pressed Chambers for details about Hiss and Hiss' connection with the Communist spy ring. Chambers provided all sorts of minute data which he could not possibly have had if he had not known Hiss quite well. This data checked with investigations made by the Committee, even though President Truman made its task more difficult by calling the entire investigation a "red herring" and refusing to allow government intelligence agencies to cooperate with the Committee. Largely through the efforts of Research Director Benjamin Mandel, Nixon and his colleagues discovered information leading them to conclude that Hiss should be questioned again. This questioning confirmed that Chambers had indeed known Hiss, even though the latter claimed he had never known Chambers. When confronted by Chambers, Hiss finally conceded that he might have known him under the name of Crosley, but never as a Communist.

The pro-Hiss entourage finally goaded Chambers into calling Hiss a Communist in public without benefit of congressional immunity. After considerable delay, Hiss sued Chambers, and Hiss' lawyers asked Chambers to produce any documents he might have which would establish that he and Hiss were Communists in the same spy ring. This maneuver turned out to be a bluff, which was called by Chambers. The latter immediately produced a thick envelope containing four pages in Hiss' handwriting and a great number of typewritten documents which he said had been typed on Hiss' typewriter. These documents contained excerpts and summaries of scores of confidential and secret State Department messages. Nevertheless, for reasons never fully made public, the Justice Department took no action against Hiss. This spurred Nixon and Stripling to request Chambers to furnish any other information which might force the hand of Justice Department. It was at this point that Chambers turned over to the House Committee the so-called "pumpkin papers"—five rolls of microfilm containing photostatic copies of literally scores of confidential and secret documents of the State Department and the Bureau of Standards. With this evidence in its possession, the Committee stirred the Justice Department into action.

On December 15, 1948, Hiss was indicted on grounds of perjury for denying that he had turned over confidential government documents to Whittaker Chambers. His first trial ended in a hung jury, with eight favoring conviction and four acquittal. The second trial, including additional witnesses to corroborate Chamber's testimony, resulted in the conviction of Hiss.

A run-down of the positions held by members of the Hiss-Chambers ring indicates the effectiveness with which the conspiracy was able to infiltrate into vital positions of government and industry—four in the State Department, two in Treasury, two in the Bureau of Standards, one in the Aberdeen Proving Grounds, one who became general counsel of the CIO, two in the Electric Boat Company, etc. Next in importance to Hiss was Harry Dexter White, former Assistant Secretary of the Treasury. Considerable evidence indicates that White exerted a substantial influence on American foreign policy, particularly in regard to the "Morgenthau Plan" for Germany and Far Eastern developments.

What was important in the Hiss case was not so much the technical crime of perjury, but rather the fact that large scale assaults on American security were uncovered; the nature and amount of top secret and confidential documents which found their way into the hands of the Soviet Government by way of American traitors was extraordinary. Three of the documents could not be made public even after the Hiss case because the State Department claimed that their disclosure would jeopardize American security. (See "The Hiss Case," speech by Senator Nixon to Congress, January 26, 1950, U. S. Government Printing Office: 1950).

COMMUNISTS IN THE UN

In June, 1948, Robert C. Alexander, Assistant Chief of the State Department's Visa Division, testified before a Senate Judiciary subcommittee that there were several hundred aliens in the United States, many of them in the UN, who were "undesirable" from the point of best interests of the United States. However, a State Department committe subsequently maintained that Alexander had been talking through his hat. Shortly thereafter, the American public was awakened to the spy danger inherent in having an international organization located in the United States, when government employee Judith Coplon was found conspiring to commit espionage with Valentin Gubitchev, a Russian UN employee.

Ultimately, the Senate Internal Security subcommittee became interested in the matter of American Communists in the UN as a corollary of the investigation into the Institute of Pacific Relations. In May, 1952, during interrogations of two top UN officials, David Weintraub and Irving Kaplan, certain evidence pointed to Communist influences. Not only had Weintraub been the official who hired Owen Lattimore as head of a UN Economic Mission to Afghanistan in 1950, but he was found implicated in Victor Perlo and Harold Ware Communist rings. Subsequently thirty-three witnesses—almost all Americans in the UN—were called by the subcommittee after it had received evidence or information that these persons had Communist connections or associations. Significantly, twenty-six invoked their constitutional privilege against self-incrimination when asked about past Communist membership. The positions held by these officials were for the most part important ones: Frank C. Bancroft (Editor, Document Control Division), Frank Coe (Secretary, International Monetary Fund), Joel Gordon (Chief, Current Trade Analysis Section, Department of Economic Affairs), Irving Kaplan (Economic Affairs Officer, Division of Economic Stability and Development), Alfred Van Tassell (Chief, Economic Section, Technical Assistance Adminstration). The subcommittee noted that most of the witnesses who refused to answer questions about party membership were persons with long records of government employment.

A distinguished UN Commission of legal experts was asked to give its opinion about American citizens who invoked the Constitutional privilege of possible self-incrimination. It held that "it does not follow that a witness claiming the privilege, whether he be a national of the United States or otherwise, suffers no ill consequences by the mere fact of his asserting the privilege. Indeed in the United States much legislation has been passed restricting . . . employment in the case of persons connected with organizations declared subversive. . . . It appears to us, therefore, that in cases where this privilege is invoked in the United States, the Secretary-General must take notice of the fact and be prepared to take the appropriate action." Subsequently UN Secretary-General Trygve Lie proceeded to weed out many American Communists in the UN.

Conclusions

The inescapable fact is that as long as the United States remains the most important non-Communist state of the world, Soviet policy will continue to exert every pressure—political, economic, and military—to weaken and ultimately destroy the government of the United States. So long as the United States adhered to the sterile containment policy based on the proposition of peaceful coexistence, the Soviets continued to hold the initiative and win victories. Repudiation of containment by President Eisenhower and adoption of certain counter-offensive measures gave promise of ultimate and complete victory.

19

Soviet Military Policy and Strength

The 19th Congress of the Russian Communist party, convened in Moscow in October, 1952, re-emphasized the military essence of Communism. Malenkov, Stalin's heir-apparent, gloated over the extension of Communist rule during the past ten years to 600 million persons in Europe and Asia. He boasted that the Soviet Union would produce, by the end of 1952, 35 million tons of steel, 47 million tons of oil, and 117 million kilowatt hours of electric power—figures indicating the Soviet economy may have roughly twice the military-economic potential it had in 1940.

That the United States was the chief enemy was underlined in the bitter attacks on it by Malenkov, Beria, and Mikoyan, among others. These Politburo (now the Praesidium) members made it clearer than ever that the main purpose of the new international Communist line was to weaken the United States and to prepare the way for the time when the most powerful bastion of "world capitalism" could be destroyed. The fact that there was to be a reversion to united front tactics in many countries did not mean that should the leading "capitalist" countries fail to destroy one another, as Stalin suggested, the Soviet Empire would not utilize its military strength to destroy the last vestiges of "imperialism." Indeed the greatest element of blackmail held over American military policy in Korea by Soviet policy-makers was the warning "not to spread the war." According to this line of thought, it was permitted to Soviet military policy to take chances and risk war (as in Berlin, Greece, and Korea), but the same offensive tactic must be denied the United States and its allies. The net result was a permanent offensive by the Soviet Empire and a permanent defensive by the United Sates which must inevitably lead to the same end as the French Maginot policy during the years of the "phony war" in the west during World War II.

Colonel William Kintner, in his incisive *The Front Is Everywhere*, pin-points the military essence of Communism. "The most distinctive feature of military organizations the world over is that they achieve their objectives by means of organized violence." (University of Oklahoma Press, 1950, p. 45). The Soviet Empire achieved its strength to a considerable degree through military strength. Operating from its initial Russian heartland, this Empire has been created through Soviet

diplomatic victories, and by means of military sweeps through east
and central Europe in 1944 and 1945, and similar sweeps by satellite
armies in China and Korea since that time. Soviet military policy in
Korea and south-east Asia has long been apparent.

"Force," said Marx, "is the midwife of every old society when it is
pregnant with the new one; force is the instrument and the means by
which social movements hack their way through and break up the fos-
silized political forms." Because military force is vital to the spread of
Communism, Communist literature reads like a military plan: Capitalism can be destroyed only by revolution; there can be no revolution
without civil war; the overthrow of capitalism is impossible without
force, without armed uprising and class warfare. "The fact that violence is inescapably associated with Communism's quest for power
affects every person in the Communist orbit. Communist legionaries
must prepare themselves psychologically for the days of armed political
conquest. Potential Communist troops are told again and again that
the Communist objective is not to be won by peaceful persuasion, by
parliamentary means, or even by the gradual progress of society, but
only by the violent use of force. Communists must be convinced of the
necessity for violence; otherwise they will fail when their supreme
political act, the armed conquest of power, is undertaken." (*Ibid.*,
p. 46).

Soviet power and its Communist parties are not content merely with
warding off blows allegedly directed against it from the capitalist
world. "In the period of world revolution its role (that of the Communist party) consists in attacking and storming the strongholds of
capitalist society." (*Theses and Statutes of the Third International*, p.
56). Stalin once told H. G. Wells: "Communists regard the substitution
of one social system for another not simply as a spontaneous and peaceful process, but as a complicated, long and violent process." (Quoted
in Kintner, *op. cit.*, p. 49).

Spontaneous and successful Communist revolutions have occurred
in no country outside Russia. Even in the case of the Bolshevik revolution, Lenin and his associates were physically transported to Russia from Switzerland by the German High Command with the express
purpose of starting a revolution against the Kerensky Government and
knocking Russia out of the war in order that Germany might turn all its
attention to the western front. Communism was established in the
satellites of eastern Europe and Asia either through military force or
through diplomacy. In a very real sense the Soviet Army and its satellite auxiliaries have been substituted for Communist revolutions that
nowhere have succeeded in themselves.

There can be no doubt that, of all the instruments of policy at the disposal of the Soviet Government, the Army is the most imposing and formidable. Although seemingly endowed with qualities of patience not possessed by Hitler, Russia's leaders must inevitably be tempted to utilize the sheer physical power which lies at hand. This they have done in the past—notably in Poland and Finland—and, working through satellite armies—in China, Korea, and Indo-China.

The impressive size of the Soviet Army, and its victories during the latter stages of World War II, encourage the Soviet Government in its uncompromising attitude, and enable it to maintain control over its colonies. Soviet leaders, at the 19th Congress of the Communist party in 1952, made plain the exceptional priority to be given to the Soviet military arm in the future. The Russian soldier is first-class military material—physically tough, used to a hard life and ignorant of many of the comforts to which western nations are accustomed. There are far less Soviet soldiers behind the lines manning officer's clubs and post exchanges than in the American Army. Military discipline is Prussian in its severity, and saluting even non-commissioned officers is strictly enforced; a single case of omission may mean five day's arrest. Absence without leave may be counted automatically as desertion, punishable by many years' forced labor. Military terminology for a soldier in the presence of an officer is rigidly laid down and adhered to.

Under the military code formulated in 1940, a soldier has no redress against an officer and no channels for an appeal against an order or a sentence. Soviet troops on occupation duty in Germany and Austria are confined to barracks after duty hours, and contact with the local population is forbidden. An officer has unlimited power over those in his command, and, in extreme cases, even in peacetime, insubordination is punishable by execution on the spot.

As a fighting force, the Soviet Army has the advantages of battle experience, self-confidence drawn from a series of victories, and experienced war leaders. The High Command is under the direction of Marshall Vasilievsky, the War Minister, who served during World War II as Chief of the General Staff and Commander of the Army Group which captured Koenigsberg in East Prussia. One of his top deputies is Marshal Zhukov, one of Soviet Russia's most distinguished officers. Vasilievsky directs the Army through four main organs: the General Staff under General Shtemenko, the Command of the Land Forces under Marshal Koniev, the Rear and Supply Services under General Khruliov, and the Political Administration under General Shikin. (J. M. Mackintosh, "The Soviet Army," *The New Leader*, December 1, 1952). The principal chain of command passes through the Headquarters of the Land Forces to the twenty-three Military Districts into which the Soviet Union is divided. Each Military District is commanded by a marshal or senior general, and, according to its geographical position, contains a large or small component of the Army's active and reserve units.

The strength of a Military District is measured in the number and types of divisions it contains. The bulk of the Army's strength lies in the rifle (infantry) divisions and motorized rifle divisions (the latter containing a greater proportion of motor transport). These divisions number 11,000 men each, and comprise normally three rifle regiments, a regiment of artillery, and an armored regiment of fifty tanks. Additionally, there are tank divisions of 10,500 men, containing three or four tank regiments and a motorized regiment. There are also larger mechanized divisions of 13,000 men containing three mechanized regiments and two tank regiments. Field artillery divisions and anti-aircraft divisions number 6,000 each, and some cavalry divisions remain at a strength of 5,000 men. As active forces, these divisions are grouped in corps or armies. A corps normally consists of two or three rifle divisions and a tank or mechanized division, and two or three such corps constitute an army. The armored formations are grouped in powerful mechanized armies comprising two tank and two mechanized divisions each.

The basis of Soviet military doctrine is the use of the Army's strength in mass formation. This was apparent in the war against Germany and the Chinese Communist's war against the Korean Republic and its American ally. Soviet armies fighting Germany in World War II regarded a superiority of eight to one over the enemy as the minimum for an offensive, and the Russians scored their greatest victories when an Army Group Commander was able to employ on one sector two tank armies of 1,500 tanks each. For the storming of Berlin in 1945 over 20,000 guns were concentrated by the Soviet commanders. The rifle armies were used to effect breaches in the enemy lines, to attack fortified positions, and to hold them against counter-attack, while the mechanized forces stood by to pour through gaps and exploit the break through. Everything is sacrificed to the aim of mobility in the mass, including the reduction of the rear and supply services to the absolute minimum. Living off the country is the rule rather than the exception. German tank commanders during World War II would often run behind the Russian lines to cut off supply lines only to find these lines non-existent. The medical, engineering, and signal services have to be content with the bare necessities; only in the branch of recovery and repair of tanks and damaged mechanized equipment is there anything approaching a satisfactory complement of technicians and equipment. During World War II and in the Korean war Soviet and satellite armies have made considerable use of penal battalions for effecting suicide breakthrough operations and running over heavily mined areas. The entire structure and outlook of the Soviet Army is that of a rough but effective machine of great brute strength.

Political indoctrination and political loyalty have long been essentials of the Soviet military system. The Soviet regime is willing and able to go to great lengths in this regard, as witness the great purges in 1937, 1938, and 1939, when Marshall Tukhachevsky and his entire staff were liquidated. The task of identifying the Russian soldier's love for his country with loyalty to the party is the duty of that unique feature of the Soviet Army, the Political Administration.

To every headquarters, from the General Staff down to battalion or company levels are attached representatives of the Political Administration with the title "Deputy Commander for Political Affairs" (*Zampolit*). The *Zampolit* normally organizes two political sessions every day—an early morning reading of the Soviet or military newspapers, and an evening session devoted to political lectures and indoctrination. There is little or no time for the reading of "funny books" or other light diversion. The main functions of the *Zampolit* are educational and propagandist; he works closely with officials of the Ministry of State Security (MGB) and the Ministry of the Interior (MVD).

The Soviet Government "frankly acts on the principal that every citizen is a potential enemy of the state, especially during Army service, when he has access to arms." (*ibid.*, p. 17). Accordingly there exist so-called "Special Sections" of Interior Ministry troops which are organized in regiments and divisions, trained and equipped to carry out decisions of the party even against the Army. These famous green-uniformed troops assist frontier guards in patrolling especially dangerous border areas, deport unruly elements, combat resistant groups, and protect and guard political officials.

Conscripts normally serve for three years, after which time they are placed on reserve. While in reserve they do a short period of training every year. Marshall Vasilievsky declared on October 7, 1952, that sixty percent of the reserve officers and ninety percent of the active duty officers from company commander upward have had battle duty, either against the Germans, or the Nationalist Chinese and Koreans and Americans.

According to a 1951 American and British analysis, the Soviet Army at that time comprised 175 full-strength divisions—rifle, mechanized, tank, and cavalry divisions, with 40 artillery and anti-aircraft divisions

in support. Of the total 110 were rifle and cavalry divisions, and 65
armored. This analysis put 32 divisions in Germany, four in Poland,
two in Austria, four in Hungary and Rumania. This added up to 42
divisions, 27 of them armored. Soviet Army strength in the Far East
was put at a minimum of 40 divisions, acting in support of the mam-
moth Chinese Communist armies. At least 100 divisions were said to
be in the U.S.S.R. proper, fifty of which were put west of a line drawn
from Leningrad to Rostov-on-Don. Well known commanders direct
these far-flung Soviet armies: General Chuikov in Germany, Marshal
Malinovsky in the Far East, Generals Antonov and Fediuninsky in the
Caucasus, Generals Pukhov and Grechko in the Ukraine, General
Galitsky in the Carpathians, Generals Bagramian and Gorbatov in the
Baltic area, and General Luchinsky and Marshal Meretskov in Leningrad and the far north.

The Soviet military pattern has been slowly but surely extended to
the satellite armies, and notably those of Communist China, Poland,
Czechoslovakia, Rumania, Bulgaria, Hungary, and more recently, East
Germany. On July 27th, 1952, Drew Middleton of the *New York Times*
wrote from Bonn, Germany: "The Soviet satellite states in eastern Europe appear to be well into the period in which industrial production,
including armaments production, is being emphasized to the point
where it has replaced Communist indoctrination as the prime objective
of the Kremlin's policy." He claimed that the satellite armies had been
transformed into forces trained, equipped, and organized on the Soviet
model. On the basis of information given him by American and British
experts on the scene, Middleton concluded: "The Soviet Union is bol-
stering the satellite states' military and industrial strength, and its own,
to meet the challenge that will be imposed on Soviet influence in eastern Europe when western rearmament is completed. The new Soviet
Empire is preparing for a great trial of strength with the West, which
the rulers of the Soviet Union are convinced is coming." At the end of
1952, the same observer declared "the Russians are carrying out me-
thodical and extensive construction to improve the potential of eastern
Europe from the Arctic Ocean to the Carpathian Mountains as a
springboard for full-scale operations against the western Powers . . ."
(*New York Times*, December 22, 1952). The end of 1952 found a
steady increase of Soviet military operations in the Baltic, beginning
with construction of an air-warning system from the island of Ruegen,
off the east German coast, eastward to Leningrad. This was followed
by stockpiling of naval stores on Ruegen and the islands of Saaremaa
and Hiiumaa off the Estonian coast and by increased construction of
light naval craft in Baltic ports from east Germany to Kronstadt. Sub-

marines, cruisers, and other Russian naval craft as well as land-based jet bombers have been known to operate as far south as Ruegen. Russia's northern flank extends to the Arctic Ocean in the Murmansk-Petsamo area near the Norwegian frontier. Year-end reports indicated railroad improvements to Murmansk and assemblage of ammunition fuel stocks along the entire front facing Norway and Finland.

In the Far East, where the war since 1950 has been hot, the Soviets were estimated to have at least 40 divisions, 27 major air bases in Russian and Chinese territory, and 11 naval bases. Soviet military forces in the Far East, aside from those in Manchuria and Korea, were said to be located in five general areas: the Russian Maritime Province, the Amur Military Zone, Sakhalin Island, the Kurile Islands, and Kamchatka Peninsula. Nine Soviet divisions were said to be scattered along the wedge of territory north of Vladivostok, with an airbase at Tetyukhe on the sea of Japan and the giant naval base at Vladivostok. Thirteen divisions were in the Amur Military Zone with headquarters at Khabarovsk, with air bases at Nikolaevsk and Sovetskaya Gavan. Sakhalin Island contained twelve divisions and the headquarters of the Soviet Tenth Air Force. The Kuriles Islands were said to be occupied by two divisions, one of which allegedly included many Japanese under General Ryuji Sejima, formerly on the staff of General Yamashita. A threat to Alaska was found in nine divisions located on Kamchatka Peninsula, with its main base at Petropavlovsk. (*Time,* November 19, 1951).

In Korea one million Communist troops were supplied from the "privileged sanctuaries" of Manchuria. Located at air bases near Mukden, Sian, and Antung, were an estimated 2100 Chinese Communist planes—almost all Russian built, and including 1200 MIG-15 jets. Air Force Secretary Finletter disclosed in September 1952, that several squadrons of twin-engined jet bombers belonging to the Soviet Air Force had arrived in Manchurian bases. He described these bombers as being comparable to the United States B-45 jet bombers. Russian bases at Port Arthur and Dairen also threatened Republic of Korea and American forces in Korea and Japan.

According to Hanson Baldwin, military editor of the *New York Times,* four principal developments indicated the potential power of the Soviet offensive striking force. These were: 1) the increasing Soviet stockpile of atomic bombs, 2) Soviet hydrogen bomb potential, 3) the increasing number of Soviet long-range bombers, and 4) evidences of Russian air reconnaissance around the northern perimeter over the Arctic, and evidence of increased Soviet air power in the Chukchi Peninsula, across the Bering Sea from Alaska. (Hanson Baldwin, " Danger

Signs in North," *New York Times*, July 21, 1952). Baldwin stated that the concensus of the experts fixed the Soviet atomic stockpile at not less than fifty "nominal" (20,000 ton bombs), and perhaps as high as 150, with a stockpile of 400 indicated by 1954. He also pointed out that it was virtually certain that the Russians would manufacture hydrogen bombs of power so immense that their destructive capabilities had to be measured in millions of tons rather than thousands of tons.

Estimates of Soviet long-range bomber strength indicate some 400 TU-4 bombers (similar to the American B-29) and 600 other bomber types. However there was evidence of an improved TU-4 being in production, which allegedly was a superior plane to the American B-50. Jane's *All the World's Aircraft*, 1952-1953 edition, stated that Soviet plane production in 1951 was double that of the United States. During 1951 "the Soviet aircraft industry is reputed to have produced 22,000 aircraft, half of them fighters, and 63,000 aircraft engines." Editor Leonard Bridgman estimated MIG-15 production during 1952 at 450 planes monthly.

Soviet military potential, in its land army aspect, was listed by the U. S. State Department in November, 1952, at 491 divisions, of which 181 were Soviet and 310 were satellite. Communist China was credited with 250 divisions. Reinforced by a large air force and a navy which included an estimated 300 submarines, here was a striking force which could extend its power from Korea to Japan; from Chukchi to Alaska; from Indo-China to Thailand and Burma; from Turkmen to Iran; from the Caucasus to Iran and Turkey; from Bulgaria and Albania into Greece or Yugoslavia; from Rumania and Hungary into Yugoslavia; from eastern Austria into Yugoslavia, Italy or Germany; from east Germany and Czechoslovakia into Germany; from Karelia into Scandinavia; and from Franz Josef Land to Greenland and Canada.

The 19th Russian Communist party Congress announced a new five year plan to strengthen the Soviet war economy. All the goals set for 1957 were well short of current American production in the key industries, but the comparison may tend to give rise to false optimism. If the new five year plan succeeds, it will make the Soviet Empire even more industrially capable of sustaining a protracted war than it was in 1952. A stepped-up geographical dispersion of industry was calculated to minimize serious crippling of any one industry. Soviet weakness in petroleum will be materially reduced by the new plan, and it must be remembered that Soviet petroleum products can be diverted to military and agricultural needs since very little is needed to support the civilian economy. The same is true of steel. It is of course a fact that if the Soviet plan succeeds, 1955 production of some 44,700,000 tons will be considerably less than half the United States production. But a far greater percentage of Soviet steel can be funneled into military uses than is possible in the United States. "Anyone who takes undue comfort from this United States leadership need only recall that it took more than three years of terrific fighting to subdue Japan, which had a steel production of only seven to eight million tons annually, yet was able to produce hundreds of fighting ships and thousands of planes." (Hanson Baldwin, "End of a Chapter," *New York Times*, August 24, 1952). Hanson Baldwin writes about the shadow of "growing military insecurity." He points out that by the end of 1953 operational hydrogen bombs will probably be so developed as to be airlifted, and that the Kremlin "may soon be in a position to launch missiles with atomic warheads against American coastal cities. . . . the air defense program of tomorrow must contemplate a time interval of only twenty minutes between the moment a submarine surfaces somewhere off the Virginia Capes and the moment an explosion occurs over Washington." (*loc. cit.*).

The Soviet military build-up is quite clearly not for defensive reasons. American leaders have repeatedly advertised that they had no intention of attacking the Soviet Empire. When it was to their advantage to do so, as in the case of Korea in the winter of 1950-1951, and they still failed to pass on to the offensive, it must have fully convinced Soviet leaders that they would be in a position to retain the initiative. On the other hand the new administration of Dwight D. Eisenhower speaks of taking the initiative away from the Soviets. It remains to be seen whether American policy will continue to be solely defensive, or whether it will take advantage of certain military and political assets which might be neutralized with the passage of time.

The Soviets have resorted to war as an instrument of national policy in Poland in 1920, Manchuria in 1929, Spain in 1936, Poland in 1939, Finland in 1939-1940, Rumania in 1941, eastern Europe in 1944-1945, Greece in 1947, China in 1945-1949, Korea in 1950, and southeast Asia since 1946. It is clear that this instrument—the most successful of all instruments in the Soviet arsenal—is ready at hand to be used again at the proper time. With the aid of diplomacy and world-wide fifth columns, Soviet military policy poses a greater threat to the free world than the combined power of Hitler, Mussolini, and Tojo. It remains to be seen which of two courses is to be followed: a continued policy of expansion and conquest by the Soviets, or a policy of liberation by the free world led by the United States. Peaceful coexistence, through Russia's choice and not that of the free world, is not a reliable alternative. Soviet behavior in international affairs

Selected Bibliography

BOOKS

Beloff, Max, *The Foreign Policy of Soviet Russia* (New York: Oxford University Press, 1949

Borkenau, Franz, *World Communism* (New York: Norton, 1939)

Budenz, Louis F., *The Cry is Peace* (Chicago: Regnery, 1952)

Burnham, James, *The Coming Defeat of Communism* (New York: John Day, 1950)

Chamberlin, William H., *Blueprint for World Conquest* (Chicago: Regnery, 1946)

Chamberlin, William H., *America's Second Crusade* (Chicago: Regnery, 1950)

Chambers, Whittaker, *Witness* (New York: Random House, 1952)

Dallin, David, *The New Soviet Empire* (New Haven: Yale, 1951)

Dallin, David, *Soviet Russia in the Far East* (New Haven: Yale, 1949)

De Toledano, Ralph, *Spies, Dupes, and Diplomats* (New York: Duell, Sloan, and Pearce, 1952)

Ebon, Martin, *World Communism Today* (New York: McGraw-Hill, 1947)

Einaudi, Mario, *Communism in Western Europe* (Ithaca: Cornell, 1951)

Fischer, Ruth, *Stalin and German Communism* (Cambridge: Harvard, 1949)

Gurian, Waldemar, *The Soviet Union* (Notre Dame: Notre Dame, 1951)

Kieffer, John E., *Realities of World Power* (New York: David McKay, 1952)

Kintner, William, *The Front is Everywhere* (Norman: Oklahoma, 1950)

Lane, Arthur B., *I Saw Poland Betrayed* (New York: Bobbs Merrill, 1949)

Lehrman, Hal, *Russia's Europe* (New York: Appleton-Century, 1947)

Lenczowski, George, *The Middle East in World Affairs* (Ithaca: Cornell, 1952)

Oliver, Robert T., *Verdict in Korea* (State College, Pa.: Bald Eagle, 1952)

Palmer, Edward E., *The Communist Problem in America* (New York: Crowell 1951)

Possony, Stefan, *A Century of Conflict* (Chicago: Regnery, 1953)

Ravines, Eudocio, *The Yenan Way* (New York: Scribner's, 1951)

Rossi, A., *Communist Party in Action* (New Haven: Yale, 1950)

Swearingen, Rodger, and Langer, Paul, *Red Flag in Japan* (Cambridge: Harvard, 1952)

Taracouzio, Timothy, *War and Peace in Soviet Diplomacy* (New York, MacMillan, 1940)

Utley, Freda, *The China Story* (Chicago: Regnery, 1951)

Van der Vlugt, Ebed, *Asia Aflame* (New York: Devin-Adair, 1953)

Walsh, Edmund A., *Total Empire* (Milwaukee: Bruce, 1950)

Weyl, Nathaniel, *The Battle Against Disloyalty* (New York: Crowell, 1951)

PERIODICALS

Intelligence Reports, Department of State, Office of Intelligence Research

The New Leader, New York

The Freeman, New York

Counterattack, New York

Stephen King-Hall Newsletter, K-H Services, London

Intelligence Digest, Kenneth De Courcy, London

News from Behind the Iron Curtain, National Committee for Free Europe

Soviet Bibliography, Division of Library and Reference Services, U. S. Department of State

Index